El Alamein

and the Struggle for North Africa

International Perspectives
from the Twenty-first Century

Edited by
Jill Edwards

The American University in Cairo Press
Cairo New York

Dar el Kutub No. 11834/11
ISBN 978 977 416 581 8

Edwards, Jill
        El Alamein and the Struggle for North Africa: International Perspectives from the
    Twenty-first Century/ Jill Edwards. —Cairo: The American University in Cairo Press, 2012
        p.   cm.
        ISBN 978 977 416 581 8
        1. World War   I. Title

1 2 3 4 5   16 15 14 13 12

Designed by Adam el Sehemy
Printed in Egypt

In commemoration of all who fought in the
Battles of El Alamein, 1942

Contents

Contributors

Mohamed Awad is director of the Alexandria and Mediterranean Research Center at the Bibliotheca Alexandrina. A professional architect and historian of architecture, Awad lectures at Alexandria University. As an ardent conservationist, he is the founder of the Alexandria Preservation Trust, an NGO for the documentation and protection of Alexandria's architectural heritage.

Niall Barr is a fellow of the Royal Historical Society and reader in military history, King's College, University of London. He is based at the Defence Studies Department, the Joint Services Command, and Staff College. Among Barr's many publications are *Pendulum of War: The Three Battles of El Alamein* (2004), and *The Lion and the Poppy: British Veterans, Politics and Society 1921–1939* (2005).

Aldino Bondesan is professor of geomorphology at the University of Padua, Italy. Bondesan is director of the El Alamein Geomorphic Project on the Alamein Battlefields, and leads teams of scientists in the comprehensive excavation, investigation, and analysis of the Alamein sites using latest technology and incorporating archival research. www.qattara.it/30-00%20Prg_files/slide0222.htm

Antulio J. Echevarria II served in the U.S. Army for twenty-three years. Echevarria is currently director of research for the U.S. Army War College. His publications include *Clausewitz and Contemporary War* (2007),

Imagining Future War (2007); and *After Clausewitz* (2001). He has published extensively in scholarly and professional journals on topics related to military history and theory and strategic thinking.

Jill Edwards is professor of international history at the American University in Cairo, and fellow of the Royal Historical Society. Edwards' publications include *Anglo-American Relations and the Franco Question, 1945–1955* (1999) and *The British Government and the Spanish Civil War, 1936–1939* (1979); she is editor of *Historians in Cairo: Essays in Honor of George Scanlon* (2002) and *Al-Alamein Revisited* (2000).

Sahar Hamouda is director of the Alexandria Center for Hellenistic Studies and deputy director of the Alexandria and Mediterranean Research Center at the Bibliotheca Alexandrina. Hamouda is professor and chair of the department of English language and literature at Alexandria University. Among her many publications is the recent book *Once Upon a Time in Jerusalem* (2010).

Glyn Harper was until recently head of the Centre for Defence and Security Studies, Massey University, New Zealand. Now Harper heads Massey's major research project in partnership with New Zealand's Defence Force for the *Centenary History of New Zealand and the First World War*. His recent publications are *Massacre at Passchendaele: The New Zealand Story* (2012) and *Letters from Gallipoli: New Zealand Soldiers Write Home* (2011).

Nick Hewitt is head of attractions and collections at the Portsmouth Naval Base Property Trust, UK. He was previously a historian at the Imperial War Museum. He has appeared in the BBC's *Coast* series, and productions for the History Channel. Among other publications is his book, *Coastal Convoys, 1939–45: The Indestructible Highway* (2008).

James Jacobs is resident military historian at the South African Army College. Jacobs lectures on the junior and senior command and staff programs at the South African National War College. He is a distinguished lecturer and writer on military history.

Alan Jeffreys is senior curator of social history at the Imperial War Museum. His publications include *The British Army in the Far East* (2005);

he is coeditor of *The Indian Army 1939–1947* (2012). He is currently work-ing on *Training the Indian Army, 1939–45*, and is coeditor of the academic history series *India at War*.

William Roger Louis is professor of history at the University of Texas, Austin, and fellow of St Antony's, Oxford. A past president of the Ameri-can Historical Association, and present director of the AHA's National History Center, Louis was chair of the Department of State Historical Advisory Committee (resigned 2008), and was elected to the American Academy of Arts and Sciences in 2011. Author of many books, he is cur-rently editor in chief of *The Oxford History of the British Empire*.

Rémy Porte is director of the research department of the Centre de Doctrine d'Emploi des Forces at the École Militaire, Paris. A lieutenant colonel in the French Army, Porte's publications include *La Mobilisa-tion industrielle: 'premier Front' de la Grande Guerre?* (2006). He was a principal speaker at the recent University of Cambridge Conference "Forgetful Allies: Truth, Myth and Memory in the Two World Wars and After," September 2011.

Thomas Scheben graduated in Islamic Studies at Mainz University. Scheben entered politics, later becoming a newspaper correspondent. He was director of the Konrad Adenauer Foundation in Cairo for five years, and is currently deputy director of the Press and Information Depart-ment of the city of Frankfurt am Main. As a researcher, he has published on Ottoman history and warfare in the Mediterranean.

Peter Stanley heads the Centre for Historical Research at the National Museum of Australia. From 1980 to 2007 he worked at the Australian War Memorial, where he was principal historian. A fellow of the Royal Historical Society, his many books include *Digger Smith and Australia's Great War* (2011); *Invading Australia: Japan and the Battle for Australia, 1942* (2008); with Mark Johnston *Alamein: The Australian Story* (2002, new ed. 2006); *Quinn's Post: Anzac, Gallipoli* (2005).

Harry Tzalas is president of the Hellenic Institute for the Preservation of Nautical Tradition, an Athens-based scientific institution specializing in marine archaeology and nautical experimental archaeology. He has organized many international conferences on Greek ship construction in antiquity. Since 1998 Tzalas has led a team of underwater archaeologists diving at Alexandria, Egypt, for ancient and medieval shipwrecks. He is author of the short story collection "Farewell to Alexandria," published in 2000 by The American University in Cairo Press.

Illustrations

Foreword

William Roger Louis

T he distance in time of seven decades provides the opportunity for balanced and comprehensive interpretation of one of the decisive events in the Second World War: the Battle of El Alamein, October 23–November 5, 1942. Each of the authors in this volume writes with authority and overall knowledge of critical events, such as the Italian entry into the war in 1940 and the British Eighth Army's victory over the forces of General Erwin Rommel three years later. By July 1942 Rommel had driven back British troops to the last defensible position before Alexandria and Cairo. At El Alamein there was a 60-km gap between the sea in the north and the vast sinkhole of Qattara in the south. Mussolini flew to Tripoli for a triumphal entry into Cairo on a white horse. It was a critical time in the war as a whole, with the Germans advancing not only in Russia but also through the Caucasus toward India.

From the vantage point of Britain and the United States, mid-1942 was the worst moment of the war. The Japanese had conquered the Malay Peninsula, Singapore, and Burma, thus arriving at the gates of India. Axis forces threatened the critical British strategic points of Malta, only 80 km from Sicily, and the Suez Canal, the lifeline to India. There were pro-Axis sympathizers in Cairo who would have greeted Rommel as a liberator. The British prepared to evacuate the city. With a different outcome at El Alamein, Britain would have lost the paramount position in the Middle East. As it transpired, the battle represented a transformation of the strategic basis of the war. The British victory stabilized the Egyptian frontier and marked the beginning of the Allied powers' sweep toward victory in North Africa. Above all, it restored British morale.

Each of the chapters challenges an element of nationalist myth that has become embedded in narratives of the war, German and Italian as well as British. Rommel emerges as an exceedingly rash though ingenious and brave commander, whose heroic stature was exaggerated in England, indeed by Churchill himself, to compensate for the failure to defeat him. On the British side, the battle represented the unified command of forces from South Africa, Australia, New Zealand, and India. The book reveals telling detail on, for example, the geographic survey of the remnants of the battlefield, including buttons and tin cans; the diet that led to the near starvation of the Maltese; and the Polish engineer who deployed landmine detectors against the Axis forces. One chapter deals with the critical part played by the Royal Navy in cutting the enemy's lines of communication in the Mediterranean. Another relates the significance of the Free French victory against Rommel at an oasis in the desert, Bir Hakim, which not only symbolized French participation but also gave the Eighth Army time to prepare a line of defense at El Alamein. Not least, British signal intelligence cracked coded messages to Rommel. Thus the new British commander, General Bernard Montgomery, knew of the state of Axis dispositions as well as Rommel's intentions.

Montgomery was tough, clear-minded, and ruthless. He prepared his forces for a war of attrition. His formative years had been those of the First World War. He had sufficient troops available to accept substantial losses, as in the precedent of 1914–18, and to hold a continuous line, thus frustrating Rommel's attempt to bounce past El Alamein. He unified the heterogeneous infantry and armored, naval, and air arms of the Eighth Army. It included Sikhs and Gurkhas as well as Poles and Greeks. There were fissiparous tendencies. The New Zealanders and Australians were critical of the British officers in the High Command and tank units. There had existed a certain defeatist attitude, but it vanished with Montgomery's meticulous and rousing planning.

British forces took part in a form of tank warfare entirely new to them. The Eighth Army fielded one thousand tanks, while Rommel commanded five hundred, only half of which were German. The American-built Sherman tanks played a critical part in the outcome. What emerges above all is the sheer scale of the battle. The British held a twofold superiority: two hundred thousand troops versus one hundred thousand commanded by the Axis, the latter plagued by shortages of supplies and fuel, the former drawing on resources in Alexandria and Cairo. Rommel's inferior forces petered out. The British took thirty thousand Axis prisoners. There were 13,500 British casualties; Rommel's troops lost eight thousand. The poem by Housman thus ends the book on an appropriately somber note.

This is a refreshingly detailed book. It refuses to accept previous accounts without reexamining the historical evidence. It questions previous assumptions even as it supports the view at the time that El Alamein was the greatest British victory since Waterloo. Church bells rang out in London. The British had defeated a bid for control of Egypt and the Middle East. They were not successful in dealing with Egyptian nationalism, as became clear in subsequent decades. Yet the victory at El Alamein enabled the British to sustain their military and political presence in the region for another quarter of a century, until the decision in 1967 to withdraw all troops east of Suez.

Acknowledgments

Acollection of this kind involves the work of many, and I am grateful to all who have helped to produce this book for the commemoration of the seventieth anniversary of the Battles of El Alamein. It has been a privilege to work with the distinguished military historians contributing to the volume, and in the process I have learned much from them. I thank them and the many other historians, archivists, and librarians who have helped along the way. I am indebted to the staff at the Imperial War Museum's Images Unit, and while not forgetting the skill of the intrepid photographers who so long ago endured the heat and dust to record the many facets of warfare, thanks are due to David Bell for his invaluable assistance. Most of the nations who fielded armies in the Desert War have embassies in this great city, and I thank their staffs and the staff of the British Embassy in Cairo for their interest and encouragement. Finally, I thank the publishing team of the American University in Cairo (AUC) Press, who labored valiantly to bring the book out in time for the October commemoration. I thank in particular Press director Nigel Fletcher-Jones, Randi Danforth, Nadia Naqib, and Noha Mohammed, the project manager who patiently sailed through the rigors of a demanding schedule. For faults surviving the Press's watchful scrutiny I am, of course, responsible.

Introduction

Jill Edwards

Over the past two years, revolutionary movements across North Africa have featured prominently in world media headlines and will continue to do so as the people strive to establish stable democracy. Seventy years ago this autumn the spotlight was also on North Africa, as the struggle between Axis and Allied forces was fought out through the Western Desert, and across North Africa, a very different place then when the region was still a vital part of the vast European imperial network. Thousands of men, mostly young, from Allied, Axis, and local forces, who gave their lives in North Africa, lie buried in dedicated cemeteries across the region, or privately in their cities. To mark the occasion of the seventieth anniversary of the Battles of El Alamein, distinguished military historians from nations represented in that struggle have contributed papers for this commemorative collection, examining the context and the battles of the Desert War, and offering food for thought on military and political the issues then and now.

The First World War had left the European democracies exhausted, bankrupt, in debt to the United States. Britain, primarily a naval power, was forced to make drastic cuts in defense expenditure. In 1922, the Washington talks on Naval Arms Reduction agreed limits on size and numbers of warships between the largest naval powers. Britain also adhered to a 'Ten-Year Rule,' ongoing annually, on the premise that there would be no war for the next ten years (and thus no need to rearm). This left Britain with largely outdated fleets and armaments, and too few new ships or aircraft being built until the mid-1930s, when rearmament was belatedly resumed.

Fig 0.1 Emir Mansur, son of King Ibn Saud of Saudi Arabia, inspecting the crew of HMS *Queen Elizabeth* with Admiral Sir Andrew Cunningham, commander in chief, Mediterranean Fleet, and Captain Barry, during the Emir's visit to the fleet at Alexandria. (Imperial War Museum [hereafter IWM]) A 9618)

Encouraged by this neglect, Mussolini began to challenge the British Navy in the Mediterranean. Flexing his military muscles and testing his international clout, Il Duce announced his intention to turn the Mediterranean into an Italian sea, '*mare nostrum*,' as part of his vision of a new Roman empire, thereby threatening Britain's vital direct sea routes to the Eastern Mediterranean, the Suez Canal, and beyond to India and the southern dominions.

The invasion and occupation by Germany of northern France, and the formation of Pétain's puppet government in central southern France, removed Britain's only continental ally and meant she would indeed have stood alone, had it not been for massive support from her dominions and colonies. That support, in matériel and men, from Australia, New Zealand, South Africa, and India, was crucial to the eventual success of the Allies in the North African campaign. As Peter Stanley, Glyn Harper, James Jacobs, and Alan Jeffreys explain, in many different respects, the impact of this war had lasting political and military repercussions in their home countries. These huge forces were supplemented with Greeks, Polish, French, and other exiled military, some temporarily based in the United Kingdom, but all now converging on the Eastern Mediterranean and Egypt.

As Rémy Porte explains, when France fell in June 1940 the outraged General de Gaulle responded immediately, issuing the call to arms that began the gathering together of what became the Free French forces, a matter that would become of great political significance for France. Governor General Eboué was the first to respond, joining de Gaulle on August 26, 1940, making Chad the first of the francophone African states to do so. Once the United States Congress had passed the Lend-Lease Act of March 1941, more desperately needed American aid in the shape of arms and other matériel began to arrive. Roosevelt's sympathy with the Allied cause was clear. Almost twelve months before the attack on Pearl Harbor in December 1941, Roosevelt's personal emissary, Col. J. Donovan ('Wild Bill,' later head of the Office of Strategic Services, OSS, forerunner of the CIA) had visited Cairo, traveling incognito with the assistance of the British Foreign Office. His mission was to study the situation in the Mediterranean region, and give the French in Syria to understand that the United States would not countenance Britain's defeat.[1]

Troops gathering in the region were conscripts with a solid core of professionals. Polish troops fought in large numbers with the British services, and at El Alamein in the Polish Brigade. It was a Polish engineer who made a major contribution to the Desert War with the invention of his mine detector, first used to pinpoint enemy mines buried in the sands of the Western Desert.[2] But there were, too, individual volunteers, their input testifying to the spirit of resistance in the many countries then under attack or occupation. One German volunteer, Franz Georg Loeser, whose parents had fled Germany for Britain, left his London school to enlist. As an alien and under age, this required persistence, but he was eventually permitted to sign up, and fought in North Africa, Europe, and the Far East.[3]

War is about many things, but first and last it is about people. Each contributor to this collection deals with the people, military or civilians, leaders or led, involved in one way or another in the battles of North Africa between 1940 and 1943. Jeffreys examines the meticulous planning that went into training the troops. Among many, the two most celebrated of the commanders in the field at El Alamein were Erwin

Rommel and Bernard Montgomery. Their roles are scrutinized first by Antulio J. Echevarria II, who measures Rommel against Clausewitz's ideal of military genius. He is followed by Niall Barr, who presents an unconventional portrait of Churchill, demonstrating just why Montgomery and the prime minister hit it off together, where other British commanders in the Desert War had failed. In contrast to these outstanding figures, the miserable conditions for ordinary soldiers, crouching for days on end in foxholes and trenches in the dusty outposts of the desert, is clearly revealed and documented in Aldino Bondesan's detailed account of the University of Padua's geomorphic project of mapping and analyzing the desert battle terrain. His photographs and charts throw new light on the implementation of strategy and tactics.

Among the hosts of courageous deeds proliferating in the intensity of war, the significance of the endurance of the Maltese people is surely outstanding. Their courage is forever saluted in the George Cross,[4] but just how did the population of the small but strategically essential rock in mid-Mediterranean manage to hold out in conditions of siege and near starvation? Thomas Scheben's scrupulous account of the summer of 1942, "Feeding the Fortress," suggests a combination of tenacity, of determination not to follow the Greeks into Axis subjection, and their difficult adherence to an organization of supply based on the success of the similar plan developed for the British, who were equally reliant on food imports. Had Malta collapsed, it would not only have been a great asset to the Axis powers, but in resisting, it stood with its naval and RAF bases directly athwart Axis supply lines to Libya, and had constantly to be reckoned in Axis strategy. Here too, as Nick Hewitt reminds us, the performance of naval and air forces was an integral aspect of the war's outcome, though with heavy loss of life and ships.

It cannot be forgotten, when writing of the Desert War, that the Allies' foremost asset at El Alamein lay not just in their ultimate preponderance of men and matériel, but in Egypt itself, in Cairo where its military headquarters were based, and especially in Alexandria, that ancient Mediterranean port where the greatest mainstay of all indubitably came from the Egyptian people. For despite the sentiments of some long-settled Italians, of Axis-leaning Egyptians, and of the small but growing number of anti-British 'Free Officers,' without the support of the government, people, and the Egyptian Army, nothing could have been accomplished, and the outcome could have been very different.

It was not only the assent but the input of the Egyptian Army that was essential in creating a sense of national participation. Around three hundred thousand military personnel were stationed in Egypt, but also in the region of half a million civilians were employed in ports around the Middle East to deal with the four hundred thousand tons of military stores arriving every month.[5] With the Mediterranean route very difficult once the German Luftwaffe arrived in force, supply was a constant problem, and getting through by sea, air, or land was equally problematic along the lengthy alternatives, the land/river route from the Belgian Congo, or around the Cape.[6]

The astonishing fortitude and cheerfulness of the Alexandrians under the most trying of circumstances shine through their reminiscences in Mohamed Awad and Sahar Hamouda's compilation of oral histories. In the more somber life of the city today, it is well to recall the truly cosmopolitan citizenry of Alexandria's first half of the twentieth century. Grown out of her long Mediterranean history, the city port was home to an extraordinary mix of nationalities and religions, with Greeks and Italians forming a sizable number of her population and contributing down the centuries to her history and literary tradition. With its large, long-settled Italian population, mothers with sons in the Italian Army were inevitably torn in their loyalty between their city and the 'old' country.

But among young Alexandrians was a small group of Greek, French, and Italian youths who formed their own embryo resistance movement, Gruppo D'Azione Antifascista e Italiani Liberie d'Egitto, to face the 'enemy' should the Allied forces collapse—as at times seemed possible. They also worked on plans for a national constitution to transform economic and political life. There was some discussion in the Foreign Office as to whether the secret services, Special Operations (SOE), or Political Warfare Executive (PWE) should offer support, but it was decided that the time was 'not yet ripe.'[7]

To Alexandrians, it must have seemed they had more than their share of the strains of war. The social and economic impact on the city was massive. The war changed lifestyles and perspectives. In some respects it was exciting and life was lived at a faster pace amid the growing crowds of servicemen in the city. But the city was bombed, and during the night of December 18, 1941, two battleships in the harbor were destroyed. Air battles could be terrifying, and yet become familiar and accommodated, to the extent that when the war moved on for some, as Harry Tzalas, the then-young schoolboy, recalls, life seemed perhaps a little dull.

In sum, these chapters do not simply follow the military progress of the North African campaigns, though they also do that. From the perspective of seventy years on it is possible to distinguish various ways in which these battles affected subsequent geo–politico–military thought. What constitutes a good military commander? To what degree did the war hasten Indian independence of 1947 or the Egyptian Revolution of 1952; or help spark the even bloodier battle for independence in Algeria— or, later, further afield, the gradual reorientation of Antipodean outlook from Europe to the Southern and Western Hemispheres? Churchill later estimated that the Desert War had been "the hinge on which our ultimate victory turned."[8] Today across North Africa the struggle for a better, different kind of victory continues.

Notes

1   The National Archives (TNA), FO371/A183/183/45, Lampson, Cairo, to FO, Telegram to Cairo, no. 44. Donovan was due in Cairo in January 1941 and would stay at the embassy.

2   My thanks to Zbigniew Mieczowski for the reference to his paper, "Poland's Battle for Freedom in World War II," at *The Polish and Franco-British Alliance in World War II*, General Sikorski Museum, December 1, 2009; and interview and correspondence, August, 2011.

3   Franz Georg Loeser, *Sag nie, du ghest den letzen Weg: Ein deutsches Leben* (Köln: Bund Verlag, 1986).

4   The George Cross was awarded to the Maltese people on April 15, 1942 by King George VI for their courage in resisting occupation.

5   Field Marshal Earl Alexander of Tunis, *The Alexander Memoirs, 1940–1945* (London, 1962), 18.

6   TNA FO371/30770, 1943, Belgium and Luxemburg, File no. 49, 2261-4796, C3361, March 26, 1942, HMG Consul General, Leopoldville, to FO, March 26, 1942.

7   TNA FO371/33223, R1937/54/2, "Anti-Fascist Activities in Egypt," Michael Wright, Cairo, and P.J. Dixon, Southern Department, FO, February 24, 1942. TNA FO371/33223, R1948/54/22, Orme Sargent to Howard, January–March, 1942.

8   Winston S. Churchill, *The Second World War*, vol. 3: *The Grand Alliance* (London, 1953), 20.

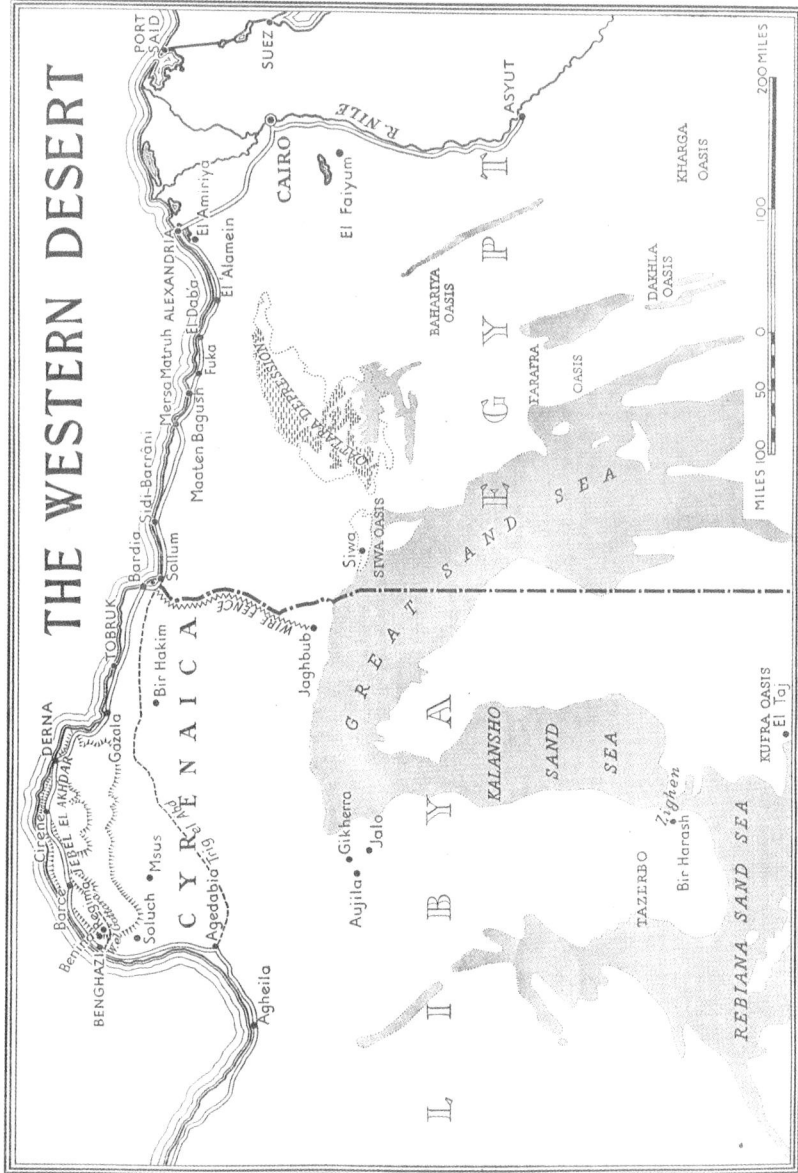

Fig 0.2 "The Western Desert" from Fitzroy Maclean, *Eastern Approaches*, ninth impression. London: Jonathan Cape, 1950 (first impression: 1949)

1

The War in North Africa, 1940–43
An Overview of the Role of the Union of South Africa

James Jacobs

Italian Entry into the War

Until Italy joined the war on June 10, 1940, the Second World War was mainly a European affair. The German war machine overran western Europe within the time span of a few months; and as the main focus of Adolf Hitler, the German dictator, was the conquest of the Soviet Union, Africa would have played virtually no role in this had it not been for the dreams of conquest by the Italian leader, Benito Mussolini. He wanted to exploit the precarious position of Britain and France in Europe to expand the Italian colonial empire in Africa. Thus on June 10, 1940, Italy declared war on Britain and France.[1]

During October of the same year, Mussolini indicated that he wanted to incorporate British colonial territory into the Italian Empire. He was especially interested in Sudan and Egypt.[2] At that stage it looked like an easy venture, as Britain was engaged in a life-and-death struggle to prevent a German invasion of the United Kingdom. The British forces in the Middle East and North Africa were small and the Arab population was dissatisfied with their presence in their territories.

British Interest in the Region

However, the British government was adamant that the territories in the vicinity of the Mediterranean would not be surrendered to the Axis forces (Germany and Italy) without a struggle, as their interest in this area was too deeply rooted. The British Empire had become involved here since the seventeenth century because of the perpetual wars between Spain and

France. Gibraltar and Malta were conquered and established as naval bases. Initially, British interests were more focused on the western Mediterranean, but the Napoleonic Wars forced them to become involved in Egypt. Even this meant only a temporary interest, but the building of the Suez Canal as a gateway to India and the dependence of British industries on the oil of the Persian Gulf in the nineteenth century meant that British interests in the Eastern Mediterranean had to be enhanced with a strong military presence.[3]

During the First World War (1914–18), Britain used Egypt as a base from which to direct military operations against Turkey. The disintegration of the Ottoman Empire in 1918 led to the establishment of British-mandated governments (under the auspices of the League of Nations) over Palestine, Transjordan, and Iraq. Egypt formally became independent in 1922, and the mandate over Iraq expired in 1928, but treaties with the respective governments allowed British military and naval bases in their territories. The British also controlled Cyprus. Thus, by 1940, British control of this region included an area from the Egyptian–Libyan border to the Persian Gulf that for its geographic position and abundance of crude oil was of cardinal importance to the British war effort.[4]

There were, however, also other reasons why the Eastern Mediterranean was of strategic importance to the British Empire. In this region, the British were geographically well placed to conduct military operations against the weaker of the Axis powers, Italy, as soon as sufficient forces were available. Together with commando raids on the European coast and strategic air attacks against Germany, the British could demonstrate that they still had the ability to act offensively in the war and thus sustain the morale of their population in spite of the seemingly unstoppable German juggernaut. Egypt was the place where the forces of the British Empire, with the exception of Canada, could be easily concentrated for operations. Forces from India, Australia, New Zealand, South Africa, and Britain itself could be transported via the Eastern Atlantic and the Indian Ocean to Egypt, outside the effective application range of the German and Italian air and naval forces that operated over the Mediterranean.

The British Prime Minister, Winston Churchill, hoped that victories over the Italian forces in North Africa would keep countries like Spain and Turkey out of the war. Furthermore, airfields in the Middle East would allow the Royal Air Force to launch attacks against the Ploesti oilfields in Romania, the only substantial source of crude oil for the Axis powers. From here British forces could also intervene in the Balkans.

British grand strategy entailed playing for time until the United States of America joined the war on the Allied side. Thus, a force could be built up to return to the European continent and defeat the Germans. In the meantime, the priority would have to be the safeguarding of the Middle East and the conquest of Italian territory in North Africa. Consequently, the British government regarded the Middle East and North Africa, next to the integrity of the United Kingdom itself, as the first priority in imperial defense.[5]

Fig 1.1 Sir Claude J.E. Auchinleck, commander in chief Middle East, July 1941–August 1942. Permission: Jacobs.

British Problems

However, by June 10, 1940 the British were in a precarious situation. Only fifty thousand troops were available for the whole Middle East region. In contrast, the Italian forces in Libya numbered five hundred thousand, and in East Africa two hundred thousand, while only nine thousand British troops were deployed in Sudan and Kenya. British reinforcements were on their way, but because of the presence of the Italian air force and navy in the Mediterranean, most of these had to be transported via the Cape sea route. Therefore, it would take some time before a substantial buildup of forces could take place to reinforce the British position in the Middle East.[6]

In spite of their sheer size, the Italian forces had certain drawbacks. The air force was obsolete and, in spite of its newer equipment, the navy was no match for the Royal Navy. The Italian Army was equipped with inferior and aged equipment and its training and morale were at a low level as the Italian population was not in favor of the war. In contrast, the British commanders in Egypt made the best use of the limited forces at their disposal. In spite of scarce resources, training standards were high. Constant training and exercises in the desert produced forces that were acquainted with the terrain and climate of the Middle East. They also possessed good maps as opposed to the inferior types available to their Italian adversaries.[7]

Both sides were faced with long lines of communication from their homelands to the theater of operations, which inhibited their ability to sustain their forces, in contrast with Europe where commanders could get fuel from civilian filling stations and receive food from the population. In North Africa, sustainment was virtually completely dependent on outside sources. The Axis forces could use Tripoli, Benghazi, and Tobruk, but the British were in control of the best harbor on the North African coastline, Alexandria.[8] Another important factor was that Axis convoys from Italy were very vulnerable due to the attacks of British naval and air forces from Malta, a small island between Sicily and North Africa. This was achieved with relatively small forces, as British cryptoanalysts exploited the carelessness of Italian Navy radio operators by breaking their radio codes. This enabled them to know exactly when logistic ships, due for North Africa, left the Italian harbors.[9]

In spite of their quantitative advantage, the Italian forces in North Africa, under command of Marshall R. Graziani, were inactive until September 1940. The small British forces in Egypt had conducted periodic raids until this time, and on September 13 the Italians halfheartedly invaded Egypt. After advancing more or less eighty kilometers, they erected a series of fortifications near Sidi Barrani. The British forces conducted an orderly withdrawal, and after Italian inactivity for two months, the arrival of reinforcements placed the British forces in a good position for a counteroffensive.[10] From the start the British counteroffensive experienced little resistance from the Italians, who were driven eight hundred kilometers westward. Reaching al-Agheila on February 9, 1941, the British conquest of the whole of Italian North Africa seemed possible.[11] In East Africa, the Italians were also driven back on different fronts. On January 19, 1941, British forces invaded Ethiopia from Sudan, and on February 10 from Kenya. By April 1941, the Italian forces in East Africa were virtually defeated. It seemed a foregone conclusion that the war in Africa would be over within weeks.

However, after the German invasion of Greece, Churchill ordered Lord Wavell, the British commander in the Middle East, to halt operations in North Africa and send some of his forces to Greece. In doing so the British forfeited an immediate opportunity to win the war in North Africa. The British forces in Greece had virtually no influence on the outcome of the Axis victory there, and it gave the latter the opportunity to recuperate and send another task force to North Africa. This time around it would include a German contingent, lengthening the war in Africa until 1943.[12]

German Involvement

Events in the Eastern Mediterranean eventually forced the Germans to become involved in this theater. The Italians' invasion of Greece in

November 1940 was as badly executed as their operations in Africa. Greece had to be occupied to safeguard the southern flank of the planned German invasion of the Soviet Union in mid-1941, and the psychological impact of the loss of Italian North Africa forced Hitler's hand into sending German forces to—according to him—a secondary theater. The German involvement immediately tipped the scales. They invaded Greece on April 6, 1941, and a month later they captured Crete by means of an airborne invasion. The last British troops withdrew to Egypt, while achieving very little.[13]

Axis control of the Balkans and Crete and the arrival of reinforcements in North Africa placed this theater again in the cauldron of events.

Lieutenant General Erwin Rommel, the newly appointed commander of the German contingent for North Africa, arrived in Tripoli ahead of his forces on February 12, 1941. Two days later a reconnaissance battalion and an antitank unit arrived. Rommel immediately dispatched them to al-Agheila to stem a possible British advance. On March 11, the first German tank regiment and a Luftwaffe contingent arrived in Tripoli. Rommel's disposition did not allow him to sit and wait to see what the enemy would do first. Contrary to instructions, he took the initiative and launched an offensive. This took the British by surprise and the pendulum swung back. By April 11, the Axis forces had reached the Libyan–Egyptian border, although they could not capture the harbor town of Tobruk. For the rest of the year, British strategy in North Africa was aimed at driving Rommel's forces back westward and relieving Tobruk, at this stage besieged by the Axis forces. Rommel tried to thwart this and capture the town. It was clear that the British faced a tough adversary and that the war in North Africa would not be over quickly.[14]

A closer look at the events reveals that the British were sufficiently reinforced to start Operation Brevity in May 1941, the first attempt to drive the Axis forces westward and relieve Tobruk. Although Rommel's forces were initially driven back, he launched a surprise counterattack on May 27, 1941 and occupied the strategic al-Halfaya pass. This placed the Axis forces in a good position to counter the next British operation, called Battleaxe (June 15–18). Both British efforts were in vain, in spite of their numerical strength. During the last operation, for example, they had a numerical advantage of 4:1 in tanks alone.

Rommel's success strengthened Churchill's resolve even more to defeat the Axis forces in North Africa. Large numbers of reinforcements were sent to Egypt, in spite of strong indications that the Commonwealth

Fig 1.2 Prime Minister and Minister of Defense Jan Christian Smuts addressing officers and men in Egypt, 1942. Permission: Jacobs.

forces in the Far East were too weak to cope with a possible war against Japan. Churchill went even further: Wavell was recalled, and Lieutenant General C.J.E. Auchinleck was appointed in his place. The name of the force in Egypt, known until then as the Western Desert Force, was changed to the Eighth Army, with command vested in Lieutenant General A. Cunningham. The four British tank regiments were increased to fourteen, while the forces in Tobruk were also reinforced by sea, with the aim of breaking out of the town to join the rest of the Eighth Army once the offensive started.[15]

British Counteroffensives

Operation Crusader started on November 18, 1941. Both sides suffered heavy losses in battles raging across the desert. The Axis forces lost 38,000 men and three hundred tanks, while the British lost eighteen thousand men and 278 tanks. By the beginning of December, Rommel realized that his manpower and logistic situation had become untenable and he withdrew to Gazala, four hundred kilometers east of al-Agheila. Realizing that they could be enveloped from the south at this position, the Axis forces started with a general withdrawal on the night of December 16–17, and by the end of the month they were back at al-Agheila.[16]

By December 1941, the war had developed into a world conflict in the true sense of the word. Germany and Italy not only had to contend with the British Empire, but since the German invasion of the Soviet Union on June 22, with that country also. On December 7, 1941, Japanese forces attacked the United States naval base at Pearl Harbor, and two days later Hitler declared war on America. In this way an alliance was established between the British Empire, the Soviet Union, and the United States of America, whose first priority was to win the war in Europe.[17] In support of operations by the Soviet Army, Anglo–American forces would make the conquest of North Africa their first priority. The aim was to establish a stranglehold on the Axis forces in Europe until their forces were within striking distance of Germany itself. After winning the war in Europe, all resources would be utilized against Japan.[18]

America's entry into the war did not immediately influence the British position in North Africa. The American armed forces were ill prepared for war and it would take a few months for their industries to convert to full-scale war production. Also, the British and American chiefs of military staff decided that Germany could still achieve victory over the Soviets, in spite of setbacks near Moscow. Consequently, aid to the Soviet Union was seen as the first priority. The British were therefore more or less dependent on their own resources for the war in North Africa.[19]

The success of Operation Crusader inflated British hopes. However, upon reaching al-Agheila in January 1942, they encountered the same problem that Rommel's forces had on the Libyan–Egyptian border, namely long lines of communication that bedeviled logistic supply. The British troops were also tired and their equipment needed an overhaul.[20] The extension of the war to the Far East also meant that urgently needed reinforcements had to be diverted to that theater, depleting the Eighth Army.[21] They were also confident that Rommel needed time for the recuperation of his forces, implying that the Eighth Army was at this stage not prepared for an Axis counteroffensive. In reality, air attacks on Malta enabled the Italians to supply the Axis forces in North Africa much more easily. Rommel now possessed shorter lines of communication and the accumulation of forces under his command proceeded rapidly. Within three weeks into the new year he launched a counteroffensive. By May 1942, the British had retreated to Gazala.[22]

South Africa Enters the War

The Union of South Africa entered the Second World War on the Allied side on September 6, 1939. As prime minister and minister of defense, General J.C. Smuts was the driving force behind South Africa's war effort. Smuts was convinced that the Union should play an important role in the war against the Axis forces, but the country and the Union Defence Force were not ready for war. A huge backlog existed in terms of military preparedness, equipment, and the manufacturing of war matériel, that would have to be rectified.[23]

During the rest of 1939 and early in 1940, three infantry divisions were created to participate in the war. The First Division, under command of Major General G.E. Brink, consisted of the First, Second, and Fifth Brigades; the Second Division, under command of Major General I.P. de Villiers, consisted of the Third, Fourth, and Sixth Brigades. The Third Division[24] was under command of Major General H.N.W. Botha and consisted of the reserve brigades for home defense.[25] A major effort was also undertaken to acquire modern equipment for the Air Force, while the South African Navy was reestablished on January 15, 1940, after this organization had ceased to exist in 1934.

In June 1940, the first South African ground forces arrived in East Africa—the First South African Brigade under command of Brigadier D.H. (Dan) Pienaar. In December of the same year, the rest of the division joined them. The division and a contingent of the South African Air Force participated in operations against the Italians until April 1941, when it was decided to send them to North Africa. They arrived in Egypt on May 4 and by the end of the month they were deployed at Marsa Matruh, where they helped with the erection of defensive works and underwent training in desert warfare. The Second Division was sent to Egypt in June 1941, and at the end of August of the same year it was deployed in the vicinity of El Alamein, where it underwent training in desert warfare and helped with the development of defensive works. In the meantime, contingents of the South African Air Force and Navy were also sent to Egypt.[26]

The New Theater of Operations

The British command in the Middle East decided not to immediately utilize the South Africans on the front, to provide them the opportunity to acquaint themselves with desert conditions such as the uninhabitable terrain, extremes in temperatures, sandstorms, and the notorious

Fig 1.3 Brigadier D.H. Pienaar, officer commanding the South African Forces in North Africa. Permission: Jacobs.

Egyptian flies.[27] D.R. Forsyth remembered measuring a temperature of 52°C. According to him, the heat was such that some men tore the skin from under their armpits and in their groins like scribbling paper. This problem was solved by drinking a mixture of salt and lime juice. He also remembered some winter nights being so cold that they put on all their clothing and wrapped themselves in up to six blankets to keep out the desert chill.[28] Even in summer, three blankets had to be used to keep warm after last light. During the day, sandstorms were unbearable. Soft sand plugged nostrils and got into wounds, retarding their healing; it jammed weapons and clogged vehicle engines. The desert also had its dangers in the form of the horned viper and the yellow scorpion. To top it all, water was perpetually scarce.[29]

On November 3, 1941, the First Division and the First and Fifth Brigades moved from Marsa Matruh to the south of Bir Istabl to conduct intensive training in desert conditions. This was done in preparation for the Eighth Army's projected offensive to relieve the garrison in Tobruk.

On November 17, the First Division crossed the Libyan border and was instructed to attack at Bir al-Gubi. Hereafter the division was supposed to advance via Sidi Rezegh to Tobruk in support of the British Seventh Armoured Division. On November 20, contact was made with the Axis forces, but the South Africans did not make any progress as heavy artillery fire from both sides made it difficult to advance. In spite of this, the Fifth South African Brigade was ordered to advance toward Sidi Rezegh and link up with the garrison in Tobruk. However, after heavy fighting, the brigade was prevented from advancing more or less five kilometers south of Sidi Rezegh, where on November 23 a strong German armored counterattack overwhelmed and destroyed this brigade as a fighting entity.

The First South African Brigade was ordered on November 22 to advance from Bir al-Gubi to the Fifth South African Brigade deployment area. The advance of the brigade did not progress far before they were beaten back by a determined German armored counterattack. Consequently this formation had to retreat to Taib al-Esem, where it beat off determined Axis attacks on November 25. On the same day, the brigade had to retreat further, but on November 28 again had to advance to support the New Zealand Division's attack on Sidi Rezegh. After being further involved in heavy fighting between November 30 and December 1, the First Brigade again had to retreat south to Taib al-Esem. On December 20 they were sent back to Egypt to recuperate.

In the meantime, the Second South African Division was detached to the Thirteenth Corps and participated in the fighting at Bardia, Sollum, Cova, and Halfaya. The Third and Fourth Brigades participated in the heavy fighting in the capture of Bardia on January 2, 1942. A total of 7,775 prisoners of war were taken, while the South Africans lost 353 men. On January 12, the Sixth South African Brigade captured Sollum and on January 17, the Axis forces at Halfaya surrendered. During the operations at Bardia, Sollum, Cova, and Halfaya, the Second South African Division lost five hundred men, killed, wounded, or taken prisoner of war.[30]

The Expansion of the War

Japan's entry into the war in December 1941, and an increase in the activities of German U-boats in the southern oceans, brought the war closer to South Africa. As indicated, there was a danger that the Axis forces could threaten traffic along the Cape sea route. Thus, the South African government again had to reconsider the country's role in the war.[31]

In spite of these developments, Smuts was adamant that the Union's largest contribution should still be in the Middle East. He agreed that the series of Japanese victories in Malaysia, Singapore, Burma, the Philippines, Indonesia, and Northern New Guinea was worrying, but he believed that they did not have the resources to fight the American forces in the Pacific and launch large-scale operations against India and Australia, until such time as an Allied counteroffensive could begin. He reiterated his point of view that a victory over Italy and Germany should be the priority and that the first step in this process was to drive the Axis forces from North Africa. He was also more concerned about the progress of the German offensive in the Soviet Union, which could make the British position in the Middle East untenable. Thus, according to him, the Union had to contribute as much as possible to the effort to defeat Rommel's forces.[32]

Between January and March 1942, the two South African divisions were used to strengthen the defensive lines of the Eighth Army in Libya. The First Division was deployed at Gazala. The division consisted of the headquarters, the First Brigade, the Second Brigade, and the Polish Carpathian Brigade. On March 21, the Third Brigade was transferred from the Second to the First Division, while the Poles were placed under command of another formation. From March 10, 1942, Dan Pienaar, now a major general, was the officer commanding the division. The Second South African Division moved to Tobruk at the end of March. A South African, Major General H.B. Klopper, was placed in command of the garrison of 33,000 men, of which more or less a third were South African soldiers.[33]

German Progress in the Soviet Union

On June 28, 1942, the German summer offensive in the southern part of the Soviet Union started. With their forces driving for the Caucasian oilfields, the possibility existed that the British position in Persia (Iran), which they and the Soviets jointly occupied, could be in danger. The Germans could even conquer Iraq, Syria, and Palestine, threatening the British hold over Egypt and the Suez Canal from two directions. The unwillingness of the Soviet government to supply any information to the British on the progress of the war in their own country made it difficult for the British command in the Middle East to determine the strength of forces to be used to defend the possible thrust from the north, as well as against Rommel.

The Far East

In the Far East, the news was also not good for the Allies. In February 1942, the Japanese captured Singapore and advanced deep into Burma, threatening the British hold over India. Commonwealth forces, including the Seventh South African Brigade, had to be sent to occupy Madagascar to prevent the Japanese from using this island to threaten the safety of the Cape sea route. South African losses during this operation were three dead and fifteen wounded.[34]

American forces would only be available for North Africa by the end of 1942. The implication of this was that British forces had to be deployed on three fronts, namely Egypt, the so-called Norther (Syria, Iraq, and Persia), and India. At the same time, any Axis success on any of these theaters would weaken the others for the British. Thus, Churchill put pressure on Auchinleck to attack as soon as possible, as victory in the Western Desert would ease pressure on the Persian Gulf region and India. It would also neutralize the series of defeats inflicted by Rommel's forces.[35]

The Gazala Gallop

Characteristically, Rommel acted first, and on the evening of May 26, 1942, his forces attacked the Eighth Army at Gazala. The Axis forces enveloped the British position to the south with the aim of destroying the British armor and cutting off the rest of their forces from Egypt. The operation lasted until June 13. Several British tanks were destroyed and the then-commander of the Eighth Army, Lieutenant General Neil Ritchie, decided to withdraw his forces to the Libyan–Egyptian frontier. However, Tobruk was not evacuated according to plan, as Churchill at the last moment decided that the fall of the fortress would be detrimental to the morale of the British forces in the theater. On June 21 Rommel captured Tobruk, together with 33,000 Commonwealth forces and large amounts of supplies.[36]

The British war cabinet expected that the Axis advance would soon continue. Because of a shortage of tanks in North Africa, permission was granted on June 21 that the Eighth Army should retard Rommel's advance on the frontier, while preparations were made to defend two hundred kilometers to the east at Marsa Matruh.

On June 25, Auchinleck relieved Ritchie of his command and, in addition to his responsibilities as commander of the British forces in the Middle East, also took personal command of the Eighth Army. In the process of this change of command, Rommel struck at Marsa Matruh and, when it became clear that the Eighth Army's position had become untenable, Auchinleck decided to withdraw further eastward. His main considerations were to keep the Eighth Army intact as a fighting entity, and the fact that the position at Marsa Matruh was too vulnerable.

Thus, the decision was made to withdraw to El Alamein, where the British forces could rest their flanks on two impenetrable obstacles with only a sixty-kilometer gap between them. These obstructions were the Mediterranean to the north and the Qattara Depression to the south. The latter consisted of a series of saltpans and soft sand that would be impassable to motorized and tracked vehicles. A defensive line here would limit Rommel's ability to maneuver, as he could not envelop the Eighth Army to either the south or the north as was done on numerous previous occasions during the Desert War. The Eighth Army's lines of communication to the Nile Delta would be very short, while those of the Axis forces were stretched to the extreme.[37]

On June 28, 1942, Rommel's tanks moved swiftly forward to prevent the Eighth Army from establishing a defensive line at Fuka. On the morning of June 30, the Axis forces were only 160 kilometers from Alexandria. By that evening they had reached the vicinity of a small, unknown railway siding called El Alamein, ninety kilometers from Cairo. At face value, it seemed a matter of time before the whole of Egypt would be under Axis control. Mussolini had arrived in Tripoli the previous day to prepare for a triumphant entry into Cairo.[38]

In the Soviet Union, the German offensives in the direction of Stalingrad and the Caucasus were making good progress and the possibility existed that these forces could, in conjunction with Rommel, execute a gigantic pincer movement to conquer the Middle East and the Caucasian oilfields.[39] The Second World War had reached a turning point.

Retreat to El Alamein

The attack by Rommel's forces on Gazala on May 26, 1942 directly impacted the South African forces. By June 13, the possibility existed that the First South African Division could be cut off by the victorious Axis forces, and on the next day the division received the expected order from Thirteenth Corps Headquarters to evacuate the Gazala line. Without suffering more significant losses, the First Division reached Marsa Matruh by the end of the month. However, the Second Division was less

Fig 1.4 South African engineers, Second Battalion, at El Alamein training for mine detection in preparation for the Second Battle of El Alamein. (IWM E 18844)

fortunate. The development of operations at Gazala caused the garrison in Tobruk to be cut off by Rommel's forces, while the rest of the Eighth Army retreated across the Libyan–Egyptian frontier.[40] Contrary to British expectations, Rommel did not besiege the town but launched an attack from the southeast. The defenses were breached and the garrison, despite heavy fighting, was forced to surrender on June 21.

The Axis forces' capture of Tobruk was a serious military and psychological setback for the Allied war effort. South Africa's military prestige in particular was tarnished, as the commander was a South African, and 10,722 of the total of 33,000 men had been taken prisoner. Nearly a whole division that formed a large part of the Union's military forces was lost.[41] It now became the task of the First Division and the air and naval contingents to restore South Africa's military pride.

However, detachments to the Second Division during May had weakened the First Division, as most of these elements had also been lost at Tobruk.[42] A compiled battalion group of the First Division was under command of the Fourth South African Brigade at Tobruk. This group consisted of companies of the First Royal Durban Light Infantry (RDLI), the First Battalion of the Imperial Light Horse (ILH), and the First Battalion of the Rand Light Infantry (RLI). This group was known as the Blake group, in deference to its commanding officer, Lieutenant Colonel E.H.R. Blake. Nearly all of them were lost at Tobruk, forcing their original formation, the Third Brigade, to cope without them for the rest of the Desert War. Another compiled battalion group of the First Division was the so-called Beer group, under command of Lieutenant Colonel J.M. de Beer. This group consisted of companies of the First Battalion of the Royal Natal Carbineers (RNC), the First Battalion of the Duke of Edinburgh's Own Rifles (DEOR), and the First/Third Transvaal Scottish Regiment. Only 240 members of this group escaped from Tobruk.[43] Another loss to the First Division was a battery of the First South African Field Regiment.[44]

On June 21, the First Division received orders to move from the border to El Alamein. The commander of the Eighth Army decided that the division needed rest and should not be deployed at Marsa Matruh. The First Brigade started moving on June 22, while the rest of the division followed the next day. By the evening of June 25, 1942, the main force of the division was deployed in the vicinity of the El Alamein station.[45]

From June 26–28, elements of the division participated in the fighting at Marsa Matruh. The Second Antitank Regiment was detached from the Second Division at Gazala. This unit withdrew with the First Division to El Alamein, but on arrival had to move back to Marsa Matruh, where it was placed under the command of the British Fiftieth Division. On June 28, the regiment broke out of the encirclement of the Axis forces at Marsa Matruh, but only 324 reached El Alamein and most of their guns were lost. A few members were detached to the First Antitank Regiment under command of the First Division, but most were sent to the Nile Delta to recuperate.[46]

From June 25, the Fifth and Eleventh Engineer Field Companies were detached to the British Fiftieth Division at Marsa Matruh. Their mission was to lay mines in the western part of the defensive line and to conduct demolition tasks in the area. While they were busy with this in Marsa Matruh harbor, the Axis forces attacked and the South African contingent had to break out. Individuals reached El Alamein, some only by July 5.[47]

At El Alamein, the South African Engineers were also tasked to support other British formations. At Deir al-Shein, the Eleventh Field Company helped troops of the Eighteenth Indian Brigade to lay mines and erect defensive positions and barbed wire. A section of this company was also sent to Bab al-Qattara, where they helped the New Zealand infantry prepare defensive positions.[48]

South African armored cars patrolled west of the El Alamein Line and informed the headquarters of the Eighth Army on the movement of the Axis forces. On arrival at El Alamein, the Fourth Armoured Car Regiment was transferred to the British Seventh Armoured Division. During July 1942, they permanently deployed one squadron with two in reserve. Their area of responsibility was from Bab al-Qattara to the Qattara Depression. The Sixth Armoured Car Regiment was still under command of the First South African Division. Their area of responsibility was the west of the El Alamein Station and north of Bab al-Qattara. They did not only report to the South African Division Headquarters, but also directly to Eighth Army Headquarters.[49]

The First Battle of El Alamein, July 1–30, 1942

Although Auchinleck was worried about a possible Axis advance to Palestine, Transjordan, Syria, Iraq, and Persia, the northern front would only be threatened by the Axis powers if their forces in the Soviet Union could break through in the Caucasus region and advance south.[50] Therefore, at this stage, stopping Rommel's forces was the first priority.

Auchinleck's decision to withdraw to El Alamein confirmed a judgment by the British General Staff that this would be the best position from which to defend Alexandria, Cairo, and the Suez Canal.[51] The so-called El Alamein Line was the last obstacle between Rommel and the Suez Canal. In contrast to the image of an impenetrable defensive line of fortifications, minefields, and barbed wire portrayed by the BBC and British newspapers, it was not much more than a line on a map.[52]

The defensive position was divided into three corps areas, with the Thirtieth Corps near the coast and the Thirteenth Corps in the south. In the Nile Delta, the Tenth Corps was deployed in depth. In the north, near El Alamein, the defensive position prepared in 1941 by the Second South African Division was in a dilapidated state. It was from here to the northern slope of the Ruweisat ridge that the First South African Division would be deployed by the end of June 1942.[53]

The Eighteenth Indian Brigade was deployed on the western part of the ridge at Deir al-Shein. They had just arrived from Iraq and had been hastily placed in prepared defensive positions. They had to cover a twelve-kilometer gap between the Thirtieth and Thirteenth Corps. The First British Armoured Division was earmarked to deploy east of this position but were still on their way from Marsa Matruh.[54]

The British Thirteenth Corps had to defend the area from the southern slope of Ruweisat Ridge up to the Qattara Depression with weakened infantry, while the Seventh British Armoured Division was also on its way from Marsa Matruh. The impassability of the Qattara Depression implied that the opposing forces would have to fight it out in the northern sector near the coast.

On July 1, Panzerarmee Afrika tried to break through between the South African positions at El Alamein and Ruweisat Ridge. The Eighteenth Indian Brigade took the full onslaught of Rommel's forces and the South Africans also felt part of this.[55] These attacks continued on July 2–3, but by July 4 Rommel was forced to deploy his forces defensively. From July 4–7, the Eighth Army conducted limited counterattacks. The Australian capture of Tall al-Makh Khad near the coast threatened Rommel's lines of communication and he responded with a counterattack against the El Alamein positions of the South African forces, but it was beaten back. From July 14–26, Auchinleck tried to regain the initiative with a series of counterattacks, but could not break through Rommel's defensive positions.[56] By July 28, he decided to postpone the destruction of Panzerarmee Afrika. The tempo of British reinforcements was so slow that a large-scale offensive could only be undertaken by September.[57]

The First Battle of El Alamein was the most crucial encounter of the war in North Africa. Had Rommel's forces not been stopped during July 1–3, the Suez Canal and Alexandria would have been under Axis control. The control of this harbor would have solved all Rommel's logistic problems and made the task of conducting a campaign to capture the Persian Gulf oilfields so much easier. South African losses were relatively light compared to the rest of the Eighth Army, but the defensive position near the station was the crucial pivot around which Auchinleck's plan turned.[58]

The Second Battle of El Alamein, October 23–November 5, 1942

During August, the command structure of the British forces in the Middle East changed drastically. Auchinleck was replaced by General Harold Alexander as commander of the Commonwealth forces in the Middle East, while B.L. Montgomery took over as commander of the Eighth Army.

In contrast to the First Battle of El Alamein, the South Africans were to play only a secondary role during this battle. The first phase entailed elaborate efforts to breach the extensive minefields that Rommel created during July–October. The First South African Division formed the left flank of four infantry divisions of the Eighth Army that moved along the lanes created by the engineers, supported by a massive artillery bombardment. During the first night alone, the artillery of the South African Division fired 62,000 rounds of 25-pounder ammunition.

At 2200h the infantry moved forward. The First Natal Mounted Rifles led the Second Brigade attack, while the First Rand Light Infantry led the Third Brigade attack. They attained their first objectives and the First and Second Field Force Battalion, the First Cape Town Highlanders, and the First Royal Durban Light Infantry and the First Imperial Light Horse continued the attack. The Third Brigade reached its objective but the Second Brigade suffered heavy casualties and was delayed.[59]

Montgomery initially planned that the infantry should breach the minefields and then British armor would move along the lifted lanes, form up, and engage the panzers from terrain of their own choosing. Eventually the British armor only reached the first of two stop lines and did not proceed to the second. Montgomery changed his plan so that the British armor would fix the panzers rather than destroy them. The focus of main effort now became a process of attrition with firepower, with artillery, aircraft, and armor to destroy as much as possible of the Axis infantry formations. Afterward, the panzers could be dealt with.

The attrition battle started on October 24 and carried on to October 31. At the start of this battle the South Africans were deployed on the Mitiriya ridge, anchoring the positions of the rest of the Eighth Army. Even before the British breakthrough, the South Africans were moved again to form part of a strategic reserve. The only active role was played by the artillery, which provided supporting fire to neighboring formations, and the armored cars, which helped with reconnaissance at different sectors of the Eighth Army. South African casualties during the Second Battle of El Alamein were 734 killed, wounded, or taken prisoner of war.[60]

Armored cars and engineers participated in the follow-up of Rommel's retreat up to Benghazi, but the rest of the division's role in the Desert War had come to an end. The decision was that conversion to an armored division would take place and that it would best be done in the Union of South Africa itself.[61] Total South African casualties in North Africa were 20,279, of which battle deaths amounted to 2,104, a total of 3,928 were wounded, and 14,247 were taken prisoner of war.[62]

Other Contributions

The first two squadrons of the South African Air Force arrived in Egypt in April 1941, and between that date and May 1943, with a total of eleven squadrons operating at one time, flew 33,991 sorties and destroyed 342 Axis aircraft. They were involved in most operations, starting with the evacuation of Crete in 1941, the first efforts to relieve Tobruk, the retreat to El Alamein in 1942, and the follow-up of Rommel's retreat, up to the fighting in the Mareth Line and the last air raids in May 1943 against the Axis forces in North Africa.

In spite of the threat of German and Japanese submarines to shipping off the South African coastline, the South African Naval Forces also participated in the Mediterranean theater. They played an important part in providing antisubmarine protection to the exposed sea route between Alexandria and Tobruk. Hence they participated in most of the operations up to the invasion of Sicily in 1943.[63]

Retrospection

In comparison to other countries, the South African contribution to the war in North Africa was small, making the country's role to be part of a larger team. Coincidentally, however, during the most crucial battle of the campaign, the South Africans played a vital role. During the first few days of July 1942, Rommel had a slight chance of disrupting the British defenses, destroying their armor still in retreat from Marsa Matruh, and occupying Alexandria and Cairo.

After the First Battle of El Alamein, the Axis forces could never again muster enough forces to win the war for possession of the Nile Delta. During the battles of Alam al-Halfa and the Second Battle of El Alamein, the strength of the Allies and the massive input of American industrial power could clearly be seen. At this stage the Germans were already bogged down in attrition warfare in Stalingrad. Thus, the Suez Canal and the Persian Gulf oilfields were safe. Subsequently, after July 1942, the South African contribution reverted to that of a minor role player, albeit one that contributed substantially—taken into account the country's small population and industrial base.

Notes

1   J. Lucas, *War in the Desert: The Eighth Army at El Alamein* (London: Armour Press, 1982), 13.

2   P. Calvocoressi, and G. Wint, *Total War* (New York: Ballantine Books, 1972), 167.

3   J.A. Williamson, *A Short History of British Expansion: The Modern Empire and Commonwealth* (New York: MacMillan, 1967), 236–38.

4   Calvocoressi and Wint, *Total War*, 181.

5   M. Howard, *The Mediterranean Strategy in the Second World War* (London: Wiedenfeld & Nicolson, 1970), 7–10.

6   B.H. Liddell Hart, *History of the Second World War* (London: Cassell, 1970), 116–17.

7   Lucas, *War in the Desert*, 14.

8   M. Van Creveld, *Supplying War: Logistics from Wallenstein to Patton* (Cambridge: Cambridge University Press, 1980), 181–82.

9   R. Lewin, *Ultra Goes to War* (New York: Pocket Books, 1978), 142–43, 196–97.

10 G. Wright, *The Ordeal of Total War, 1939–1945* (New York: Harper & Row, 1968), 35–36.

11 Calvocoressi and Wint, *Total War*, 173.

12 Liddell Hart, *History of the Second World War*, 124, 125, 134.

13 Calvocoressi and Wint, *Total War*, 175–79.

14 Liddell Hart, *History of the Second World War*, 127.

15 Liddell Hart, *History of the Second World War*, 183–91.

16 P. Young, ed., *Atlas of the Second World War* (London: Pan Books, 1970), 41.

17 D. Irving, *Hitler's War, 1939–1942* (Hong Kong: Paper Mac, 1977), 352.

18 Howard, *Mediterranean Strategy*, 16–17.

19 Howard, *Mediterranean Strategy*, 21–23.

20 Liddell Hart, *History of the Second World War*, 277.

21 M. Wright, ed., *The World at Arms: The Reader's Digest Illustrated History of World War II* (London: Reader's Digest, 1989), 95.

22 Liddell Hart, *History of the Second World War*, 277; Young, *Atlas*, 42.

23 C.F.J. Muller, ed., *Vyfhonderd Jaar Suid-Afrikaanse Geskiedenis* (Pretoria: Academica, 1984), 452–53.

24 W.A. Dörning, "A Short Chronicle of the South African Defence Force, 1912–1987," *Militaria*, 17/2 (1987): 34–38.

25 C.J. Beyers, ed., *South African Biographical Dictionary*, part 3, 92–93.

26 Dörning, "A Short Chronicle," 34–36.

27 I.S.O. Playfair et al., *The Mediterranean and Middle East*, vol. 3, 59.

28 Interview with D.R. Forsyth, Pretoria, June 9, 1987.

29 S.G. Hyslop et al., *Afrika Korps* (Richmond, Virginia: Time-Life Books, 1991), 129.

30 C.J. Nöthling, *Geskiedenis van die Suid-Afrikaanse Weermag* (Pretoria: SAM-HIK, 1995), 48–49.

31 D.W. Krüger, *The Making of a Nation: A History of the Union of South Africa, 1910–1961* (London: MacMillan, 1971), 209.

32 W.K. Hancock, *Smuts*, vol. 3: *The Fields of Force, 1919–1950* (Cambridge: Cambridge University Press, 1962), 364–67.

33 *Official Year Book of the Union of South Africa and of Basutoland, Bechuanaland Protectorate and Swaziland*, no. 23 (1946): 5–7.

34 Nöthling, *Geskiedenis*, 50.

35 Calvocoressi and Wint, *Total War*, 397–98.

36 J.R.M. Butler, ed., *History of the Second World War*, vol. 3: *Grand Strategy*, 606.

37 General Sir Claude J.E. Auchinleck, "Despatch to the Secretary of State for War on January 27, 1943." Supplement to *The London Gazette* (January 15, 1948): 328.

38 Liddell Hart, *History of the Second World War*, 290–91.

39 R.D. Cornwell, *World History in the Twentieth Century* (London: MacMillan, 1970), 61.

40 Dörning, "A Short Chronicle," 36.

41 Krüger, *Making of a Nation*, 210.

42 SANDF Archives, Divisional Documents, no. 68, File 64: Operational Report, First SA Division: El Alamein Defensive Battle, 29 June–30 September, 1942, p. 2.

43 J.A.I. Agar-Hamilton and L.C.F. Turner, *Crisis in the Desert, May–July 1942* (Cape Town: Juta, 1960), 130–31; 234.

44 "Springboks Take Revenge," *Pretoria News*, July 7, 1942; SANDF Archives, Divisional Documents, no. 88, File 1, Div 81/A2: Strengths, July–October 1942.

45 SANDF Archives, Divisional Documents, no. 68, File 64: Operational Report, First SA Division: El Alamein Defensive Battle, 29 June–30 September, 1942, p. 2.

46 SANDF Archives, War Diary 347, File A3/ME 37: War Diary of First SA Division HQ, June 1942; SANDF Archives, Union War Histories no. 376, Précis of Evidence no. 3: The Crisis at El Alamein, 30 June–4 July 1942, p. 4; SANDF Archives, Union War Histories Narep and Info List VII, File no. 1: Gunning through Africa (Report on the role of the South African Artillery in the Second World War by Major E. Millen, p. 238).

47   Agar-Hamilton and Turner, *Crisis in the Desert*, 265.

48   N. Orpen, *War in the Desert* (Cape Town: Juta, 1971), 344.

49   H. Klein, *Springboks in Armour: The South African Armoured Cars in World War II* (Cape Town: Juta, 1971), 277–78.

50   Calvocoressi and Wint, *Total War*, vol. 1: *The War in the West*, 397–98.

51   Auchinleck, "Despatch to the Secretary of State for War" (January 15, 1948): 328.

52   C. Barnett, *The Desert Generals* (London: Pan Books, 1983), 195.

53   Agar-Hamilton and Turner, *Crisis in the Desert*, 271.

54   E. Dorman O'Gowan, *1ˢᵗ Alamain—The Battle that Saved Cairo* (London: Purnell's History of the 2nd World War, no. 7, vol 3/6, 1967) 1062.

55   SANDF Archives, WD 358, File A7/ME 52: War Diary, Third SA Bde HQ, July 1, 1942.

56   General Sir Claude J.E. Auchinleck, Commander in Chief Middle East Forces, "Operations in the Middle East from 1 November 1941 to 15 August 1942" (despatch to the Secretary of State for War on January 27, 1943); Supplement to the *London Gazette* (January 13, 1948).

57   Butler, *History of the Second World War*, UK Military Series; Playfair, I.S.O. et al., *The Mediterranean and Middle East*, vol. 3, 359.

58   Total Eighth Army losses were 12,700 killed, wounded, or taken prisoner of war, while the First SA Division lost 164 killed, 253 wounded, and 8 taken prisoner of war. (*Roll of Honour, World War II, 1939–1945*; SANDF Archives, Div Docs 105, File 1 SAD/A2/2: Battle Casualties, July 1–30, 1942.

59   *Official Year Book of the Union of South Africa and of Basutoland, Bechuanaland Protectorate and Swaziland*, no. 23 (1946), 8.

60   *Official Year Book of the Union of South Africa and of Basutoland, Bechuanaland Protectorate and Swaziland*, no. 23 (1946), 9.

61   Orpen, *War in the Desert*, 454–76.

62   *Official Year Book of the Union of South Africa and of Basutoland, Bechuanaland Protectorate and Swaziland*, no. 23 (1946), 9.

63   *Official Year Book of the Union of South Africa and of Basutoland, Bechuanaland Protectorate and Swaziland*, no. 23 (1946), 14, 18.

2

Training the Troops
The Indian Army in Egypt, Eritrea, and Libya, 1940–42

Alan Jeffreys

Introduction

This chapter examines the 'approach to battle,' the battles, and lessons learnt by the Indian Army formations in the North African and East African campaigns, concentrating mainly on the experience of the Fourth Indian Division. For as Lieutenant General Sir Francis 'Gertie' Tuker, commanding the Fourth Indian Division from 1942–44, remarked in his study of the Eighth Army, "If the approach to battle is good, then the battle will be easy."[1] On taking over the Fourth Indian Division, he immediately introduced training instructions to improve the fighting effectiveness of the formation. The Fourth Division produced over forty training instructions in North Africa and Italy, which were in constant use by the formation, learning and integrating their lessons into training.

The Indian Army was the biggest volunteer army during the Second World War. Indian Army divisions fought in the Middle East, North Africa, and Italy, and made up the overwhelming majority of the troops in the Far East. In fact, 2.3 million personnel served in the Indian Armed Forces. India also provided the base for supplies for the Middle East and Southeast Asian theaters. The Fourth, Fifth, and Tenth Indian Divisions all fought in North Africa, with the Fourth Indian Division fighting through almost the entire campaign, first with Western Desert Force (WDF) and then in the Eighth Army. The Eighteenth Indian Infantry Brigade of the Eighth Indian Division was instrumental in the delaying action at Deir al-Shein during the First Battle of El Alamein, and the Third Indian Motor Brigade also fought briefly in North Africa. Indian

31

Army officers such as General Sir Claude Auchinleck, Commander in Chief (C in C) Middle East, and his Chief of General Staff (CGS) Lieutenant General Tom Corbett held important posts in the theater. At the beginning of the Second World War, Indian Army infantry divisions consisted of three brigades: one battalion in each brigade would usually be British and the other two Indian or Gurkha. As Major General Henry 'Taffy' Davies, who commanded the Twenty-Fifth Indian Division, commented in his memoir

> The Division, as all soldiers know, is the basic fighting formation in practically every army in the world. It is large and powerful enough with its establishment of about 17,000 men, to effect a decisive influence in any military operation, irrespective of the scale of the campaign. At the same time, it is sufficiently compact to enable its commander to exercise a personal leadership and control and to permit its functioning as a well coordinated team. In the British Army, during two world wars, the Divisional spirit has been something which has been fostered and nourished as an important matter of principle.[2]

The artillery units in the division were all British with the exception of the Indian Mountain Batteries. The sappers were Indian, as were the signals and other administrative services, with British Non-Commissioned Officers (NCOs) in technical appointments. Indian Army formations shared the same training and organization as the British Army, and therefore regular units could fight alongside British Army units with little disruption. However, unlike Dominion formations in North Africa, the Indian Army had no right of appeal to General Headquarters (GHQ) India, but all Commonwealth formations were responsible for their own training with little direction centrally.[3] In both WDF and the Eighth Army, with the exception of the Fourth Indian Division, most British formations were not given the opportunity to train together.[4]

Battle of Sidi Barrani

Two brigades, the Fifth and Eleventh Indian Brigades of K-4 force, soon to be the Fourth Indian Division, left India for Egypt in 1939. Indian troops quickly adapted to the conditions in North Africa and immediately began training for desert warfare. Training pamphlets were issued and weekly training programs for all units were instigated. Eleventh Infantry Brigade concentrated on collective training whereas the Fifth Brigade embarked on individual training. Collective training was from company up to brigade level whereas individual training involved all ranks concentrating on such matters as weapon training and drill. Troops underwent Tactical Exercises Without Troops (TEWTS); lectures on armored divisions, desert warfare, the Egyptian Army, and the Italian opponents were organized. Exercises in the desert were planned as early as October and November 1939.[5]

The Fourth Indian Division along with the Seventh Armoured Division fought at the Battle of Sidi Barrani. They were designated WDF and commanded by General Richard O'Connor under the overall command of General Archibald Wavell, C in C Middle East.[6] Neither formation was at full strength, with the Seventh Armoured Division consisting of two regiments in its brigades instead of the usual three. The Fourth Indian Division comprised two infantry brigades rather than three and lacked much of its artillery. However, both divisions had trained in the desert as Lieutenant General Sir Geoffrey Evans, brigade major in the Eleventh Indian Infantry Brigade at the time, wrote: "We were sent out into the desert in July 1940. Before and since then our training for desert warfare had been hard and continuous. We were fit, we were tough and we were ready for battle."[7] Niall Barr compares both formations to the British Expeditionary Force of 1914 "in terms of quality, training and expertise."[8]

The Italian forces, the Tenth Army, under the command of Marshal Rodolfo Graziani, had advanced to Sidi Barrani, ninety-six kilometers inside Egypt, on September 13–16, 1940. They were dispersed into fortified camps that were incapable of supporting each other. The plan for Operation Compass was that the Fourth Indian Division would advance through the twenty-four-kilometer gap between the camps at Solfafi and Nibeiwa, and then attack the Italian camps at Nibeiwa, Tummar East, and Tummar West from the rear, supported by the Seventh Armoured Division with artillery support. The Fourth Indian Division Operational Order no. 2, written by Colonel Thomas 'Pete' Rees, general staff officer grade 1 (GSO1) with that division, instructed the artillery to create thick smoke and high explosive (HE) to cover the approaching tanks, keeping their fire on the targets as long as possible.[9] "In short," as the official British historian commented, "quantity was going to be challenged by quality."[10] A replica of Nibeiwa was made in the desert. Exercise no. 1 took place on November 25–26, led by the Fourth Indian Division commanding officer Major General Sir Noel Beresford-Pierse following tactics from the training pamphlet *The Division in the Attack* based on First World War experience.[11] The training included attacks on dummy camps with live artillery and machine-gun fire.[12] Because the exercise was of "the greatest value" and "showed clearly that alterations would have to be made in some tactical methods," it was included in later training, as was true of other methods in the training manual that experience showed to be sound.[13] In training, tanks advanced under artillery cover with the infantry twenty minutes behind. O'Connor and his commanding officers thought the advance was too long-winded, and added a diversionary attack by a battalion on the eastern face of Nibeiwa. Exercise no. 2 was the next planned training that was in fact the actual attack.

On December 9 at 7 a.m., the division having crossed 160 kilometers of desert undetected, the Eleventh Indian Brigade led by Brigadier Reginald Savory, supported by the Seventh Royal Tank Regiment with forty-eight Matildas and the Fourth Indian Divisional Artillery with seventy-two guns, advanced in 'desert formation' that Geoffrey Evans likened to "a large fleet of small ships at sea."[14] The formation slipped through the gap undetected and formed up around Nibeiwa. The diversionary attack on the eastern face led by the Fourth/Seventh Rajput Regiment had begun at 5 a.m. By 7 a.m. the main attack on the camp included an artillery bombardment and tank advance on the northwest entrance followed by the Second Queen's Own Cameron Highlanders and the First/Sixth Rajputana Rifles. The Italian antitank weapons were unable to penetrate the tanks but their artillery fought well. By 10.40 a.m., two thousand prisoners and thirty-five tanks had been taken for a loss of eight officers and forty-eight men.

Brigadier Lloyd, commanding the Fifth Indian Brigade again supported by the Seventh Royal Tank Regiment, attacked Tummar West. The artillery attack was at 1.35 p.m. and twenty tanks attacked at 1.50 p.m., with the First Battalion Royal Fusiliers following twenty minutes later, followed by the Third/First Punjab Regiment. This time, no Italian tanks were met, only artillery. Again the tanks were immune, and took the gun positions with infantry support. They then attacked Tummar East supported by the Fourth/Sixth Rajputana Rifles. The Italians launched a counterattack on Tummar West but were caught by the machine-gun fire of the Rajputana Rifles and the First Battalion Royal Northumberland Fusiliers. There were some four hundred Italian casualties in the ten-minute action. The Sixteenth Brigade and the Eleventh Indian Brigade isolated Sidi Barrani, marking the end of the thirty-six-hour battle.

The battle went according to plan, helped by the fact that soldiers of the WDF were prewar regulars properly trained in the desert in close cooperation with infantry, tanks, and artillery as well as having naval and air support. It showed what could be achieved with good training, intelligence, all arms cooperation (called combined arms at the time), high morale, and the fighting ability of the two regular army divisions at a very early stage of the Second World War. At Sidi Barrani the Italians lost 38,300 prisoners, 237 guns, seventy-three tanks, and more than a thousand vehicles for British losses of 624 killed, wounded, or missing. Training was very important, in particular the training exercise. According to the battle report the exercise "was an excellent full-scale rehearsal for the forthcoming operations."[15]

Other battle lessons included successful secrecy surrounding the operation so that the second training exercise was the real operation, because the operations "were favored by good fortune. Generally speaking, everything went according to plan as far as 4 IND DIV was concerned; the enemy was undoubtedly surprised."[16] Brigadier Savory, commanding Eleventh Indian Infantry Brigade, reported that the victory was due to high morale, the training exercise, reconnaissance, air support, and the importance of night training where he stated: "It is no exaggeration to say that the battalions could work as well by night as by day, either on foot or in M.T."[17]

Battle of Keren

Further experience was gained when the Fourth Indian Division together with the Fifth Indian Division were instrumental in the defeat of another Italian force, at the Battle of Keren. The East African campaign, from July 1940–November 1941, really is a forgotten Second World War campaign. Seventy thousand British, Commonwealth, and Allied forces fought against three hundred thousand Italians. The Allies ultimately captured fifty thousand prisoners, and occupied 932,400 square kilometers at a cost of five hundred casualties and 150 killed.

The Allied forces had some advantages over the enemy, as the Fourth Indian Division had come straight from defeating Italian forces in the Western Desert at the Battle of Sidi Barrani, and the RAF had air superiority. The regular Italian forces were numerically superior, had mules for mountain warfare, and mountain guns; whereas the Indian troops had been mechanized and left their mule companies on the northwest frontier. They were armed with 25-pounders that had low trajectories,

Fig 2.1 Soldiers of the Fourth Indian Division decorate the side of their lorry "Khyber Pass to Hellfire Pass"—the nickname for the strategic al-Halfaya Pass, fortified by the Germans and attacked unsuccessfully by the British during Operation Battleaxe, June 21, 1941. (IWM E 3660)

making them less useful for mountain warfare. Instead of mules, carrying parties needed to be formed, which meant that battalions were depleted by as much as a quarter of their strength. The campaign is important according to Andrew Stewart because "The British Commonwealth forces . . . proved far more adept at overcoming the resulting logistical challenges, showing themselves time and again to be able to move over poor terrain at great speed and keep their opponent uncertain of their strategy."[18] At Keren, in contrast to later campaigns in North Africa, the Indian divisions fought alongside each other, learning from one another, and employed as complete divisions rather than as individual brigades under differing commands.

Operation Battleaxe

After Keren, the Fourth Indian Division was short of men and equipment, and not ready for battle. However, the division was earmarked for Operation Battleaxe. Again they trained for desert as well as night training and also studied German methods and organization.[19] WDF, now commanded by Beresford-Pierse, was to seize the Halfaya passes and secure the Bardia–Sollum–Capuzzo area. Both the Fourth Indian Division and the Seventh Armoured Division needed retraining, reequipping, and reorganization. The plan was for the Armoured Brigade and the Fourth Indian Division (comprising Eleventh Indian Infantry Brigade and Twenty-Second Guards Brigade), to attack the Halfaya–Sollum–Capuzzo–Bardia area on June 12. Fort Capuzzo was captured and defended against German counterattack, and the barracks at Sollum were also captured. But a German attack on June 17 forced Messervy to order a general retreat, a third successive defeat of British and Commonwealth forces by General Rommel. Paddy Griffiths commented that Operation Battleaxe "stands as a classic early example of all those difficulties of reconnaissance, navigation, and terrain analysis that proved such pitfalls for tacticians throughout the whole desert war."[20] There were also problems of inadequate training time—particularly for reinforcements—as when the Second Queen's Own Cameron Highlanders received two hundred reinforcements on June 12, 1941.[21]

Operation Crusader

After the failure of Battleaxe, Wavell, C in C Middle East, was replaced by General Auchinleck, an Indian Army officer who had been C in C India. After much harrying by Winston Churchill, Auchinleck and his army commander, General Alan Cunningham, instigated their first attack on Rommel's forces: Operation Crusader. WDF was replaced by the Eighth Army in September 1941, with WDF HQ becoming XIII Corps comprising the Fourth Indian Division and the Seventh Armoured Division. By October, the Fourth Indian Division was still in XIII Corps along with the Second New Zealand Division and the First Army Tank Brigade. Although the Fourth Indian Division was the most experienced infantry division in the desert, it was depleted after Sidi Barrani, Keren, and Operation Battleaxe.[22] There had been no divisional training since returning from Eritrea. There had been some limited training but most of the time had been taken up with the preparation of defenses. The

Seventh Indian Brigade was the only formation that had actually carried out any formation training.[23] The main objectives of Crusader were the recapture of Cyrenaica and the relief of Tobruk. The Fourth Indian Division's role was to cover the Egyptian border from Sidi Omar to the coast: the Eleventh Indian Infantry Brigade carried out this holding role on the coastal sector but sent patrols out into no man's land to establish ascendancy. The Fourth Indian Division was also meant to cover the advance of the Second New Zealand Division and the Seventh Indian Infantry Brigade attacking the Omars position on November 22. By November 28, the Fourth Indian Division had control of the area up to and including Bardia.

On December 1, the Fourth Indian Division took Omars. However, it was becoming clear that the standard of training within the division was not what it had been. On the night of November 30, the Third/First Punjab Regiment attacked Omars from the north but made limited progress. An account of the Fourth Indian Division's action during Operation Crusader commented

> With a trained and experienced battalion, this attack would in all probability have succeeded; but the battalion, through no fault of its own, lacked training and experienced leaders, with the result that fire was opened prematurely, and the enemy roused.[24]

The Division went on to fight as a complete formation at the battles of al-Gubi and Alam Hamza and then advanced toward Bengazi. The account concluded that the successful actions by the Fourth Indian Division were due to "its high standard of training, and the very intimate teamwork and cooperation existing among all ranks."[25] However, when the division was out of the line for rest and reorganization in late December 1941, a divisional report on operations and training noted that the success of the formation was down to the original standard of training and that it must be reestablished.[26] Thus it can be seen that although the Fourth Indian Division fought well at Crusader, it was becoming apparent that units were not as effective as before due to the lack of time for suitable training. As the Division was more involved, Crusader battles were more important for the Indian Army than El Alamein. Indeed, as Paddy Griffiths concluded, these were an important series of battles that are often overlooked in modern historiography, arguing that "The 'Crusader' battles represented a British victory that in itself was as significant as Second Alamein in late 1942. . . . But the key difference is that in 'Crusader' Eighth Army was unable to sustain its follow-up."[27]

Major General Tuker and the Fourth Indian Division

The arrival of Major General Francis Tuker brought a fresh impetus to training. On December 30, 1941 he took over from Messervy, who was made commanding officer of First Armoured Division. Tuker was one of a small number of Indian Army officers who had taken training seriously in the late 1930s. On taking command of the First Battalion, Second Gurkha Rifles, he instigated a new training regime for the battalion. In a paper on training infantry written in 1934, Tuker remarked that, "All is most certainly not well with the training of our infantryman."[28] Within the battalion he issued training circulars, orders, and instructions, and some of his ideas were absorbed into Indian Army doctrine and published in *AHQ India Training Memorandum no. 17* (1938).[29] The battalion trained for night work, patrolling, and forest fighting. As a result of his thorough training of the battalion, Tuker came to the attention of GHQ India and was made deputy director of staff duties, GSO1 in 1939, and in October 1940 was appointed Director of Military Training (DMT). Under his command the directorate produced a huge number of manuals. Much was based on existing experience: for example, a doctrine was finally produced for internal security with the publication of Military Training Pamphlet (MTP) no. 11 (India), *Notes on Training for Duties in Aid of the Civil Power, 1941*.[30] The directorate also produced new training manuals for Indian Army formations stationed in various parts of the Empire at the beginning of the Second World War. For example, MTP no. 9 (India) on *Forest Warfare*, 1940, was based on Tuker's experience in Assam in 1919, and training with the Second Gurkhas in 1933. It acted as a corrective to Malaya Command's training pamphlet that noted the difficulty of operating in the jungle, and suggested keeping to tracks and roads.[31] As Tuker noted in the DMT's address of September 23, 1941

> It has always been our object on the training side to try and get everybody under one hat. We do not wish this so as to control them but to get their help in order to devise our various tactical doctrines, and in order that they may be able to spread the news abroad whenever we have built up new methods and produced new ideas.[32]

Fig 2.2 Indian patrols: Here a Sikh corporal, a member of an Indian patrol, is wearing his bandolier. (IWM K 3366)

These training pamphlets were not meant to be the last word and were revised in light of further experience.

Tuker conducted a tour of the Middle East in 1941 as DMT, learning valuable lessons and assessing how useful the directorate's material had proved in theater. The Indian troops were regarded as well-trained. He noted that "Training is the main thing that wins battles, for it is the only thing that makes soldiers out of common citizens. GHQ India as a whole has yet to realise this and to realise that we will never reach a standard that is high enough for today."[33] An officer of the Second Queen's Own Cameron Highlanders, whom Tuker interviewed, commented that standards dropped whenever the training had dropped off or was unsuitable, as at Halfaya and Keren respectively.[34]

The Directorate produced Army in India Training Memoranda (AITM), a development of the prewar AHQ Training Memoranda, with the first one appearing in May 1940. The second AITM, published in November 1940, clearly shows the importance of patrolling and 'infiltration' for infantry, a lesson that had repeatedly to be learned in most theaters of war throughout the Second World War. It also showed that training was proving difficult at this early stage of the war due to the large number of inexperienced officers, Viceroy Commissioned Officers, and NCOs in the Indian Army, plus the reorganization, mechanization, and change of tactical methods within it, and the added problem of the further expansion of the army.[35] AITM no. 3 listed all twenty-one War Office MTPs available in 1940, and eight Indian MTPs stating that MTPs (India) "cover special subjects and forms of war, on which no other guidance is readily available."[36] In contrast, the British Army had different series of training pamphlets, including *Current Reports from Overseas*, *Notes from Theatres of War*, and *Army Training Instructions*. None of these seems to have been distributed in India, or even mentioned in the Indian training material, although lessons learned from all theaters including northwest Europe were mentioned in the AITMs. British Army formations were forbidden to issue training instructions, whereas Indian formations in all theaters produced them.[37]

GHQ India concentrated on open warfare for training. One of the first Indian divisions to produce training directives and instructions in the Middle East was the Fifth Indian Division in summer 1941 on its arrival in North Africa from Eritrea where it trained for desert warfare.[38] Training Instruction no. 2 commented that, like mountain warfare, training for the desert "is a specialist job but it is a job that can be learnt, if not mastered, by well trained troops quickly, if training is practical and intense." The instruction had sections on desert navigation, night movement, dispersion, wireless communication, and minefields.[39] The next training instruction was on the all-important role of infantry/tank cooperation in desert warfare.[40] The Division was rushed to Iraq in August 1941. They returned to North Africa when Major General Briggs took over as divisional commander, but he had little time to retrain the division for desert warfare before the defeat at the Gazala Line, and a defending role at Ruweisat Ridge. The formation returned to Iraq in late 1942 and began training for a new role as a mixed infantry and armor division. The Fifth Indian Division issued over ten training instructions and revisions, together with General Briggs' General Officer Commanding (GOC) training directives for this new role.[41]

The Fourth Indian Division issued training instructions when Tuker took over command in December 1941, and he, of course, sent copies back to the DMT India. Indeed, as DMT he had sent copies of all GHQ India training material to Auchinleck as C in C Middle East.[42] Training instruction no. 2, on desert fighting, promulgated drill, tactics, and organization for battle groups, stating "to operate successfully in the manner indicated in this Instruction requires the highest possible training of all arms." The battle groups were organized mainly for defensive operations except for night attacks with battle drills of "simplicity and speed."[43] Tuker regarded the use of 'Jock columns'[44] for all actions as tactically unsound, although useful for harassing the enemy, raiding, or establishing ascendancy in no man's land; but concentration of force was the only way to defeat the enemy: "Concentration as opposed to 'Swanning.'"[45]

Training Instruction no. 3 was based on Tuker's experience with sections on mountain warfare from MTP (India) no. 7, infantry tank cooperation, and night training—all subjects that he had been studying since the 1930s. Theater training materials were adopted as the lessons of Middle East Training Pamphlet no. 5 were assimilated into this training instruction as well as lessons from Crusader. The division now had two months to retrain, in contrast to many British and Commonwealth divisions in North Africa.[46] The last Tuker personally wrote was Training Instruction no. 6, *The Infantry Night Attack on a German Armoured Leaguer*, giving the battle drill for a night attack on an armored leaguer the division could do any time from April 1942 onward.[47] Mine laying and disarming were very important, with at least three early Training Instructions devoted to them.[48]

Tuker's old battalion joined the Fourth Indian Division in April 1942, and Tuker wrote in a confidential note at the end of the war

> By now I had a Goorkha Bn in 7 Bde for I had found when I took over the Division in Jan 42 that the infantry was not up to the standard to which I was accustomed. Frankly, I built the infantry of the Division round that Bn for it had been mine and I had put into it the whole of my knowledge of training and war, and after me, Lovett, a very fine CO, took on my work and brought the Bn to the highest pitch of battle skill I have ever seen. With this new example the standard of British and Indian Infantry in the Division rapidly rose.[49]

Tuker had problems trying to keep his division together under the commands of both Auchinleck and Montgomery. The formation was withdrawn from the desert and split up, one brigade going to Cyprus, one to Palestine, and the third to the Canal Zone, even though the division had trained as an infantry division in a mobile role to work within an armored division for desert warfare.[50] In a letter to Brigadier Glyn Gilbert, commandant of the infantry school, he wrote that "As a Divisional Commander I have always found it a far greater trouble to fight for the keeping in existence of my Division as a Division and then for its equipping and opportunity to train than I have to fight the enemy." On taking command of the Eighth Army, Montgomery had declared that divisions would not be broken up. He had stressed the need for training and for time to be made available for it.[51] Writing to General Sir Alan Hartley, Tuker lamented the breakup of the Indian Army Division

It was the most experienced Div[ision] in Mid[dle]-East and all it needed and asked for was to get out for 2 months *as a Div.*[ision] with about 4500 reinforcements and to train on certain new lines as a result of its experience of last winter's fighting. I asked for this and that we sh[oul]d be back in May for the fighting. You know the result. All our Ind Div[ision]s are fed up and feel a bit humiliated at the break up of their Div[ision]s and their squandering piecemeal. 10 Div[ision] has virtually ceased to exist; 5 Div[ision] has practically none of its art[iller]y left. I'm afraid the prestige of the Indian Div[ision]s has dropped sadly and the sorrow of it is that it wasn't their fault. They were taken from their Div[isional] Com[man]ds and sent here, there and everywhere. They'd no knowledge of this type of fighting. How could they have any? 5 & 10 Div[ision]s hadn't seen the Western Desert and the German armour. Its v.[ery] sad. It's a wearing game trying to get one's Div[ision] together. I've been at it since March. But we *must* do it and we've got to restore the name of the Ind Div[ision]s out here.[52]

Battles of El Alamein

Although Indian Army formations played a much smaller part in the Battles of El Alamein than Operation Crusader, there were important actions by Indian infantry brigades, such as the delaying action at Deir al-Shein by the Eighteenth Indian Infantry Brigade. Deir al-Shein was saucer-shaped, and its choice was largely dictated because it was the only place in the area that it was possible to dig in. It was six kilometers northwest of Ruweisat Ridge, which was solid rock and as a result was important to the defense of the Alamein position. The brigade was unprepared for desert warfare, having arrived from Iraq under the temporary command of Lieutenant Colonel C.E. Gray of Second/Third Gurkhas; the remainder of the brigade consisted of the Second/Fifth Essex Regiment and the Fourth/Eleventh Sikh Regiment. Gray had just spent a year in the Adjutant's Branch, and the Essex battalion and Gurkhas had never been in action. The brigade had not even been trained in the use of the 2-pounder antitank guns.

They spent their first two days digging, wiring, and mining. Only dry rations had been brought and the water allowance was a mere three-quarters of a gallon per day. A defensive 'box' might have been possible had there been time to build it, but the compressors arrived too late to dig emplacements, and the full quota of mines arrived too late to be laid. Three different types of mines were delivered, but often without fuses, as there was no Royal Engineers Officer in charge of issuance. According to Colonel Bamfield, commanding officer (CO) Fourth/Eleventh Sikh Regiment

> Guns did not exist when we first arrived but there were rumours of some coming from various sources. Eventually, the Commander, 121 Field Regiment RA arrived and after a reconnaissance sited the guns we expected. These were eighteen 25-pounders, sixteen 6-pounders and twenty 2-pounders A-tk. There was little time to dig them in and they later suffered accordingly.[53]

The brigade had no signal equipment and was short of ammunition, and the supporting artillery regiments, the Seventy-Ninth and 121st Field Regiments, had been fighting all the way back from Tobruk. The 'box' itself was about 3,650 by 1,820 meters. The brigade took up positions, with the Sikhs on the northwest side, the Essex on the northeast side, and the Gurkhas in a semicircular front of about 5,460 meters on the east, with the Sixty-Sixth Field Company Sappers & Miners holding the southwest. There were gaps in the perimeter due to the lack of mines. There were also four medium machine guns manned by men of the Cheshire Regiment, and seven Matilda tanks with crews from the

Forty-Second Royal Tank Regiment. The 2-pounders were manned by South African units together with personnel from the Welsh Regiment, and the 6-pounders by various units. The Advanced Dressing Station was from Thirty-Second Field Ambulance, and lastly there were some South African sappers with compressors.

On July 1 at 9 a.m. the German shelling began for an hour on the Essex positions and then over the whole box. At 11.15 a.m., two men dressed as British prisoners were sent in to offer surrender terms to the Eighteenth Indian Brigade that were refused. In the afternoon, under the cover of a heavy dust storm, the enemy advanced through the gap in the minefield and formed up behind the Essex and the Gurkhas. This move was followed by twelve Mark IV tanks and some light tanks—of which the Essex antitank guns and 25-pounders destroyed two before surrendering. The tanks moved on toward the Sikhs, where a troop of 2-pounders destroyed two panzers. The tanks destroyed the four remaining 25-pounders. Some of the Sikhs managed to escape, but seven officers and five hundred men were missing. The tanks then attacked the Gurkhas, who withdrew from the position but two companies ran into a tank park. The Gurkhas and the Sikhs were the most heavily hit. The Gurkhas lost twelve officers and 580 men and their CO was captured, and the Sikhs lost three officers and 370 other ranks.

At the same time there was heavy shelling of brigade headquarters, which was overrun by five tanks supported by infantry guns. The brigade CO was injured and the HQ captured, although some did manage to escape. At about 7 p.m. the Battalion HQ of Second/Third Gurkhas evacuated the area. A and C Companies were cut off but also managed to escape through a gap in the area as did the remainder of the brigade, particularly after the diversion created by an Allied bombardment. Most of the survivors managed to get to the El Alamein box. Delayed by the 'fog of war,' support eventually came in the early evening with the Twenty-Second Brigade and its eighteen tanks, and then withdrew after dark. The brigade destroyed eight Panzers for the loss of four tanks. New Zealand's official historian recognized the importance of this delaying action

Contemporary records do not do justice to 18 Brigade. Auchinleck mentions its 'stalwart resistance' and that 'the stand made by the brigade certainly gained valuable time for the organisation of the Alamein

Line generally' (Despatch, p. 364). Post-war revelations of all the facts show that the brigade did much more than this. Tactically and administratively insecure though it was, the brigade fought with a vigour that upset Rommel's battle plan. Just as the fighting in July marked the turn of Allied fortunes in the Middle East, so the action of 18 Brigade on July 1 may be said to have marked the turn of the battle on the Alamein Line. Had Eighth Army been able to avail itself of the opportunity created by the brigade, a crushing defeat might have been imposed on Rommel.[54]

This delaying action meant the destruction of Eighteenth Indian Infantry Brigade; but due to this and similar defensive actions the Afrika Korps suffered significant losses in armor that meant further advance was impossible. Lieutenant Colonel K.F. May (CO Second/Fifth Battalion, Essex Regiment), having escaped captivity, reported that if the Sikhs had fought, the brigade could have broken off the attack under cover of darkness. But due to its lack of acclimatization to desert warfare and training, the brigade was unable to break off from the action and the majority were captured.[55] Jonathan Fennell has recently suggested that at this period, morale was low among all British and Commonwealth forces, including the Indian units.[56]

In contrast, the Fifth Indian Infantry Brigade was a seasoned desert-trained formation. But from June until September the brigade had come under command of the Fifth Indian Division, then the Tenth Indian, back to the Fifth Indian, rejoining the Fourth Indian Division in September. In October 1942 it was to act as reserve to XXX Corps with the Seventh and 161st Brigades to hold the El Alamein position, and was then placed under the command of the Fifty-First Highland Division on November 3–4. The formation's role in Operation Supercharge was to cut a pathway through the enemy minefields south of Tall al-'Aqqaqir. They quickly achieved their objective of the Rahman track that helped the armored divisions pass through, taking 351 prisoners for eighty casualties. On November 7, 1942, the Fourth Indian Division was withdrawn from offensive operations to do battlefield salvage. The Fifth Indian Infantry Brigade had learned from the action, and a training instruction was immediately produced updating the drill for breaking through organized defenses, replacing Training Instruction no. 16, which was not based on experience and too detailed for practical application.[57]

The Fourth Indian Division within the Eighth Army

The Fourth Indian Division continued training after El Alamein. Training Instruction no. 19 on desert movement gave basic formation for brigade groups moving during the day that would be capable of all-round defense against tank attack.[58] The Seventh Indian Infantry Brigade trained accordingly between November and December, with the first week consisting of mobile training, the next couple of days desert movement, and the last few days on a training exercise prepared by GHQ Training Team no. 2 for day and night formations.[59] This resulted in a further divisional instruction on desert movement issued on December 16, 1942 that laid down "the formations that will be adopted by units and Bdes. In order that attached arms can know their relative pos[itio]n in whatever formation they may be working."[60]

With the onset of the Tunisian campaign, Tuker realized that the Division would have to retrain for mountain warfare. He wrote to General Horrocks that the Fourth Indian Division had "more experience than most in this type of warfare," due to service on the northwest frontier and the fighting at Keren.[61] Training in mountain warfare started in January 1943 with the issue of Training Instruction no. 28. It required a "true appreciation of the tactical value of ground and features. It is an art which has become generally rusty as a result of much desert fighting." It needed a high standard of physical fitness and individual training, requiring a high level of junior leadership as "in mountainous countries initial errors are not easy to rectify."[62] The success of this mountain warfare training was demonstrated by the divisional night attacks on the Matmata mountains in March 1943, and the Battle of Wadi Akarit, April 5.[63] But Montgomery did not rate the Fourth Indian Division highly—or the Indian Army generally—and he used them sparingly after he took over command of the Eighth Army.[64] Tuker noted

> Monty disliked Indian Div[ision]s Matmata and Akarit were a shock to him. Akarit w[a]s won by 4 Ind Div and no-one else. We'd licked the Axis army by 0830 hours on 6 April completely and utterly, while other Div[ision]s were still struggling and fighting, and being driven back and attacking again.[65]

After these actions the division joined the First Army for the remainder of the campaign in North Africa. The Fourth Indian Division was hugely successful at Majaz al-Bab with its night approach, mountain warfare experience, and all arms support. Tuker, along with General Allfrey, V Corps commander, accepted General von Arnim's surrender in North Africa.

In addition to infantry training and tactics, the Fourth Indian Division was innovative in its use of supporting artillery. For example, heavy artillery support was used in the second battle for Keren, but as at El Alamein much surprise was lost due to pre-battle ranging and too much rigid control. The Fourth Indian Division counteracted this by giving the Commander Royal Artillery (CRA) his own signal section, whereas other British divisions were still deploying the barrage and dispersion of firepower.[66] After the Tunisian campaign, Tuker was sent to England to lecture to the Army Council, and the CRA, Brigadier H.K. Dimoline, became an instructor at the gunnery school at Larkhill so his methods spread throughout the British and Indian armies. He later became CRA in the Seventh Indian Division in the Burma Campaign in 1945.[67]

Tuker saw the importance of training for a particular type of terrain such as desert or jungle warfare. He wrote to General Sir Alan Hartley, Deputy C in C India

> No formation can come straight into the show and do well. 1st Armd has been written off twice in 12 months. Most of our Indian Bdes from Cyprus and Iraq were written off out here. The fact is that it is a different sort of fighting just as jungle fighting is different. I would not take 4 Div into Malaya or Burma as it is. It would need and I would need at least a months hard training in the jungle with some instructors who know their job.[68]

He also told Hartley that his own defensive system from India had now been adopted in the Middle East tactical schools.[69]

The Indian Army divisions were not the only formations to undergo training programs and issue training instructions. Commonwealth formations did too. The Ninth Australian was a well-trained and battle-hardened division.[70] The Second New Zealand Division trained for six weeks before Crusader, and whereas the First South African Division did not have time to train, the New Zealanders were retraining in September 1942 as nearly all the battalion commanders were new.[71] The Fifty-First Highland Division underwent training exercises and issued training instructions as they had two months to train from September 1942. The Fifty-First Highland

Division Training Instruction no. 2, September 13, 1942, indicated that the division would train for breaking through prepared defenses, night attacks, wireless communication, cooperation with tanks and the RAF, and navigation for desert operations and mobile operations assisted by the Ninth Australian Division.[72] Several historians have stressed the poor level of training of troops for the Middle East, and an informal approach to training with little uniformity of doctrine.[73] This problem was recognized by Auchinleck. When he took over as C in C Middle East, he requested the appointment of a DMT Middle East at major general level, whose main job would be to increase cooperation between armor, artillery, and infantry.[74] Major General John Harding was appointed DMT in January 1942. Auchinleck and Harding also wanted all the training establishments to be concentrated in southern Palestine, just as in India they had been in Southern Command. Harding, summarizing the training situation in the Middle East, recommended setting up a Middle East war school and expansion of the junior staff school, as the tactical training of junior officers was "the most important part of all training and is not, in my opinion, on a satisfactory basis."[75] Noting that time for training time was short, and wartime officers were not at the same standard as prewar regulars, he recommended battle drill to cover the common circumstances of battle. He also recommended units and formations be trained by two training teams in designated areas that could hold a whole division and to go into battle only after inspection by the DMT. Other ideas included the setting up of a senior staff college, and training at all establishments only by instructors with battle experience. The directorate was divided into two sections, as in India, with Military Training 1 (MT1) responsible for training pamphlets, and MT2 in charge of the training schools. Another Indian Army officer, Brigadier Bateman, was appointed first commandant of the Middle East Training Centre (METC). As GSO1 in the Fourth Indian Division he had written and issued training instructions and continued to issue training memoranda for METC.[76] Thus Auchinleck, Harding, and others began the reorganization of training and the issue of training material with a common tactical doctrine for the Middle East theater, before the great trainer, General Montgomery, took over command of the Eighth Army, and immediately issued the Eighth Army Training Memorandum no. 1 on August 30, 1942.[77] Lessons learned from the later battles of El Alamein were published as *Lessons from Operations Oct. and Nov. 1942*, Middle East Training Memorandum no. 7 and distributed army-wide.[78]

As Chris Mann has pointed out, "The Indian Army in its approach to war differed somewhat to the Montgomery dominated British Eighth Army."[79] In Africa, Indian Army formations were more successful when they were employed as a whole division rather than brigades under differing commands. When both the Fourth and the Fifth Indian Division fought and trained together at Keren, the formations had worked well to adapt to the terrain and the tenacious Italian defense, and to overcome being equipped for mechanized rather than mountain warfare. In conclusion, therefore, the Indian Army formations in Egypt, Eritrea, and Libya were most effective when, well . . . trained, as at Sidi Barrani and Keren, and as the Fifth Indian Infantry Brigade was in the breakthrough during Operation Supercharge.

Notes

1   Lieutenant General Sir Francis Tuker, *Approach to Battle* (London: Cassell, 1963), 6, 85, 366.
2   Major General H.L. Davies, "Small Green Men" (unpublished memoir),126, IWM 66/82/1.
3   See Niall Barr, *Pendulum of War: The Three Battles of El Alamein* (London: 2004), 46.
4   See Tim Moreman, "From the Desert Sands to the Burmese Jungle: The Indian Army and the Lessons of North Africa, September 1939–November 1942" in *The Indian Army in Two World Wars*, ed. Kaushik Roy (Leiden: Brill, 2011), 231–32.
5   See Fourth Indian Division Training Conference, October 11, 1939, TNA WO 169/602.
6   As well as Matruh Garrison and Seventh Royal Tank Regiment.
7   Lieutenant General Sir Geoffrey Evans, *The Desert and the Jungle* (London: Kimber, 1962), 11. See also Lieutenant Colonel G.R. Stevens, *Fourth Indian Division* (Toronto: McLaren, nd.), 7, 10, 13.
8   Barr, *Pendulum of War*, 46.
9   Fourth Indian Divisional Operational Order no. 2, *Rees Mss*. Papers of Major General T.W. Rees, OIOC Mss Eur F 274/13.
10   Major General I.S.O. Playfair, *The Mediterranean and Middle East*, vol. 1: *The Early Successes against Italy* (London: HMSO, 1954), 260.
11   See SS 135 *The Division in the Attack—1918*, reprinted as a Strategic Combat Studies Institute Occasional Paper no. 53 (Shrivenham: Strategic and Combat Studies Institute, 2008).
12   See Fourth Indian Division Instructions nos. 1 & 2 for WDF Exercise no. 1, November 1940, TNA, WO 169/602.

13   Middle East Training Pamphlet no. 10, "Lessons of the Cyrenaica Campaign December 1940–February 1941," 3.

14   Evans, *The Desert and the Jungle*, 15.

15   Report on Capture by the Fourth Indian Division of Enemy positions at Nibeiwa, the Tummars, etc south of Sidi Barrani culminating in the capture of Sidi Barrani itself 9, 10, 11 December 1940, 3, *Rees Mss*, Papers of Major General Thomas 'Pete' Rees, OIOC, Mss Eur F 274/13. See also same report TNA, 169/602 and *Bateman Mss.*, Papers of Major General Donald Bateman, IWM, 72/117/2/1.

16   Capture by the Fourth Indian Division of Enemy positions, 28.

17   An Account of the Operations Carried out by the Eleventh Indian Infantry Brigade of the Fourth Indian Division in the Western Desert of Egypt from 6th to 12th Dec. 1940, Appendix—Lessons from the Operation 6–12 December 1940, *Savory Mss.*, Papers of Brigadier Reginald Savory, NAM 7603-93-44.

18   Andrew Stewart, "'Speed and Dash': The British Commonwealth's Campaign in East Africa, 1940–41," *Global War Studies* 7, no. 2 (2010): 161.

19   See the Eleventh Indian Infantry Brigade, Notes on Brigade Commander's Conference, 15 May 1941, TNA, WO 169/5351.

20   Paddy Griffiths, *World War II Desert Tactics* (Oxford: Osprey, 2008), 29.

21   See report by Commander Fourth Indian Division on Operations in the Western Desert, June 15–18, 1941, TNA WO 169/3289.

22   See Michael Carver, *Dilemmas of the Desert War: The Libyan Campaign 1940–1942* (Staplehurst, Kent: Spellmount, 2002), 32.

23   See Account of Operations in Cyrenaica, November 18 to February 28, 1942, 3–4, *Bateman Mss.*, Papers of Major General Donald Bateman, IWM 72/117/2/6; and *Tuker Mss.*, Papers of Lieutenant General Sir Francis Tuker, IWM 71/21/4/5.

24   Account of Operations in Cyrenaica, 22.

25   Account of Operations in Cyrenaica, 90.

26   See Operations & Training, Fourth Indian Division, December 26, 1941, TNA, WO 169/3289. See also Training Note by Brigadier Donald Bateman, January 14, 1942, *Tuker Mss.*, IWM 71/21/2/7.

27   Griffiths, *Desert Tactics*, 42.

28   The Training of Infantry 1934, *Tuker Mss.*, IWM 71/21/2.

29   See AHQ Training Memorandum no. 17: Notes on Individual Training Period 1938, 15–17, *Tuker Mss.*, IWM 71/21/5.

30   See Military Training pamphlet no. 11 (India), Notes on Training for Duties in Aid of the Civil Power, 1941 (Delhi: GSI, 1942), OIOC L/MIL/17/2252. See also Srinath Raghaven, "Protecting the Raj: The Army in India and Internal Security c. 1919–1939" in *Small Wars and Insurgencies* 16, no. 3 (December 2005).

31   See Military Training Pamphlet no. 9 (India), IWM. See Attack on Aihang Village, Assam, May 1918, *Tuker Mss*, IWM, 71/21/2/1, Letter from Tuker to Lieutenant Colonel A.E. Cocksedge, Defence Department, Combined Inter-Services Historical Section, Simla, dated July 26, 1947, *Tuker Mss.*, 71/21/4/5. See also Malaya Command, *Tactical Notes for Malaya* (Malaya, 1940).

32   Director of Military Training's Address, September 23, 1941, 1, *Tuker Mss.*, IWM 71/21/2/5.

33   DMT's tour of the Middle East, Note C, 5–6, *Tuker Mss*. IWM 71/21/2/6.

34   See DMT's tour of the Middle East Note C, 8, *Tuker Mss.*, IWM 71/21/2/6.

35   See AITM (*Army in India Training Memorandum*) no. 2, 17, 25, OIOC L/MIL/17/5/2240.

36   AITM no. 3, 22, OIOC L/MIL/17/5/2240.

37   See ATM no. 25, 16, IWM.

38   See also the Ninth Indian Division in Malaya, who produced two Training Instructions in April 1941, quoted in Tim Moreman, *The Jungle, the Japanese and the British Commonwealth Armies at War, 1941–45: Fighting Methods, Doctrine and Training for Jungle Warfare* (London: Frank Cass, 2005), 21.

39   Fifth Indian Division Training Instruction no. 2, August 19, 1941, TNA WO 169/3301.

40   See the Fifth Indian Division Training Instruction no. 3, "Some Principles Regarding Co-operation between Infantry and 'I' Tanks in Desert Warfare," October 1, 1941, TNA, WO 169/3301.

41   See Fifth Indian Division War Diaries, TNA WO 169/7541 and WO 172/1936. See also Antony Brett-James, *Ball of Fire* (Aldershot: Gale & Polden, 1951), 244–47.

42   See Letter from Auchinleck to Tuker, July 13, 1941, *Tuker Mss.*, IWM 71/21/1/8.

43   Fourth Indian Division Training Instruction no. 2, May 2, 1942, *Tuker Mss.*, IWM 71/21/2/7.

44   Jock columns were offensive all-arms units (except tanks), first organized by Lt. Col. J.C. 'Jock' Campbell, that looked to attack enemy soft-skinned transport.

45   Training, Infantry Tactics, March 27, 1942, TNA CAB 106/776.

46   See Fourth Indian Division Training Instruction no. 3, April 29, 1942, *Tuker Mss.*, IWM 71/21/2/7.

47   See Fourth Indian Division Training Instruction no. 6, June 8, 1942, and a letter from Tuker, January 19, 1961, *Tuker Mss.*, IWM 71/21/2/7.

48   See Fourth Indian Division Training Instruction nos. 4–5, 7, May–June 1942, *Tuker Mss.*, IWM 71/21/2/7.

49   Notes by Major General F.S. Tuker, October 6, 1945, 12, *Tuker Mss.*, IWM 71/21/1/6.

50 See Tuker, *Approach to Battle*, 98–99.

51 Letter to Brigadier Glyn Gilbert, 7 Jan 1967, *Tuker Mss.*, IWM 71/21/2/7 and notes by Tuker for the History of Fourth Indian Division, December 1943, *Tuker Mss.*, IWM 71/21/2/9.

52 Letter to General Sir Alan Hartley, August 27, 1942, *Tuker Mss.*, IWM 71/21/2/9.

53 Major P.C. Bharucha, *Official History of the Indian Armed Forces in the Second World War 1939–1945: The North African Campaign 1940–43* (India & Pakistan Combined Inter-Services Historical Section, 1956), 548.

54 Lieutenant Colonel J.L. Scoullar, *Official History of New Zealand in the Second World War 1939–45: Battle for Egypt: The Summer of 1942* (Wellington: War History Branch, 1955), 159.

55 See Lt. Col. K.E. May, report on action of the Eighteenth Indian Infantry Brigade at Deir al-Shein, July 1, 1942, written April 1, 1944, TNA WO 106/2233.

56 See Jonathan Fennell, *Combat and Morale in the North African Campaign* (Cambridge: Cambridge University Press, 2011), 49.

57 See Fourth Indian Division Training Instruction no. 16, *Tuker Mss.*, IWM 71/21/2/7 and Fifth Indian Infantry Brigade Training Instruction no. 2, November 1942, TNA WO 169/7611.

58 See Fourth Indian Division Training Instruction no. 19, November 12, 1942, *Tuker Mss.*, IWM 71/21/2/7.

59 See Seventh Indian Infantry Brigade, Training Programme Nov–Dec 1942, Training Exercises November 27–29, and Training-Drill for Desert Formation, November 25, 1942, *Holworthy Mss.*, Papers of Major General A.W.W. Holworthy, IWM 91/40/2 AWWH 1/14-16 and AWWH 2/3-4.

60 See Fourth Indian Division Training Instruction no. 25, December 16, 1942, *Tuker Mss.*, IWM 71/21/2/7.

61 Stevens, *Fourth Indian Division*, 201.

62 Fourth Indian Division Training Instruction no. 28, Mountain Warfare, January 16, 1943, TNA WO 169/14735.

63 See Tuker, *Approach to Battle*, 311–32.

64 See Chris Mann, "The Battle of Wadi Akarit, 6 April 1943: Fourth Indian Division and Its Place in 8th Army," in *The Indian Army, 1939–47: Development and Experience*, ed. by Alan Jeffreys and Patrick Rose (Farnham: Ashgate, 2012).

65 Letter to General Sir Alan Hartley, February 21, 1944, *Tuker Mss.*, IWM 71/21/2/9.

66 Royal Artillery—Fourth Indian Division, note by Brigadier H.K. Dimoline, CRA, April 1946, *Tuker Mss.*, IWM, 71/21/2/7.

67 See unpublished biography of Tuker by John Smyth, 40, *Smyth Mss.*, Papers of Major General Sir John Smyth, IWM.

68 Letter to General Sir Alan Hartley, October 16, 1942, *Tuker Mss.*, IWM 71/21/1/3.

69 Letter to General Sir Alan Hartley, October 16, 1942.

70 See Allan Converse, *Armies of Empire: 9th Australian Division and 50th Division in Battle, 1939–1945* (Cambridge: Cambridge University Press, 2011), 101–103.

71 See Fennell, *Combat and Morale*, 225, 238–39.

72 See Fifty-First Division Training Instruction no. 2, September 13, 1942 and Fifty-First Highland Division Training Exercise no. 1, November 26–27, 1942, TNA WO 169/4164. See also Fennell, *Combat and Morale*, 238 and Barr, *Pendulum of War*, 262–64.

73 See Barr, *Pendulum of War*, 50, 157–59, and David French, *Raising Churchill's Armies* (Oxford: Oxford University Press, 2000), 232–35.

74 See letter from Auchinleck to General Alan Brooke, January 15, 1942, *Auchinleck Mss.*, Papers of Field Marshal Sir Claude Auchinleck, John Rylands Special Collections (JRSC), AUC 640.

75 Major General A.F. Harding's Appreciation of Training Situation, February 28, 1942, 2 *Corbett Mss.*, Papers of Lieutenant General Thomas Corbett, Churchill Archives Centre, CORB 4/10.

76 See letter from Auchinleck to Brooke, June 2, 1942, JRSC, AUC 894. See also Despatch on Operations in the Middle East from November 1, 1941 to August 15, 1942, 368–69. TNA WO 32/10160.

77 See Eighth Army Training Memorandum no. 1, August 30, 1942, *Briggs Mss.*, Papers of Major General Raymond Briggs, IWM, 99/1/2/5 and Notes on Five Months as CGS, MEF, *Corbett Mss.*, Churchill Archives Centre CORB 4/16.

78 See *Lessons from Operations* Oct. and Nov. 1942, METM no. 7, IWM.

79 See Mann, "The Battle of Wadi Akarit, 6 April 1943."

3

"The Part We Played in This Show"
Australians and El Alamein

Peter Stanley

U nderstanding the significance of the Battle of El Alamein holds for Australians involves placing the Ninth Australian Division's part in the battle in a broader context, one that will probably be unfamiliar to non-Australian readers.[1] This discussion of El Alamein's importance for Australia therefore necessarily begins a long way from the desert of Egypt.[2]

Australia has a long record of participating in wars, all but two of which have been fought exclusively overseas. (The exceptions are the protracted frontier conflict that accompanied European settlement, which saw fighting in many parts of the continent from 1788, and the Second World War, when Australia itself came under attack briefly in 1942 and 1943.) For the most part, then, Australia has been a part of coalitions presided over by either Britain or the United States. Since a Victorian colonial warship served in New Zealand in 1860, up until the continuing war in Afghanistan, Australia has been a staunch—indeed, an unduly enthusiastic—minor player in larger alliances. This has been the case in several colonial wars (in New Zealand, Sudan, China, and South Africa), in the two world wars (and the war against communist Russia), in wars fought during the Cold War (in Korea, Malaya, Borneo, and Vietnam), and in wars as part of the American alliance (in the Gulf, Iraq, and Afghanistan).

In only two campaigns in those fifteen conflicts might Australia's contribution be regarded as decisive, or even significant. The first was on the western front in 1918, when the Australian Corps played a significant part both in halting the German spring offensive and in advancing to victory in November 1918. The second was arguably the part played by the Ninth Australian Division in the Second (but not the first) Battle of El Alamein, in October 1942. Whether the British Expeditionary Force in 1918 or the Eighth Army in 1942 would have gained victory without their Australian formations remains, of course, hypothetical. But it is certainly justifiable for Australians to regard the contribution of their national contingent in these coalition forces as significant, if not decisive.

Australians continue to be mesmerized by the disaster of the Gallipoli campaign of 1915, in which the Australian Imperial Force lost some eight thousand dead in an eight-month campaign. The anniversary of the initial landing on Gallipoli, April 25, is marked annually by ceremonies of remembrance and a national public holiday. Anzac Day has become the de facto national day, far more popular than Australia Day—January 26—the anniversary of the first permanent British settlement in 1788, a date clouded by the tragic fate of Australia's indigenous peoples. While Anzac Day ostensibly offers an opportunity to remember the dead of all of Australia's wars (or at least its overseas wars—the frontier wars remains largely excluded from commemoration), Gallipoli remains its focus.

The great project of Australia in the twentieth century was to establish a nation and to come to terms with what nationhood meant. The six Australian colonies achieved federation by an act of the British Parliament, forming the Commonwealth of Australia on January 1, 1901. But federation meant only formal or legal nationhood. Through the rest of the century, Australians worked out what nationhood entailed, especially through their relations with Britain. While this gradual recognition and adjustment to the nature of nationhood had constitutional, political, diplomatic, economic, cultural, sporting, and demographic dimensions, Australia's experience in a series of wars decisively challenged, changed, and redefined the relationship between Australia and Britain.

The experience of war altered the relationship between the two from the very first months of the century when (for example) British military authorities executed two Australian officers convicted of murdering civilians in South Africa. Regarding Peter Handcock and Harry 'Breaker' Morant as criminals (rightly: they killed a dozen people between them), British authorities declined to contact the Australian government in advance of their executions, because the two were members of an imperial unit, the Bushveldt Carbineers. While this aroused nationalist angst later in the century, at the time the only condemnation was directed

Fig 3.1 Australian troops occupy front-line position at Tobruk. The garrison comprising Australian, Polish, and British troops was under siege by Rommel's forces from April 1941. (IWM E 4702)

toward the two Australians for so flagrantly breaking the usages of war. The episode is significant because it would in time become a leitmotif for British perfidy in a developing nationalist historiography, and a reminder that Australia's experience of war has increasingly been interpreted in a nationalist framework.[3]

In the Great War, British mishandling of Australian troops aroused unease at the time, beginning with the failed invasion of Gallipoli in 1915. While the dominant tone of public reportage was pride in sharing an imperial campaign, Australian citizen soldiers began to express disquiet at the source of military failure. On the western front, what was seen as costly bungling gave Australians pause: admiration of the British army and its leaders turned to disillusionment. Botched attacks, such as at Fromelles (in July 1916, when a diversionary attack virtually destroyed the Fifth Australian Division) or at Bullecourt (in April 1917, when mistakes cost the Fourth Australian Division dearly), brought Australians to look suspiciously at an imperial power whose army had previously been the subject of unalloyed admiration. That British command failures cost the lives of many more British troops did not signify: such failures fueled the fervent Australian desire in the last year of the war to see Australian formations under the command of Australian generals. The successes of the Australian Corps in the war's final campaigns especially (in which, ironically, they suffered losses comparable with those incurred under British command) gave Australians confidence in their own command. It was to became a preoccupation in Australian military history but, more importantly, also a concern among Australian military officers.[4]

The experience of the Great War imbued the generation of Australian officers who became generals in the Second World War with a determination not to place their forces under the command of British senior officers. When in 1939 a Second Australian Imperial Force (AIF) was formed and dispatched to join imperial forces in the Middle East, its commanders (who had been regimental or staff officers in 1918) were determined not to repeat the errors of the Great War. While a close part of a British imperial military system, and therefore serving under British operational control, they nevertheless insisted on a degree of national autonomy. General Sir Thomas Blamey, a senior staff officer in the Australian Corps in 1918, became the commander of the AIF force sent to the Middle East in 1939. He insisted on taking with him what became known as the AIF Charter: a statement of intent empowering him to refer to the Australian government decisions by British superiors that Blamey considered contravened Australian prerogatives. Blamey's charter explicitly stipulated that "No part of the Force is to be detached or employed apart from the force without his consent."[5] It gave him "the right to disobey his [British] superior in command of the theatre," a right Blamey exercised several times.[6]

The Second AIF soon formed a substantial part of British imperial strength in the Middle East theater. The Sixth Australian Division took part in the capture of Italian Cyrenaica in early 1941, and the failed defense of Greece and Crete in April and May. (Churchill and Wavell duplicitously circumvented Australian attempts to retain discretion in the deployment of Blamey's troops, resulting in Australians being committed

Fig 3.2 Australians and South Africans with distinctive headgear playing cards in gun post. (IWM E 14671)

to a campaign that was likely to fail, and did so, with the loss of six hundred Australian dead and five thousand men captured.) The newly formed Ninth Australian Division, under Major General Leslie Morshead, became the mainstay of the garrison of besieged Tobruk from April 1941 until the Australian government insisted on its weary troops being relieved in the autumn. Again, the division's relief reflected both military and political wariness over the costs of accepting British command without question. The loss of most of the Eighth Australian Division in the surrender of Singapore in 1942 (a disaster feared or foreseen by more acutely nationalist officers in the 1930s) reinforced Australian suspicion that Dominion forces could not necessarily expect that imperial commanders would use them in Australia's best interests.

The war in North Africa gave this climate of mutual incomprehension, suspicion, and occasional hostility free rein. Despite a generally harmonious relationship, in crises clashes between senior Australian officers and their British superiors exposed the differences in understanding and trust between the two. The gulf of sympathy makes the fact of their cooperation on the battlefield of El Alamein all the more impressive.

The protagonists in this British–Australian contest came from equally justifiable positions. From the British point of view, Australian formations, and their commanders, were part of a unified command structure; effectively an empire army. Except for the small metal 'Australia' on their epaulettes, and their tan boots, Australian officers were virtually indistinguishable from the British. They were trained using the same manuals, equipped with the same weapons and vehicles, and often even sounded similar, so much were Australian middle-class officers facsimiles of their imperial counterparts. Integrated as they were into the Eighth Army's command, logistic, medical, and operational structure, Australian units and formations appeared to British commanders and staffs to be interchangeable with their British equivalents.

Australian commanders took a different view, especially those who dealt directly with British superiors—Blamey (until he went home in March 1942) or Morshead (who remained in command after the Ninth Division's relief from Tobruk). While they accepted that the Ninth Division formed part of an integrated imperial army, they reserved the right to appeal to their own government on matters affecting the coherence or well-being of their own force. By the early twenty-first century the coexistence of independent national components in coalition forces—in Bosnia, East Timor, Somalia, Iraq, or Afghanistan, say—is the rule rather than the exception; but seventy years ago the sort of assertiveness that was to disturb imperial relations at El Alamein was both novel and uncomfortable. This uneasy partnership underpins the Australian involvement in the Battles of El Alamein in 1942.

After Churchill sent home the Sixth and Seventh Australian Divisions early in 1942, in order to meet the Japanese advance through southeast Asia, the Ninth Australian Division remained the sole Australian formation in the Middle East. (The circumstances of the transfer of the Sixth and Seventh divisions remain the subject of distorted nationalist myth in Australia, suggesting the power of nationalism as a motive force in Australian

Fig 3.3 Westland Lysander Mark II JVE, 6 Squadron RAF, Ramleh, Egypt, makes low-level 'attack' on Australian infantry during an antiaircraft exercise in the Western Desert. (IWM AUS 143)

historiography. It is widely and popularly believed in Australia still that the divisions were 'recalled' by the Australian Prime Minister John Curtin, and that Churchill attempted to divert one of the convoys carrying them to hold the Japanese advance on Burma, a unilateral action that Curtin resisted, defying both Churchill and Roosevelt. In fact, while Curtin did stand up to the two to insist on the convoy returning to Australia, they had been dispatched from the Middle East at Churchill's order.)[7]

The Ninth Division, recovering and retraining after its time in Tobruk, and positioned in Lebanon and Syria (in case German forces broke out of the Caucasus to advance southward toward Palestine), was called forward to Egypt late in June, when Rommel's forces broke through the Gazala Line and advanced eastward toward El Alamein. The Ninth Division's men were distressed to learn that the fortress of Tobruk, which they had largely held through most of the previous year, had fallen so easily. Allied fortunes were in decline, and the Australians joined the desert army at its lowest point. The division joined the Eighth Army in the first week of July, the first time Australian troops had served in the

Western Desert since the Second/Thirteenth Battalion was relieved at the end of the siege of Tobruk in December 1941.

The 'British' force opposing Rommel was in fact a Commonwealth or an Empire army. The Eighth Army comprised what Rommel described to Hitler as "the finest troops of the British Empire."[8] In July 1942, besides British formations such as the Seventh Armoured and Fiftieth Divisions, it included divisions from India (two), South Africa, New Zealand, and Australia. This mixed force created what its deputy adjutant general judiciously described as its "special problems . . . i.e. mixed forces, mixed races, etc."[9] Its commander, General Claude Auchinleck, found that the Australians, drawing their own conclusions from their experience of Tobruk, were "tending to draw away from us [i.e., the British army] in matters of principle and doctrine."[10] This in itself caused anxiety: the desert campaigns demonstrated that an army lacking cohesion was more easily beaten. In 1941, Auchinleck's apprehension over the Australian government's insistence that its troops be relieved from besieged Tobruk induced him to threaten resignation. In 1942, confrontations with the commander of the Ninth Australian Division threatened his force's cohesion during its most crucial battle. The story within the Australian contribution to the two Battles of El Alamein is the story of dealings between British and Australian commanders and troops, as a significant stage in the long evolution of that relationship through a century of wars.

The Ninth Australian Division joined the Alamein battle just as British, Indian, New Zealand, and South African defenders had halted the eastward advance of the Panzerarmee Afrika around the little desert railway station at the end of the first week of July. Contrary to persistent belief in Australia, the division's arrival did not actually halt the Axis advance, but it did allow Auchinleck to make counterattacks that denied Rommel the initiative and contributed to his giving up attempting a breakthrough.

In the very first days of the July battle, Auchinleck and Morshead clashed over the way in which the Ninth Division would fight. Eager to use the first of the Australian brigades to arrive, Auchinleck wanted to send it forward to operate independently of the rest of the division, which was still in convoys stretching back toward the Nile Delta. Morshead confronted Auchinleck, telling him that he could not use the brigade in this way. "Why?" asked Auchinleck. "Because," Morshead replied, invoking the AIF charter bequeathed by Blamey, "they are going to fight as a formation with the rest of the division." "Not if I give you orders?"

Auchinleck countered. "Give me the orders and you'll see," said Morshead, calling his superior's bluff. Auchinleck's angry reply was to observe that Morshead was "being like Blamey. You're wearing his mantle."[11] In the event, given the gravity of the situation before El Alamein, the two compromised. Auchinleck gained the use of the Twenty-Fourth Brigade alone, but on the strict understanding that the loan was temporary. The argument was no isolated event. Two days later Morshead intervened to prevent his brigade being used in an attack Morshead thought unjustified, while in the following week his British corps commander, Lieutenant General William Ramsden, twice complained to Auchinleck that Morshead had objected to him using Australian troops as he wished.[12]

In the July battle, Australian brigades halted further German attacks (notably at Tall al-Eisa) and made successive attacks on Axis-held ridges—some startlingly successful, others disastrous. The Australian contribution to the July battle was arguably critical. The seizure by the Australian Twenty-Sixth Brigade of the Point 26-Trig 33 ridge on July 10 was later seen as the hinge of more than just Auchinleck's holding battle against Rommel. The verdict of the writer of the Australian official history volume (himself a Ninth Division officer) was that the event was "the turning point in Africa"—indeed of the western allies' war against Germany.[13] But it was not just an Australian judgment on an Australian success. As Auchinleck's chief of staff, Eric Dorman-Smith, wrote, the July 10 attack delivered "a shattering, and almost decisive blow."[14] But only 'almost decisive': the Eighth Army lacked the ability to convert local successes into victory.

Throughout the three weeks of fighting, relations between Australian and British formations remained tense. Though obliged to cooperate (all of the Eighth Army's armor and much of its artillery was British, as was most of the supporting Desert Air Force) operational arrangements repeatedly broke down. Cooperation between British tank units and Australian infantry especially became fraught. Lieutenant General William Ramsden again complained of Morshead's "bloody-mindedness" when Morshead passed on his men's lack of confidence in British armored units.[15] Auchinleck's response was to invite the two to tea. Morshead was mollified, but the subsequent British–Australian infantry attack on 'Ruin' (also Mitiriya) Ridge on July 26–27 failed, partly because of the plan's complexity, but partly because cooperation with British armor foundered yet again. Such disasters fueled misunderstandings and resentments that prevented British and Dominion commanders cooperating effectively. A line in a letter from Auchinleck to Allanbrooke reveals the unconscious British condescension in late July. Complaining that some Dominion officers "say quite openly that we are incompetent," he dismissed their strictures with "the enemy has his 'Wops' to contend with, so the difficulties are not all on our side!"[16]

Fighting a determined and skillful enemy, whom he just held in a series of scrappy fights, Auchinleck had been frustrated that his Dominion subordinate commanders repeatedly questioned or opposed his orders. Nor was Morshead his only 'difficult' subordinate. South Africa's Dan Pienaar and New Zealand's Bernard Freyberg also contested his decisions. The disagreements exposed a rift between tactical and national understandings. Auchinleck, like all commanders in the Desert War, recognized that the brigade had become "the real tactical unit" in the desert.[17] But his desire to employ brigades flexibly and interchangeably ran up against the Dominions' wish for national cohesion and autonomous command. Auchinleck complained of how it was "damnably difficult to get any real flexibility" because of "the impossibility of detaching subordinate Dominion formations" where they were needed operationally.[18] While the Eighth Army's component forces cooperated imperfectly in the July fighting, by the time it opened the offensive battle in October, under a new commander, that relationship had been transformed.

While the Australian part in the July fighting had generated friction between the two, the October fighting saw much greater cooperation and harmony. This reflected both the new spirit that Bernard Montgomery infused into the Eighth Army, but also determined efforts by both protagonists to rectify the relationship. Montgomery, who replaced Auchinleck in mid-August, deliberately fostered a more cohesive ethos. His adoption of an Australian slouch hat, festooned with badges of units from most of his national contingents, exemplifies the change. (Montgomery, who had grown up in Tasmania, claimed an Australian hat as a right. The hat is today on display in the Australian War Memorial museum in Canberra, captioned to remind Australian visitors of the Eighth Army's multinational character.[19]) Morshead, impressed with Montgomery and his talk of winning, told one of his brigadiers "things are going to be different." (But Australian gunners thought their new general "a prize galah" for wearing a slouch hat "jammed down on top of his head," and British officers, appalled at the sight of their general in a slouch hat, persuaded him

Fig 3.4 Men of the Fifty-First Highland Division ('The Ladies from Hell') charging with fixed bayonets during training practice in the desert, September 23, 1942. (IWM E 17348)

to adopt the famous beret.[20]) Regardless of what Montgomery said or what hat he wore, it was what he did to the Eighth Army's confidence, competence, and cohesion that mattered.

That relations between Australians and British troops would be better is indicated by the way in which British formations new to the desert were 'fostered' or 'affiliated' by experienced Dominion divisions. Morshead's units looked after Major General Douglas Wimberley's Fifty-First (Highland) Division, an encounter that exposed the contrasting command styles and military culture of the two forces. While grateful for the Australians' advice as "efficient and helpful mentors," Wimberley felt constrained to point out to his commanders that though their Scotsmen had learned a great many practical skills from their hosts, he hoped that

Fig 3.5 Australian reinforcements arriving at the battle front, greeted by British troops. (IWM E 1403)

they would not emulate the Australians' more casual approach to discipline. But while the ways of each took "a bit of getting used to," the effect of the affiliation was to strengthen the relationship between the two.[21] Even more importantly, Australian infantry mingled with British armored units, and the misunderstanding and animosity of the July fight gave way to a more positive collaboration.

On October 23, Morshead's division held the crucial coastal sector of the Eighth Army's line, and it became the 'hinge' on which Montgomery's plans for the battle swung. The Ninth Division attacked on the evening of October 23 and remained in action for a further twelve days. It bore the brunt of further advances and repeated German counterattacks, as

Montgomery wore out the German strength in the north while preparing for an armored breakthrough in the south.[22] The battle cost the Eighth Army some 2,350 dead, with others 'missing.' The bulk of the casualties—almost 60 percent—were in proportion to those suffered by British formations. But the Ninth Australian Division, one of eleven in the Eighth Army, suffered 20 percent casualties.

The sites of the Ninth Division's fights—Trig 29, the Fig Orchard, Thompson's Post, the Blockhouse, the Saucer, Barrel Hill, Ring Contour 25—did not become household names in Australia. Virtually none of them are known now outside of the thinning ranks of veterans and a small band of operational military historians. Australians generally have a hazy idea of El Alamein's location and significance. In Melbourne it is the name of a railway line, and the connection with the battle is tenuous; Sydney has an El Alamein memorial fountain in King's Cross, but the place is more associated with the war on drugs than the war against Nazism. Extraordinarily, even some of the individual record cards in the national Roll of Honour held at the Australian War Memorial still read "El Alamein, Libya."[23]

Even at the time, and even though El Alamein represented the only place where troops of the western Allies faced German troops in battle, Australians had expressed reservations about the use of their troops in this place against this enemy. Private John Butler of the Second/Twenty-Third Battalion recorded in his diary his belief that his unit would soon enter the fight. Butler, a British migrant, also wrote that he thought that this would be "against the wish of Australia," surmising that Australians would prefer the Ninth Division to be returned to Australia to face the seeming Japanese threat against it.[24] Private Butler was more prescient than he knew. The Australian prime minister John Curtin, at the urging of the American supreme commander of the Southwest Pacific area, General Douglas MacArthur, had already asked Churchill to agree to return the division. Rebuffed in May, Curtin reiterated his request in July, August, September, and October. MacArthur's machinations and Curtin's representations eventually bore fruit, and the Ninth Division left the Eighth Army early in 1943. Whether it was sensible to retrain a division experienced in fighting Germans equipped with tanks in the desert to fight Japanese infantry in tropical jungle remains debatable. Certainly on the eve of D-day in 1944, Montgomery wished he had been able to bring the Ninth Division with him from North Africa to Italy and on to Normandy, as he did the Seventh Armoured, Fiftieth, and Fifty-First (Highland) divisions.

The Ninth Division's contribution to the victory at El Alamein in October and November 1942 was undoubtedly critical. Senior British officers generously acknowledged its contribution. Oliver Leese, in a private message to Leslie Morshead, wrote that he was "quite certain that this breakthrough was only made possible by the homeric [sic] fighting over your Divisional sector." (Morshead, knowing of the power of such praise, published the compliment in unit orders.[25]) Perhaps the greatest compliments came from senior British commanders. Just before Christmas 1942, the Ninth Division's survivors paraded at an airstrip at Gaza, in Palestine, where the commander in chief in the Mediterranean, Field Marshal Earl Alexander, addressed them. Ninth Division veterans cherished Alexander's farewell address, in which he spoke glowingly of their part in the battle ("the Battle of Alamein has made history, and you are in the proud position of having taken a great part in that great victory"). Alexander assured the assembled ranks that there was "one thought I shall cherish above all others—under my command fought the Ninth Australian Division." Arguably, as Mark Johnson and I suggest in *Alamein: The Australian Story*, some men present may not have realized that the Eighth Army came under Alexander's command. Had the address been delivered by Montgomery (by then far to the west, pursuing the defeated Panzerarmee in Libya) perhaps the effect might have been greater. "As it was," we wrote, "Alexander's presence at Gaza arguably began the slide from Australian consciousness that has gradually occurred."[26]

El Alamein's gradual eclipse was not, of course, just Alexander's fault. It began because it coincided with campaigns closer to Australia that were seen at the time as more important and have, if anything, grown in retrospect. The fighting against Japanese forces invading Australian New Guinea in 1942 has always tended to dominate Australian remembrance of the Second World War. The two Battles of El Alamein, between July and November 1942, almost exactly matched the duration of the Kokoda campaign in Papua. Japanese troops landed at Gona on July 21, and the village of Kokoda was liberated on November 2. 'Kokoda' remains a much more potent word in Australian memory than does 'Alamein.' Indeed, for every book published on El Alamein in Australia there must be at least four dealing with the Papuan campaign.[27] For all that El Alamein cost more Australian lives, identified and articulated an Australian stance in relation to a major ally, and, not least, decisively influenced a battle regarded as a turning point of the war (at least in North Africa), El Alamein remains under-acknowledged in Australia.[28]

In the aftermath of the battle, all Australian troops were invited to write to their families through an 'airgraph' service that would deliver messages by microfilming standard forms. A Victorian gunner wrote to his mother in Gippsland, asking, "I guess you have heard about the part we played in this show?"[29] She certainly would have, grateful that he had survived the largest battle Australians fought in the Second World War and hopeful that he might soon be returning home. No one can be confident of that question being answered positively today. Given the contribution the Ninth Division made to the outcome of the battle, the casualties it incurred in doing so, and the plaudits men attracted at the time, Australia's effacement of regard of 'the part we played in this show' is ironic and profoundly sad.

Notes

1   Peter Stanley is a prolific war historian. His recent work includes *Bad Characters: Sex, Crime, Mutiny, Murder and the Australian Imperial Force* (2010) and *Digger Smith and Australia's Great War* (2010). He is involved in several projects marking the centenary of the Great War, 2014–18.

2   This essay is based largely on research conducted for Mark Johnston and Peter Stanley, *Alamein: The Australian Story* (Melbourne: Oxford University Press, 2002 repr. 2006).

3   While Australian historiography is increasingly dominated by an unquestioning nationalism, it is hard to find examples that demonstrate where El Alamein and the AIF's service in the war in North Africa fit within it. El Alamein itself is given the briefest of mentions when it is not ignored. This contrasts with the treatment of both the war in the Southwest Pacific (which is of course dealt with in detail) but also with the 1941 siege of Tobruk, when the Australian government's determination to withdraw its force from the besieged fortress is portrayed approvingly.

4   For an examination of the high standing of the British Army in Australia before 1915, see Craig Wilcox's *Red Coat Dreaming: How Colonial Australia Embraced the British Army* (Melbourne: Cambridge University Press, 2009).

5   Gavin Long, *To Benghazi* [vol. 1, Series 1 (Army) of the official history *Australia in the War of 1939–1945*] (Canberra: Australian War Memorial, 1961), 100–101.

6   John Robertson, *Australia at War 1939–1945* (Melbourne: William Heinemann, 1981), 29.

7   For a discussion of the facts and the myths of this episode, see Peter Stan-
     ley, *Invading Australia: Japan and the Battle for Australia, 1942* (Melbourne:
     Penguin, 2008), 136–39.
8   Basil Liddell Hart, *The Rommel Papers* (London: Hamlyn, 1953), 289.
9   Syllabus, GHQ, Middle East, Military Training Branch, War Diary, TNA
     WO 169/3901.
10   Auchinleck to Dill, October 13, 1941, Auchinleck Papers, 377, John
     Rylands Library, Manchester, UK.
11   Barton Maughan, *Tobruk and El Alamein* [vol. 3, Series 1 (Army) of the offi-
     cial history *Australia in the War of 1939–1945*] (Canberra: Australian War
     Memorial, 1966), 552.
12   David Horner, *High Command: Australia and Allied Strategy 1939–1945*
     (Sydney: Allen & Unwin, 1982), 282–83.
13   Barton Maughan, introduction to Everard Baillieu, *Both Sides of the Hill:
     The Capture of Company 621, a German Wireless Intercept Unit by the Sea near
     Tel el Eisa, Egypt 10 July 1942* (Melbourne: Second/Twenty-Fourth Battal-
     ion Association, 1985), ix. Maughan was able to acknowledge in 1985—as
     he had not been in 1968—that the capture of Company 621 helped divulge
     German coded communications.
14   Eric Dorman-Smith, "Alamein—July 1st–July 17th: The Decisive Battle,"
     O'Gowan Papers, GOW1/2/17, John Rylands Library, Manchester, UK.
15   Corelli Barnett, *The Desert Generals* (London: Kimber, 1960), 212–13.
16   Auchinleck to Brooke, July 25, 1942, Allanbrooke Papers, 6/2/12, Liddell
     Hart Centre for Military Archives.
17   Auchinleck to Brooke, 12 January 1942, Allanbrooke Papers, 6/2/12, Lid-
     dell Hart Centre for Military Archives.
18   Auchinleck to Brooke, July 25, 1942, Allanbrooke Papers, 6/2/12, Liddell
     Hart Centre for Military Archives.
19   "Australian Army Slouch Hat: Lieutenant General B.L. Montgomery, Eighth
     Army," RELAWM30701. I can testify to the intent of the caption, because I
     wrote it when curating the Memorial's Second World War gallery in 1999.
20   Fred Majdalany, *The Battle of El Alamein: Fortress in the Sand* (London: Wei-
     denfeld and Nicolson, 1965), 37; David Goodhart, *We of the Turning Tide*
     (Adelaide: F.W. Preece, 1947), p. 109. For details of the British officers'
     coup in divesting Montgomery of the slouch hat, see Johnston and Stanley,
     Alamein: The Australian Story, 129.
21   Memoirs of Major General D.N. Wimberley, p. 30, PP/MCR/182, Impe-
     rial War Museum.
22   For detailed accounts of the Australian part in the battle, see Mark John-
     ston and Peter Stanley, *Alamein: The Australian Story*, and Mark Johnston,
     *That Magnificent 9th: An Illustrated History of the 9th Australian Division,
     1940–46* (Sydney: Allen & Unwin, 2002).

23 See, for example, a random selection of cards in the Roll of Honour (www.awm.gov.au) that disclose that Captain Wilton Cobb, Second/Fifteenth Battalion, Private Joseph Cheong, Second/Twenty-Fourth Battalion, Private Leslie Dawson, Second/Seventeenth Battalion, or Private Norman Talintyre, Second/Twenty-Third Battalion—all of whom died in the opening attack on October 23, 1942—are all recorded as having died in "Libya," an error that has gone uncorrected since 1942.

24 Diary, July 9, 1942, Pte John Butler, 3 DRL 3825, Australian War Memorial.

25 Leese to Morshead, November 6, 1942, Appendix H to 9 Aust Div Report on Operations Alamein, CAB 106/777, The National Archives, UK.

26 Mark Johnston and Peter Stanley, *Alamein: The Australian Story*, 268.

27 The National Library of Australia's catalog suggests that it holds ninety-eight books with "Kokoda" in the title, almost all published in Australia, and twenty-four with "Alamein," many of which have been published overseas.

28 This relative ignorance or disregard has arguably intensified in the decade since our *Alamein: The Australian Story* was first published, in 2002. In the meantime, revisionist partisans have constructed a saga of 'the Battle for Australia,' exaggerating Japanese operations against or near Australia to claim that Australia had been their main objective. See my *Invading Australia* for a critique of this new interpretation.

29 Airgraph 3288, ORME0077, Reel 1, Australian War Memorial.

4

"No Model Campaign"
The Second New Zealand Division and the Battle of El Alamein, October–December 1942

Glyn Harper

On the evening of October 23, 1942, just after 2200h, as the first enemy artillery rounds passed over his forward headquarters, Lieutenant General Bernard Freyberg, General Officer Commanding (GOC) of the Second New Zealand Division, received news that the "Infantry are off—both bdes [brigades] are away to a good start." General Freyberg turned to his G1, the principal staff officer, and remarked

> If there was ever justice in a cause this is it. I don't think the Itys will stick it and I don't think the Boche will either—they didn't in the last war. . . . Auchinleck could have won the war by putting in Blamey instead of Ritchie. Mind you this is going to be a stiff fight.[1]

Freyberg was right. The Eighth Army did have a stiff fight ahead in what would be a turning-point battle in the North African campaign. The New Zealanders, like their Dominion brethren from Australia and South Africa, played a key role in defeating the Axis forces during this battle. Freyberg was right in that the Italians and Germans on the Alamein position could not "stick it" against the weight of manpower and matériel wielded against them by an army commander who demonstrated considerable skill in their use. But while this Second Battle of El Alamein has been praised by some commentators as a great and important victory, the pursuit of the defeated Axis forces after the battle, especially the famed Afrika Korps, has attracted less attention but considerable criticism. In the immediate aftermath of the Alamein battle the New Zealanders again played a key role.

The Hard Road to El Alamein

In October 1942, the Second New Zealand Division was an experienced, battle-hardened formation with an impressive reputation. But this experience had been hard won through a series of costly defeats and limited successes. The division's war had started poorly with the two disasters of Greece and Crete. This had been followed by its first military 'success' in Operation Crusader in November 1941, a success that cost the Second New Zealand Division more casualties than its two previous military disasters: some 4,620 men and its heaviest casualty toll of the war.[2] The New Zealanders then moved to garrison duty in Syria, at Freyberg's request. Freyberg was anxious to have his division away from the Eighth Army and a commander whose doctrine of dispersion of formations into 'Jock columns' and brigade groups was "a menace and a danger both in attack and defence."[3] How much of a menace and danger was revealed when the Second New Zealand Division was rushed back to Egypt in June 1942 to help stem Rommel's latest advance. Abandoned by neighboring formations, the Second New Zealand Division was left isolated on the Minqar Qaim escarpment where it was quickly surrounded by the Afrika Korps, and Freyberg was seriously wounded. Only a daring night breakout prevented its capture, leaving a disappointed Rommel to lament

> Unfortunately, the New Zealanders under Freyberg had escaped. This division, with which we had already become acquainted back in 1941–42, was among the elite of the British Army, and I should have been very much happier if it had been safely tucked away in our prison camps instead of still facing us.[4]

Two further disasters followed Minqar Qaim. In July 1942, New Zealand infantry captured two key objectives in the southern sector of the El Alamein Line. These were part of Ruweisat Ridge and al-Mreir Depression. On both occasions, armored protection that had been promised failed to materialize and the isolated, vulnerable infantry were soon overrun by Axis tanks. The New Zealand brigadier Howard Kippenberger later described Ruweisat Ridge as "a tragedy of misdirection and mismanagement."[5] In a letter to his wife he complained that things were not being done right in the Eighth Army; that his wife could have run the Ruweisat battle better than General W.H.E. 'Strafer' Gott, and that General Claude Auchinleck was more like a sergeant major than a general.[6]

Fig 4.1 A machine gun post in a rocky part of the Allied positions in the Alamein area. (IWM E 014536)

Unfortunately Kippenberger's letter was intercepted by the British censor and passed to Auchinleck. Kippenberger was soon in hot water, as Freyberg was informed that the letter "shows a complete disregard of censorship regulations and discloses information that might be of value to the enemy if it fell into the wrong hands."[7] The constant failure of British armor to coordinate their actions with the infantry left a legacy of "a most intense distrust, almost hatred of our armour," recalled Kippenberger.[8]

The situation improved with the arrival of generals Harold Alexander and Bernard Montgomery to take command of the allied campaign in North Africa. Montgomery was something of an unknown quantity. Prior to his arrival, Kippenberger was informed by his 'unenthusiastic' English friends that Montgomery "was understood to be mad and . . . that he would certainly get rid of some dead wood."[9] His first meeting with Montgomery left Kippenberger "feeling very much stimulated,"[10] while Freyberg was especially pleased to learn from Montgomery that the "mania for breaking up military organisations" was over.[11]

Montgomery's first encounter with Rommel in the battle of Alam al-Halfa at the end of August 1942 was a considerable success, thanks primarily to Ultra intelligence decryptions and the efforts of the Desert Air Force. A counterattack launched by the Eighth Army against the flank of a faltering Axis force, which used a New Zealand and a British infantry brigade, was again poorly coordinated and costly for those infantry taking part. Its failure convinced Montgomery that his army needed more time and intense training before he could launch his own offensive.

Before looking at the Second New Zealand Division's role in the October battle, one point needs to be stressed. The year 1942 had been a long, tough campaign for the New Zealanders with several disasters and heavy casualties. Since November 1941 and continuing into early 1943, the Division had not received a single reinforcement because of New Zealand's commitments elsewhere. As a result, Second New Zealand Division was desperately short of infantry and "incapable of fighting a sustained action."[12] All its infantry battalions were about half their nominal strength. Freyberg noted in his diary three days before the attack: "Men in good form—our trouble is we are short of men now—weapons all right—guns and tanks must do what infantry have done before."[13] The New Zealand Division had been allocated key roles in the battle ahead and would be taxed to its limits to achieve them.

Mitiriya Ridge

Prior to the El Alamein attack on October 23, 1942, the Second New Zealand Division commenced an intensive period of hard training. Attached to it was the Ninth Armoured Brigade, as one of its infantry brigades was in the process of converting to an armored formation. Additional regiments of field and medium artillery were also added to the division.

The training was very tough, and the live firing exercises used on many occasions resulted in some casualties. As Kippenberger later commented about this training, "It was not going to be easy and we spared no pains. I have never worked or thought harder than in these weeks, nor have I ever worked troops so hard; and all commanders and staff did the same."[14] This training culminated with a full-scale divisional rehearsal under conditions as similar as possible to the actual attack it would carry out later to capture Mitiriya Ridge. During moonlight on September 26, the simulated attack involved the infantry brigades 'laying up' during the day and crossing live minefields under an artillery barrage. At long last the New Zealand Division (and the Eighth Army) was tailoring its training exercises to the plan of attack. It was to make a critical difference.

More than just training occurred. Freyberg, now back in command and still recovering from recent wounding at Minqar Qaim, made every effort to fully integrate the British Ninth Armoured Brigade, with its new Sherman and obsolete Crusader tanks, into the New Zealand Division. Each infantry brigade carried out brigade and battalion exercises with the armored regiments, and social events were held at which officers of all brigades mixed freely. The regiments of the Ninth Armoured Brigade put the New Zealand Division's distinctive fern-leaf emblem on their tanks, mixed ceremonial parades were held, and joint exercises and tactical exercises without troops were conducted. Before the battle commenced, Freyberg assured the New Zealand government that the New Zealand Division with its three tank regiments was now "more powerful than a Panzer Division" and said that the days of New Zealand infantry being overrun by enemy armor "are I hope past."[15] Kippenberger recalled after the war that while the New Zealanders were only "moderately confident of much better things" from the British armor before El Alamein, they had "complete and justified confidence" in the Ninth Armoured Brigade.[16] Rommel was under no illusions about what lay ahead, and he expected the Australians and New Zealanders to play a key role in the attack. He wrote prior to El Alamein

> the British would first have to try for a break-through. We had no doubts about the suitability of the British Army for such a task, for its entire training had been based on the lessons learnt in the battles of material of the First World War. In this form of action the full value of the excellent Australian and New Zealand infantry would be realized and the British artillery would have its effect.[17]

Writing to his wife on the eve of the battle, the commander of the 'excellent' Australian infantry, Lieutenant General Sir Leslie Morshead, accurately predicted

> A hard fight is expected, and it will no doubt last a long time. We have no illusions about that. But we shall win and I trust put an end to this running forward and backward to and from Benghazi. It is the supreme effort to finish this war in North Africa, and if successful as we feel it will be, it should have a material influence on the war.[18]

Fig 4.2 Lieutenant General Freyberg and Brigadier Kippenberger in the desert on the Alamein Line, August 1942. The scars left by the wound Freyberg received at Minqar Qaim in June 1942 are still clearly visible. Reproduced with kind permission of Glyn Harper.

Kippenberger made a similarly prescient statement to Angus Ross, the adjutant of the Twenty-Third Battalion, at about the same time Morshead was writing his letter, "You know Angus, when the history of the Second World War comes to be written this night of 23–4 Ocober will be seen as the very beginning of the turning of the tide. We are privileged people to be here tonight."[19] The objective the New Zealanders were expected to seize was Mitiriya Ridge, the scene of an Australian disaster the previous July, and a key feature of the Alamein position. Freyberg believed that this battle, unlike previous ones during the desert campaign, "approximates the battles fought in 1918," and he turned to the techniques developed in that war to plan the New Zealand attack.[20] Of the attacking infantry divisions on the night of October 23, 1942, the Second New Zealand Division was alone in using a quarter of its 104 guns to provide a creeping barrage for the infantry to 'lean on' during their advance, while the rest of its artillery fired concentrations on known strong points. There is some debate as to how effective the creeping barrage was, although its effect on morale was high. The New Zealand official historian of the divisional artillery wrote that a creeping barrage, when combined with counterbattery concentrations, were the "correct artillery tactics" but that the number of guns was "too few to be fully effective."[21] Lieutenant General Sir Francis Tuker was blunt in his assessment of the use of artillery at the second El Alamein battle. He described the creeping barrage as "wasteful" and believed that the dispersion of the artillery effort prolonged the outcome of the battle.[22]

On the right of the New Zealand sector, the Fifth Brigade was to advance 6,400 meters while the Sixth Brigade on their left advanced 4,570 meters. This would bring both brigades to their final objective, Mitiriya Ridge, which they were to hold in equal portions. Once the two brigades were established on the ridge, the support weapons and Armoured Brigade were to move forward to join them, the latter to take up defensive positions in front of the infantry. Freyberg noted that the "Armoured COs were full of confidence and very cheerful—maybe they will be 'sadder and wiser' men but it is good to see them in such fine form."[23] Freyberg, an old warrior, knew the cost of what lay ahead.

Each brigade had decided to take its first objective with only one battalion, and then push through two more battalions onto the final objective of Mitiriya Ridge. The Twenty-Eighth Maori Battalion was allocated to 'mop up' any opposition in both brigade areas—an important role given what had occurred at Ruweisat Ridge, but one they felt demeaned their status. A recent history of the battalion records this frustration

> It is difficult to determine or understand why the Maori were left out of the main attack. Their pre-eminence in attack and their outstanding ability to capture their objective was indisputable. Perhaps their failure to obey orders at Munassib the previous month may have worried Kippenberger.[24]

On the eve of the attack, Kippenberger delivered a stirring piece of oratory to the Twenty-Third Battalion, who were keyed up for action

> I told them that this was the turn of the war and the greatest moment of their lives: they had the duty and the honour of breaking in, on which everything depended; our hats were in the ring and I expected them to do it, whatever the cost. 'Reg' [the Commanding Officer], called the men to their feet and they gave three fierce, thunderous cheers. As I went away someone remarked that our first objective was as good as taken.[25]

The decision to use the 'fiery' Reg (Lt. Col. Reginald Everard Romans) and his most reliable battalion in the initial advance nearly caused disaster. Romans's battalion easily carried the first objective, but dissatisfied at the scanty resistance and unsure as to whether they had reached the objective (those counting the paces were dead or wounded), they pushed on. In the words of their adjutant: "But there was no standing barrage. Reg and I discussed it and we agreed that we hadn't seen anything like the fighting that the break-in battalion had every right to expect. Reg said 'Push on! Push on!' and so we went on to take what we thought was our objective."[26] It was, in fact, Mitiriya Ridge, the brigade's final objective.

Meanwhile, Kippenberger and Brigade HQ had been driven frantic trying to locate or contact the Twenty-Third Battalion. The brigade's war diary contains repeated references to the battalion's disappearance: "Still NO report from 23 Bn." An entry made as late as 0115h on October 24 recorded: "Capt Coop reported he had been right up to barrage and could NOT find 23 Bn. Presumed 23 Bn ahead of the barrage."[27] Word was finally received of the battalion's actions at 0235h, when its adjutant reported to Brigade Headquarters.[28] Little wonder that he received "a rather frosty reception" from Kippenberger, and the blunt instruction: "You go back and tell Reg to pull back to his proper, initial objective."[29]

Kippenberger's brigade had easily secured all its objectives, and he wrote proudly back to New Zealand: "Very hard fighting in this attack, but the troops were simply magnificent and my Bde got the whole of its objective on the first night. We lost a lot of good chaps though."[30] On the left, the two battalions of the Sixth Brigade had pulled up 450 to 700 meters short of their final objective: the result of faulty map reading rather than enemy resistance. The rest of the ground was taken in another night attack on October 26–27. Its commander, William Gentry, wrote home to his family on October 28: "We have just fought a battle in which the lads did magnificent work in an operation which, whatever the final outcome, will go down in military history as a model of its type."[31]

The Second New Zealand Division had been the most successful of all the infantry divisions used on the opening night, thanks to a combination of experience in night fighting in the desert, excellent military leadership, hard realistic training prior to the battle, and the 'new' creeping barrage. But Kippenberger was right: losses in both brigades had been heavy. To have made such a dent through a belt of densely sown minefields in terrain so well suited for defense, and to have the infantry, armor, and support weapons in position by dawn was, according to Nigel Hamilton, "inconceivable to Rommel" and "a magnificent infantry performance."[32]

There was still much hard fighting to be done before El Alamein was won, but little of it was carried out by the Second New Zealand Division. At one point it was planned to make another large infantry assault in the New Zealand sector. Both New Zealand infantry brigadiers were aghast at this prospect

> Kippenberger: Another infantry attack means 5,000 yds [4570 meters] at least—very hard to do. Must be regarded as serious as we can't pin his positions as before. It is not a soft spot opposite us.
> Gentry: Have we not to consider very carefully this further attack. Bns after similar casualties in another attack will be little more than coys[companies]. If we take them in again and lose 50% it would take a very long time to build up.
> Kip: The 5,000 reinforcements on the water are not the men to fill the gaps. I have had 11 Officers killed and they are all old hands. We have only 1,200 bayonets left.
> Gentry: They are the survivors of god knows how many battles.[33]

Freyberg overruled his brigadiers, and offered to launch another New Zealand infantry attack 3,650 meters beyond Mitiriya. Montgomery turned the proposal down, fully aware that such an attack would cripple the New Zealand Division and make it incapable of further action.[34] After the Sixth Brigade reached its final objective on the night of October 26–27, both New Zealand brigades moved into reserve in anticipation of the pursuit phase. After October 26, the bulk of the infantry fighting was done by the Ninth Australian Division to the north.

Operation Supercharge

With Rommel's attention focused on the north of the El Alamein Line by the Australian 'crumbling operations,' which drew in the last of his reserves, Montgomery prepared to deliver his *coup de grace*—Operation Supercharge—in the center of the Alamein position. The New Zealanders again played an important role in this phase of the battle. Allocated two British infantry brigades to make the main assault, in addition to the Ninth

Armoured Brigade, Freyberg and the New Zealand Division's headquarters staff planned and directed the initial break-in phase of Operation Supercharge. Its low numbers and recent losses restricted the New Zealand infantry to being used as flank protection.[35]

Commencing at 0105h on November 2, Operation Supercharge took Rommel by surprise, as he had been expecting the counterattack to be launched from the Australian sector in the north. The operation was a limited success and was especially costly to the Ninth Armoured Brigade, which lost seventy-five of its ninety-five tanks. It served its purpose, though, and broke Afrika Korps' and Rommel's will to resist. At 0327h on November 2, the Fifteenth Panzer's War Diary recorded that the "new enemy penetration had given rise to a very dangerous situation. . . . The enemy threatened to break through." A counterattack on this new breach in the line failed and left 8 Panzer Regiment with only eight tanks and no commanding officer. Its War Diary recorded the effect: "The division's backbone for future operations has been broken."[36] Down to just thirty-five German and twenty Italian tanks at the end of the day, Rommel was left with no choice but to withdraw. He wrote a very gloomy letter to his wife on November 3 that accurately assessed his situation

> The battle is going heavily against us. We're simply being crushed by the enemy weight. I've made an attempt to salvage part of the army. I wonder if it will succeed. At night I lie open-eyed, racking my brains for a way out of this plight for my poor troops.[37]

That evening, Rommel issued the order to withdraw from the Alamein positions but was prevented by Adolf Hitler from implementing it for another twenty-four hours. On November 4, the Axis forces at El Alamein were in full retreat.

The Pursuit and Left Hooks

On November 4, the time had come for the Eighth Army to pursue a retreating Axis force. Montgomery, aware that Rommel's army was now "completely crippled," launched two armored divisions—the First and the Tenth—and the New Zealand Division with its attached armored brigade, in pursuit.[38] Afrika Korps' withdrawal presented Montgomery with a priceless opportunity because, according to the German sources, it was poorly conducted. Afrika Korps' War Diary reported

Officers of all ranks had lost their heads and were making hasty and ill-considered decisions, with the result that confidence had been lost, and in some places panic had broken out. Some vehicles were set on fire on or beside the road, and guns were abandoned or destroyed because there were no tractors for them. A large number of vehicles had left their units and were streaming back without orders.[39]

The War Diary of the Ninetieth Light Division noted that there was "very little discipline during the withdrawal" and claimed whole units were "fleeing in wild panic."[40]

The pursuit phase of the Alamein battle has been strongly criticized by many writers who believe that Montgomery acted with undue caution. Alexander McKee has accurately stated that "There was no pursuit, merely a follow up."[41] Correlli Barnett has been most critical of Montgomery's performance, believing that he "signally fail[ed] to take advantage of this

Fig 4.3 Battle commanders largely responsible for the El Alamein victory. From left: Brigadiers Gentry and Kippenberger, General Freyberg, and General Morshead, March 1943. Source: DA 13870, Queen Elizabeth Army Memorial Museum, Waiouru. Permission: Harper.

astonishing flow of precisely accurate intelligence, which removed all guesswork from generalship," and that his failure to destroy Afrika Korps at El Alamein "calls in question Montgomery's generalship at this stage of his career."[42] As early as the evening of November 3, Freyberg had warned Lieutenant General Herbert Lumsden, Tenth Corps commander, that Rommel "will slip away if they are not careful."[43] The cautious pursuit ensured that this happened.

There was one overriding factor, however, that explains and perhaps excuses Montgomery's caution, and this was the state of his armored corps, his prized *corps de chasse*. So far in the Alamein battle, Tenth Corps had failed in every task allocated, demonstrating excessive caution and an inability to follow even the simplest directives. As it was this corps that would be unleashed during the pursuit, it was only natural that Montgomery would want to keep it on as tight a leash as possible to ensure that it did in fact accomplish even the most limited of tasks assigned to it.

Montgomery planned to use the New Zealand Division, augmented by an armored brigade, as the main pursuit force, and directed them to the Fuka escarpment some seventy-two kilometers to the west, while the British armor of Tenth Corps made a series of shorter wheels to the coast of some sixteen to twenty-four kilometers. Just after 1000h on November 3, Kippenberger had been told to prepare his brigade for a rapid pursuit, but it was not until 1430h the next day that the brigade began to move slowly forward. As Freyberg commented about the delay: "The congestion of vehicles in the forward area would have done credit to Piccadilly. Fortunately the RAF ruled the skies."[44] Montgomery's fears proved justified as the armor 'swanned' about the desert out of coordinated control in several fruitless encircling movements. Nor did the New Zealand Division (Montgomery's "mobile shock troops" according to his chief of staff,[45] and the only substantial infantry force used in the pursuit) demonstrate much dash or daring. Freyberg was especially concerned not to have his division mauled by the Afrika Korps for a fourth time. He also erroneously believed Rommel had a powerful armored force under command. He warned his subordinate commanders not to get heavily involved with the German armor and told Lumsden on November 3: "We may have to fight to get out. We are not going to take casualties as that would knock us out. His [Rommel's] difficulties are enormous. We know. We have done it often!"[46] To his subordinate commanders, Freyberg had stated that "the policy is not to fight but to position our force to bottle him."[47] Freyberg,

Key to Maps

Symbol	Meaning	Symbol	Meaning
	High ground		Road or track
	Depression		Anti-tank ditch
	Minefield		Minefield breach
	Swamp		Enemy movement
	Wood		Allied movement
	Inundation		
I	Company	AS	Australian
I I	Battalion	FR	French
I I I	Regiment	HL	Highland
X	Brigade	IN	Indian
XX	Division	NZ	New Zealand
XXX	Corps	SA	South African
XXXX	Army	UK	United Kingdom
		US	United States

Friendly unit	Infantry	Paratroops	Armour	Recon	Motorised Infantry
Enemy unit	Armoured recon	Mountain troops	Defensive positions	Position to be occupied later	

Headquarters

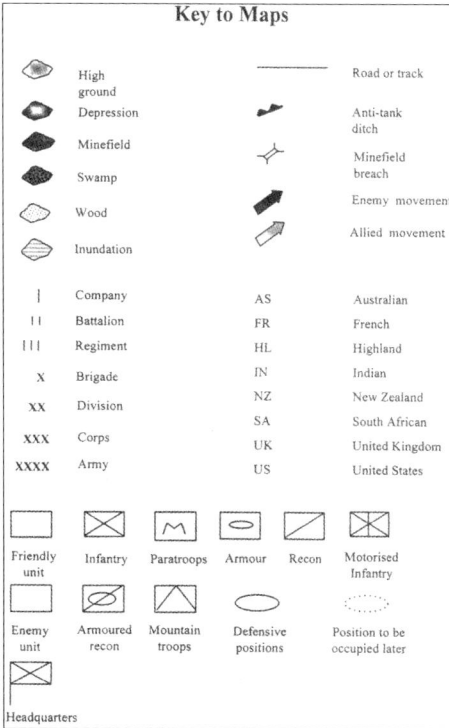

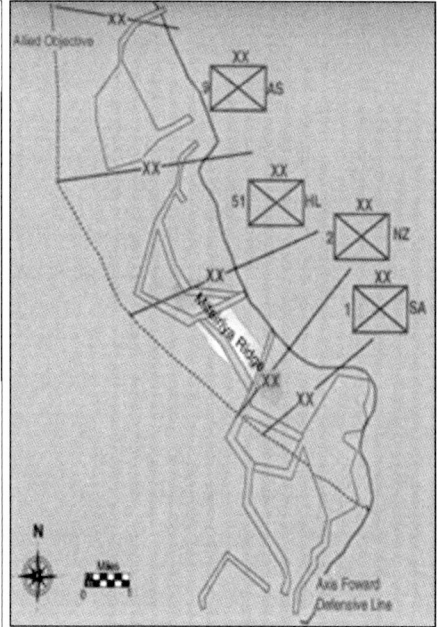

Fig 4.4.1 The plan of attack, showing the corps at El Alamein, October 23, 1942. Permission: Harper.

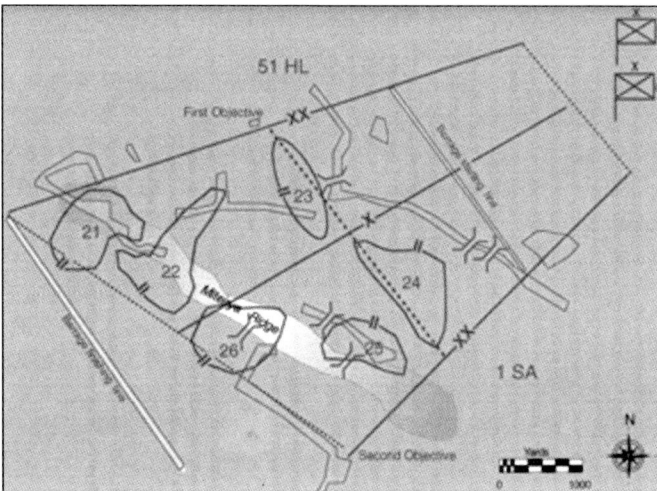

Fig 4.4.2 Map showing the situation at first light on the New Zealand sector: El Alamein, October 24, 1942. Permission: Harper.

the commander of the three left hooks carried out by the New Zealand Division, was in no doubt as to the purpose of a left hook and tended to view it as a substitute for heavy fighting, a way of achieving a victory with minimal casualties.

The first two left hooks were attempted at al-Agheila between December 13 and 15, and then at Nofilia four days later. The third and largest was Montgomery's attempt to outflank the Mareth Line by sending a reinforced New Zealand Division, numbering 25,600 men, 112 pieces of field, medium, and antiaircraft artillery, 172 antitank guns, and 150 tanks, in a wide outflanking movement to Tebaga Gap behind the Axis force's main positions. The reason for its failure is beyond the scope of this chapter.

All three outflanking movements followed a similar pattern. Initial opportunities were promising, and it looked as if the chance to place Afrika Korps 'in the bag' were good. Such opportunities soon evaporated because of Freyberg's excessive caution and some poor command decisions. At al-Agheila, the New Zealanders failed to cut the main coast road and left a large gap between their two blocking positions. It did not take the Afrika Korps long to find the gap and slip away.[48]

However, both Panzer divisions ran out of petrol when they reached Nofilia and another left hook was possible. But the New Zealanders waited a day before trying it. Then on December 17 they tried to cut the coastal road again, using the Fifth Brigade, but Freyberg ordered the brigade to turn too early. It came up against Rommel's flank guard, the Thirty-Third Reconnaissance Unit, which held them off until the Afrika Korps escaped. An attempt by Twenty-Eighth Maori Battalion to mine the coastal road ended in disaster when this battalion ran into a German minefield.[49]

Kippenberger, writing to one of the official historians, was scathing in his assessment of these failures

> You have one or two tricky questions to deal with in this volume, particularly the conduct of the three 'Left Hooks' which seem to me to have been clumsily and rather timidly executed. I thought so at the time and am inclined to the same opinion still.[50]

Freyberg's caution is understandable but it did see opportunities to destroy the Afrika Korps after the October battle being lost. Freyberg above all wanted to avoid the heavy casualties of the past and saw the left hooks as the means to achieve this. This is certainly the view of the New Zealand official historian, who stated that Freyberg's chief concern, still being 2,400 men short even after the absorption of the Eighth Reinforcement at Tripoli, was to limit his casualties as much as possible.[51] As one of Freyberg's key staff officers admitted fifty years later

> But we had all had so much experience of being exposed to German armour, of getting our formations overrun that we were all very cautious. This went on for a long time. It takes a long time to get that sort of apprehension out of the system.[52]

Kippenberger's private opinion—one he never publicly stated—gives another reason

> The trouble was that General Freyberg was naturally an extremely cautious general, and that all the time he had the business of the Charter in his mind. It was the same trouble in Crete which we should have held against the first attack if vigorously commanded. Always he had in mind that New Zealand Division must not be risked. . . . It is heresy to talk like this . . . and you cannot write it . . . the only sort of battle in which General Freyberg was any good was the encadred set-piece battle, on which he was a master . . . these are candid opinions . . . which you will keep to yourself, but should have in the background.[53]

Freyberg's 'extreme caution' ironically was to prove more costly in the long run. As Rommel pointed out, if Montgomery had abandoned his caution after El Alamein, it "would have cost him far fewer losses in the long run than his methodical insistence on overwhelming superiority in each tactical action, which he could only obtain at the cost of his speed."[54] This comment could equally apply to Freyberg in his conduct of the left hooks. Their failure meant much hard fighting and one more military disaster lay ahead for the New Zealanders in North Africa.

'The End of the Beginning?'

There were many reasons for the defeat of the Axis forces at El Alamein, not the least important being logistics and firepower. An Afrika Korps division, Fifteenth Panzer, was emphatic about the cause of their defeat

The English did not win the battle of Alamein by superior leadership or dash. On the contrary, after their original plan of attack failed they worked their way systematically forward, always probing ahead with the greatest care choosing limited objectives. Often, particularly after our withdrawal from the Alamein line, the enemy failed to perceive or take advantage of good opportunities to destroy German troops.[55]

There is little doubt, though, that the primary responsibility for breaking the El Alamein line had been with the experienced infantry divisions backed by heavy artillery support. Freyberg's report on the El Alamein operations concluded that the "value of well-trained infantry, capable of attacking by night with the bayonet against any form of defence, was fully proved."[56] Fifteenth Panzer admitted too that one of the reasons for the Eighth Army's success had been because its infantry were "superior to the Germans, and still more to the Italians in night fighting" and had made "skilful use of darkness, artificial smoke and creeping barrages."[57] El Alamein could not have been won without the contributions of the two elite infantry divisions in the Eighth Army, identified earlier by Rommel as the Ninth Australian Division, operating in the north, and two brigades of New Zealand infantry plus supporting units in the center, and later in the pursuit. That the New Zealanders played a vital role was uncharacteristically recognized by Montgomery

> The Battle of Egypt was won by the good fighting qualities of the soldiers of the Empire. Of all these soldiers none were finer than the fighting men from New Zealand. . . . Possibly I myself am the only one who really knows the extent to which the action of the New Zealand Division contributed towards the victory.[58]

New Zealand losses had been heavy. More than 1,700 New Zealanders became casualties during this Second Battle of El Alamein. Among the 7,350 graves of Allied servicemen in the Alamein cemetery are those of 1,049 known and fifty-six unknown New Zealanders.[59] After the October battle, the New Zealand division was now below strength by 3,600 men, a deficiency felt especially keenly in the infantry, the artillery, and the engineer corps.

The Second Battle of El Alamein was an important tactical victory for Montgomery and the Eighth Army. As Stephen Bungay has concluded, "However one looks at it, in the third round of fighting at El Alamein Rommel was decisively defeated."[60] And there was a strategic effect to the battle as well. One senior German staff officer at their Supreme Command, the Oberkommando der Wehrmacht (OKW) recalled after the war that this battle was indeed "the turning point at which the initiative passed from German into Allied hands." Generalmajor Eckhardt Christian admitted that the OKW "doubtlessly underestimated Africa's strategic importance" and that by November 1942 "The realization of the enemy's strength and our own weakness came too late to avert disaster. The enemy now had the initiative and retained it."[61] Winston Churchill was correct when he stated in a speech that a new phase of the war had been entered: one he labeled "the end of the beginning."[62]

Despite this strategic effect, Montgomery's innate caution during the pursuit phase—a caution shared by Freyberg, his left flank specialist—prevented this battle being transformed into the decisive strategic victory it could have become. The astute General George Marshall was never impressed with the British campaign in North Africa. In some off-the-record comments made in 1949, his interviewers noted

> He [Marshall] explained that our [the US military leaders] opinion of the British at that time was not very high in that the President thought the Eighth Army at El Alamein would lose again in the desert. FDR said to have them attack at night. The General discussed what was wrong with British command in Africa at some length. He said that the British in the Middle East [the Eighth Army] had committed about every mistake in the book. It was no model campaign. The pursuit of Rommel across the desert was slow. The British even laid a minefield in front of them which benefited the Germans more than it did the British. Here Marshall formed an opinion that Montgomery left something to be desired as a field commander. The experience with Montgomery in northwest Europe confirmed Marshall's opinion about that.[63]

But, as stated above, the Second Battle of El Alamein was an important tactical victory for the British Eighth Army and the Desert Air Force. It also signified, as Alexander McKee noted, a crucial shift. McKee wrote of the battle: "At long last the British were learning how to make war—which is not the same thing as fighting."[64] It had taken them some time.

Notes

1   Freyberg's war diary, October 23, 1944, Archives New Zealand (hereafter ANZ) WA II 8/44.
2   Glyn Harper, *Kippenberger: An Inspired New Zealand Commander* (Auckland: HarperCollins, 2005), 129.
3   Freyberg, letter to Barrowclough, C2310, August 4, 1942, ANZ WA II 8/AA Miscellaneous 1942.
4   Rommel, letter to Lu (his wife, Lucia Maria), June 29, 1942, in *The Rommel Papers*, ed. B.H. Liddell Hart (London: Arrow Books, 1987), 240.
5   Howard Kippenberger, letter to J. L. Scoullar, November 10, 1953, Correspondence of Howard Karl Kippenberger 1947–55, ANZ WA II 11/6.
6   Howard Kippenberger, quoted in a letter to Scoullar, May 2, 1951, ANZ WA II 11/6.
7   DAG GHQ MEF to HQ NZEF CRME 62340/4/AG2(a), memo, September 5, 1942, ANZ WA II 8/AA.
8   Howard Kippenberger, *Infantry Brigadier* (Oxford: Oxford University Press, 1949), 180.
9   Howard Kippenberger, draft of New Zealand *Listener* article, July 1947, the personal collection of Bill Glue.
10 Kippenberger, *Infantry Brigadier*, 196.
11 Freyberg to Fraser (NZ PM), cipher message p. 130, October 3, 1942, General Papers "Lightfoot" and "Supercharge," Freyberg Papers, ANZ WA II 8/25A.
12 Oliver Leese, "Impressions of the Part of 30 Corps in the Battle of Egypt," attached to letter to Scoullar, April 30, 1953, ANZ WA II 11/6.
13 Freyberg's diary, October 20, 1942, ANZ WA II/45.
14 Kippenberger, *Infantry Brigadier*, 222.
15 Freyberg, cipher message to Fraser p. 130, Oct 3, 1942, General Papers "Lightfoot" and "Supercharge," Freyberg Papers, ANZ WA II 8/25A.
16 Kippenberger, letter to Latham, May 24, 1949, ANZ WA II 11/6.
17 Liddell Hart, *The Rommel Papers*, 298–99.
18 Morshead, letter to Myrtle, October 23, 1942, Personal Records, Morshead Papers, A1 File 3, 3DRL 2632, Australian War Memorial, Canberra.
19 Professor Angus Ross, interview with Glyn Harper, Dunedin, January 17, 1995.
20 Freyberg, comments on conference regarding "Lightfoot," September 21, 1942, ANZ WA II 8/25 A.
21 W.E. Murphy, *Official History of New Zealand in the Second World War 1939–45, Second New Zealand Divisional Artillery* (Wellington, War History Branch, 1966), 377.
22 Francis Tuker, *Approach to Battle: A Commentary; Eighth Army, November 1941 to May 1943* (London: Cassell and Co., 1963), 220, 242.

23 Conversation, conference of Brigadiers, 1100h October 23, 1942, recorded in Freyberg's Diary, ANZ WA II 8/44.

24 Wira Gardiner, *Te Mura o Te Ahi: The Story of the Maori Battalion* (Auckland, NZ: Reed Publishing, 1992), 103.

25 Kippenberger, *Infantry Brigadier*, 225

26 Angus Ross, interview, Dunedin, 17 January, 1995.

27 War Diary 5 NZ Inf. Bde, October 23–4, 1942, ANZ WA II 1, DA 52/1/34.

28 War Diary 5 NZ Inf. Bde, October 23–4, 1942.

29 Angus Ross, interview, Dunedin, January 17, 1995.

30 Kippenberger, letter to Jim Fraser, October 31, 1942, the personal collection of Bill Glue.

31 Brigadier William Gentry, letter to his family, October 28, 1942, in Sally Mathieson (ed.), *Bill Gentry's War, 1939–45* (Palmerston North: The Dunmore Press, 1996), 160.

32 Nigel Hamilton, *Monty: The Making of a General 1887–1942* (London: Hamish Hamilton, 1981), 777.

33 Freyberg Diary, October 26, 1942, ANZ WA II 8/44.

34 Hamilton, *Monty*, 802.

35 Ian McGibbon, *New Zealand and the Second World War: The People, the Battles and the Legacy* (Auckland, NZ: Hodder Moa Beckett, 2003), 123.

36 Panzer War Diary, November 2, 1942; GMDS File 24902, Afrika Korps Records, ANZ WA II 11/2215.

37 Rommel, letter to Lu, November 3, 1942, *Rommel Papers*, 320.

38 Mark Johnson and Peter Stanley, *Alamein: The Australian Story* (Melbourne: Oxford University Press, 2002), 259.

39 Afrika Korps War Diary, November 6, 1942, ANZ WA II 11/22, GMDS File 2586/1, Afrika Korps Records.

40 90th Light War Diary, November 11, 1942, ANZ WA II 11/23, GMDS File 288761, Records of 90th Light and 164th Light Division.

41 Alexander McKee, *El Alamein, Ultra and the Three Battles* (London: Souvenir Press, 1991), 176.

42 Correlli Barnett, *The Desert Generals*, 2nd ed. (London: Pan Books Ltd., 1983), 312, 310.

43 Freyberg, conversation with Corps Commander 2130h November 3, 1942, Freyberg's War Diary, ANZ WA II 8/44.

44 Freyberg's War Diary, November 3, 1942, ANZ WA II 8/44.

45 Francis De Guingand, *Operation Victory* (London: Hodder and Stoughton, 1947), 467.

46 Freyberg's War Diary, November 3, 1942, ANZ WA II 8/44.

47 Freyberg's War Diary, November 6, 1942, ANZ WA II 8/44.

48 Harper, *Kippenberger*, 199.

49 Harper, *Kippenberger*, 201.

50 Kippenberger to J.L. Scoullar (the author chosen for the official history of the 'Left Hooks'), June 7, 1955, ANZ WA II 11/6.

51 W.G. Stevens, *Official History of New Zealand in the Second World War 1939– 45. Bardia to Enfidaville* (Wellington: War History Branch, 1962), 249.

52 Sir Leonard Thornton, interview with Glyn Harper, Wellington, January 25, 1993.

53 Kippenberger to Scoullar, 'very personal' letter, June 21, 1955, ANZ WA II 11/6.

54 Liddell Hart, *The Rommel Papers*, 360–61.

55 Panzer War Diary, Preliminary Remarks, GMDS File 24902, Afrika Korps Records, ANZ WA II 11/2215.

56 Freyberg, "The New Zealand Division in Egypt and Libya. Operations 'Lightfoot' and 'Supercharge.' Part 1, Narrative and Lessons," 27. Freyberg's Secret After-Action Report, November 20, 1942, copy in author's possession.

57 Panzer War Diary, Preliminary Remarks, ANZ WA II 11/22, GMDS File 24902, Afrika Korps Records.

58 Montgomery, Foreword to "The New Zealand Division in Egypt and Libya. Operations 'Lightfoot' and 'Supercharge.' Part 1, Narrative and Lessons," p. iii, Freyberg's Secret After-Action Report, December 1942, copy in author's possession.

59 Ronald Walker, *Official History of New Zealand in the Second World War 1939–45, Alam Halfa and Alamein* (Wellington: War History Branch, 1967), Appendix 3, 481.

60 Stephen Bungay, *Alamein* (London: Aurum Press, 2002), 196.

61 Eckhardt Christian, "The El Alamein Crisis and Its After-effects in the OKW," 1, 9, MS D-172, Army Heritage and Education Center (AHEC), Carlisle, PA.

62 Winston Churchill, speech at the Lord Mayor's luncheon banquet, London, November 10, 1942, quoted in Bungay, *Alamein*, 200.

63 George Marshall, interview with Dr. Matthews, Majors Lemson and Hamilton, and Dr. Howard Smith, July 23, 1949, Verifax 530, Item 5008, Marshall Library, Lexington, VA.

64 McKee, *El Alamein*, 112.

5

The Free French
in the Battle for North Africa, 1942
Military Action and Its Political Presentation[1]

Rémy Porte

*"Lorsqu'à Bir Hakim un rayon de sa gloire renaissante
est venu caresser le front sanglant de ses enfants, le monde
a reconnu la France."*[2]

—Charles de Gaulle, 1942

By the time General Koenig's[3] First Division Free French forces
(DFF)[4] received orders to relieve the 150th Indian Brigade's advance
position in the Libyan Desert at Bir Hakim,[5] General de Gaulle's
men had been fighting nonstop since August 1940, in Africa and along
the Mediterranean coast, in fact, ever since the Folliot Company of the
First Marine Battalion had first been integrated into the British Seventh
Armoured Division on the Libyan border.

In Africa, Ethiopia, northern Chad, the Levant, and the Egyptian
Western Desert, French units were incorporated into the British and
Commonwealth forces,[6] retaining as far as possible their identity as the
Free French. The distinction was important because it underlined the
degree to which de Gaulle was willing to participate in operations against
the Axis forces, in regions where France's historic reputation still com-
manded respect. So it was not particularly surprising to find his troops in
Cyrenaica in the Western Desert.

Slowly Increasing Numbers of the Free French Forces, 1940–42

Their sudden and unexpected defeat in June 1940 left most French shocked
and refusing to believe in either the legality or legitimacy of Marshal Pétain's

puppet government. De Gaulle was then a minor official only recently promoted to the provisional rank of general, and his call to arms on June 18 over the BBC radio at first made little impact in metropolitan France, except perhaps on a tiny handful of compatriots. The core of those who joined the Free French included French troops on their way to Britain at the time of the capitulation, who chose to remain there rather than go back to France,[7] groups from French territories overseas, and a few individual stalwarts.[8]

In North Africa, bloody confrontations between *pétainistes* loyal to the 'hexagon'—mainland France—and *gaullistes*, now under British command, were inflamed by events such as those in Dakar in October 1940, in Gabon that November, and the Syrian campaign of 1941. These deepened the split between opposing sides of the French Army of North Africa. Morocco and Tunisia had been the first to accept the Franco–German armistice of June 1940, though they remained cautious with regard to engaging their forces and equipment, preferring to reserve them for combat later. At over two hundred thousand men, these were the true inheritors of the Nineteenth Corps and the Army of Africa, kept back and carefully dispersed between two cantons. The remaining troops bitterly opposed erstwhile comrades in arms so ready to obey a government collaborating with the enemy. They therefore began to regroup in East Africa and Egypt. These, the Free French, numbered around fifty thousand men. Many were from the French colonial forces, others drawn from the various theaters of war, from Britain, the Middle East, Africa, and the Pacific, and from all three branches of the military: army, air force, and navy (FFL, FAFL, FNL). Though inevitably with limited arms, encouraging waves of response to de Gaulle from French colonial territories gave the Free French their solid base. The effect of this gathering to the tricolor, even if at times only symbolic, proclaimed to the world that France had not yet been knocked out of the war. Even when total numbers of troops in the global war swelled, the relatively small size of the Free French was always less important than its political impact.

Forces in Cyrenaica in 1942 and the Position at Bir Hakim

From the beginning of this war, as in 1914–18, the importance of the Suez Canal as the great arterial 'jugular' of the empire came to the fore. To secure it and to defend Egypt against Italian–Libyan forces, over 240,000 troops were stationed along the Nile Valley, transforming the country into an enormous military camp. In early 1941, among the multitude of

British and Commonwealth troops there were no more than a few thousand French. Even so, embedded within the support unit of the Seventh Armoured Division, the French had played so important a role in reconnaissance that in his speech following the victory at Tobruk, Churchill chose to emphasize that the Allied success was owed to both British *and* Free French.[9] Never one to miss an opportunity to promote Free French action, General de Gaulle followed suit, declaring: "*L'empire italien s'écroule sous les coups de nos alliés britanniques aidés par des troupes françaises.*"[10]

By early 1941 the situation had become critical for the Allies in the Eastern Mediterranean. Greece and Crete were under German occupation. In Baghdad, nationalist Arabs had rebelled, seizing power; and in Palestine the Grand Mufti, too, called for revolution, though the French Levant as a whole remained loyal to Vichy. This context explains why the armistice of Saint Jean d'Acre, which concluded the Syrian campaign of June and July 1941, brought a surge of four thousand extra men to the ranks of the Free French forces.[11]

Meanwhile across the Egyptian–Libyan frontier, enormous forces flowed back and forth, east–west, west–east. In February General Rommel arrived in Tripoli, followed shortly by the first German troops in support of the Italians. His reconquest of the whole of Cyrenaica in the spring directly threatened Egypt. General Wavell counterattacked in June, and his replacement, General Auchinleck, with the Free French in 'Jock columns,'[12] took the initiative in the autumn. By early 1942, the Allies were once more on the defensive, with the frontline fixed provisionally from Gazala on the Mediterranean coast to Bir Hakim, some seventy kilometers south.[13] The major part of the Eighth Army was now deployed in an extended rectangle between Gazala, Bir al-Harmat, Bir-Bu-Maafes, and Tobruk, and strategically placed to secure the direct coastal route into Egypt. However, in desert terrain it proved impossible to form a continuous frontline, and defense was therefore organized around a series of positions thirty to fifty kilometers apart, patrolled by mobile units and interspersed with minefields.[14] Markers were set every five to ten kilometers across these huge desert spaces. Each marker was constructed from three 200-liter barrels stacked up and painted with a number for easy identification—but set in sand, and under a searing sun, not easy to locate.

Having been reinforced with tanks and petroleum stocks in January 1942, Rommel's strategy was to take the offensive locally early in the year, then hold the line. His plan for May was simple but bold: on May 20 and

21 an Italian corps would lead a diversionary attack against the Allied lines in the north, while he, commanding a German–Italian army, would cut around the Eighth Army's southern flank, attack from the rear, crush them, and take Tobruk. The success of this plan depended on speed of execution in no more than four days. Within this framework, the outlying position of Bir Hakim seemed of little importance to either the British (situated as it was at the far end of their southernmost position) or the Germans, who to start with took only some elements of an Italian division to deal with it. Yet Bir Hakim lay at the center of six camel tracks fanning out in all directions, and from that point of view presented a uniquely strategic desert position, as it had for the Turks who had once fortified it.

The entire terrain was in fact set on an immense plain of sand and rock, crested by a single ridge. The official history of the BN2 Battalion describes it thus: "During daytime the whole landscape is warped by mirages, the sun's heat causing the air to quiver so that it becomes impossible to judge distances." Nevertheless, for three months the Free French worked nonstop improving and fortifying the site. More or less triangular in shape, and with a battalion stationed at each point around a perimeter of roughly sixteen kilometers, its outer limits were protected by vast minefields, seeded particularly to the north, where they extended in a 'V' shape pointing west toward Gazala and east toward 'Knightsbridge.' All around the site were trenches and antitank devices. Around the inner area, gun posts were set close together every 100–150 meters, giving cover from every possible angle of approach, with foxholes and trenches offering mutual support, and extra cover and shelter from air attack for men and equipment.[15] While all the time coping with the sand, meticulous preparation of the terrain was achieved through a judiciously selected range of obstacles to check the enemy, and carefully coordinated firepower. Every possible combination of camouflage was cunningly placed, and firing strictly controlled without in any way cramping the Free French 'style' that occasionally startled the British command, and in some quarters was deemed lacking proper respect for formal military tradition. One soldier noted in his diary: "RAS, apart from the hard slog and morale."[16]

Battle and Siege
Under General Koenig's command, the First Free (Libre) French Brigade (BFL) had a lineup of around 3,700 battle-ready men, five infantry battalions, three of which were colonials,[17] and two legions of the Thirteenth

Fig 5.1 From Bir Hakim in the desert, Free French legionnaires rush to attack an enemy strong point, June 12, 1942. (IWM E 13313)

Demi-Brigade. For the antitank units there were four batteries of six 75-mm canons, with smaller 47-mm gauge artillery. There were additionally a detachment of engineers reinforced with some British, one complete signals company, plus a trained nursing detachment with an ambulance equipped for surgery. Transport and supply personnel made up the complement. The troops shared a wide range of occupations between them, matching the equally wide national range of these men drawn from the four quarters of the globe.

Toward the middle of April German advance patrols appeared, come to size up the Bir Hakim position, but these alerts were not followed up. Then, suddenly, patrols reported that enemy units were beginning to gather. On May 25, Jock column Tomcol (BN2) was recalled urgently to Bir Hakim, and the order for the general attack was given for the following day. The engagement of May 26 lasted all day in an extended holding operation, stalling the enemy advance. But the following morning, May 27, German–Italian units forced the Free French back to their core position.

There are many works[18] covering these protracted battles that were fought furiously from May 27 to June 10, so no need for details here. But overall it is possible to distinguish three main phases. The first lasted from May 27 to June 2, when the French position was assaulted by successive waves of attack, chiefly by the Italians whose attempts to break through the defenses became increasingly persistent. The second phase was from June 3–7, when the real siege began. Artillery exchanges and fighting right at the barricades became more and more frequent. Both air forces, the German attacking, and the Royal Air Force defending, played an increasingly important role. Then the third phase ran from June 8–10, when Rommel launched continuous daytime bombardment against Bir Hakim. The French position began to weaken, water and munitions reserves were becoming dangerously low, defenses slowly were worn down, and the German–Italian forces began to break through the nearest minefields.

The Seventh Armoured Division tried to attack from the east and southeast to draw the German–Italian pressure from the Free French.[19] However, from the British point of view, the way the general state of the battle was evolving meant the position had to be evacuated. For the French, June 9 was particularly bad as wave upon wave of German aircraft flew continuously overhead, bombing the French lines.[20] The battle continued until 9.30 that evening, while Koenig and his staff officer were negotiating with the British how to carry out the evacuation over the night of June 10–11. "I must ask," demanded General Koenig, "for . . . complete fighter air cover starting at six a.m., bombarding the enemy batteries . . . at dusk I shall need a strong attack from the seventh motor brigade in the south to cover our exit from the fort. . . . I repeat. I must insist these demands be met. These are the only concessions I ask for the First Free French Brigade. I do not think the British army will refuse this last request."[21] In the small hours of June 10, Koenig ordered his officers and unit commanders to spend the day preparing to destroy all matériel that could not be transported with them. The general order to evacuate

Fig 5.2 Colonial troops man outposts: a colonial machine gunner receiving orders by telephone at a Western Desert outpost. (Photograph by Cecil Beaton IWM K 3538)

was given at 5.00 p.m. It took the form of a sudden southwesterly break-out, compass direction 213°30' toward Base 837 which was about seven kilometers away, where British columns were waiting for them.

Despite the site commander's efforts, in the end no amount of careful planning could actually have prevailed under that ceaseless enemy bombardment. For Capt. Graviers' sappers, too few in number, pushed for time, and operating under such heavy attack, there was no hope of opening the 200-m passage Koenig had requested. By 11.30 that evening when the operation should already have begun, only a few dozen meters of one branch of the 'V' had been partly prepared, too narrow to allow passage for the surging exodus of motorized vehicles.[22] Worse still, the final preparations attracted the attention of Axis forces, which immediately opened fire. "I must admit," Koenig recorded, "the game was played out, but played out badly—too late now for recriminations." As they left the site, the men had

Fig 5.3 A British signaler at work in a radio truck in North Africa. (IWM E 16501)

at first hesitated, then followed the general, who charged ahead shouting, "Forward, into battle!" The trucks followed in an increasingly disorderly fashion. To get their bearings, staff officers had to rely on visual memory because the plans had been destroyed. It took more than three hours before all units were evacuated from the site. In the darkness of night and fighting all the way, units became disorientated, and motor transport was frequently ablaze, demanding many courageous acts. "This is turning into ghastly and appalling chaos and tragedy, for it cannot be otherwise."[23]

On June 11 at around 0400h, the first survivors reached Base 837, yet by 1100h there were still fewer than a thousand of them, and the divisional commander was pessimistic: "Very tough retreat, men became separated, scattered and wounded, and patrols had to be sent out to assist them, still no news of the general."[24] All day long, together in small groups or alone, the men gradually joined up with the British. Koenig himself had become separated and only turned up at Gabr al-Ari halfway through the morning.

First, as Koenig later recalled, "Their bold break-out was met by a blistering counterattack. . . . The First Free French Division was obviously unable to continue the battle." In the end, 1,150 officers and men were lost during the exodus, plus as many as 168 dead and wounded during the two weeks of tough resistance. In terms of human life the cost had been exceptionally severe, and yet the garrison had not surrendered. And it did provoke a response from Berlin.

In General de Gaulle's account of the row over his troops' military status, recorded in the first volume of his *Mémoires de guerre*, Radio Berlin announced that according to the laws of war, Free French troops did not meet the definition of regular military and, in consequence, if taken prisoner would be executed. The Free French leader immediately requested permission to respond over the BBC, that in that case he would be obliged to mete out the same punishment to German prisoners of war. The German response came swiftly to assure de Gaulle that his men would indeed be treated as regular troops according to the laws of war.

In fact, the prolonged resistance of the Free French at Bir Hakim created a real headache for Rommel, since it severed his forces from their principal supply line, forcing the Afrika Korps commandant to lose precious time salvaging his position. Tactically, the chief impact fell into three categories: disruption of the German lines of communication, attrition of German–Italian forces,[25] and delay in Rommel's main strategy of looping around the Allied forces from the south. Beginning with an army of 3,700, the final total of Free French survivors was 2,500, with the wounded regrouping with those in the rear. Not only had the Free French not been wiped from the battlefield, but one of their major units had proved capable of holding off an enemy of clearly superior numbers through two whole weeks.[26]

The chronology of events demonstrates the importance to the Allies of the Free French resistance at Bir Hakim. Even after May 27—when troops of the Italian Ariete division arrived and the position should have collapsed—the fight was sustained until June 11, preventing Rommel from reaching the Alamein front until July 1, and thereby giving the commander in chief of allied British forces in Egypt the time needed to coordinate his reinforcements west of the Nile Delta and muster his troops there.

Participation in the Battle of El Alamein

But still nothing was decided. Tobruk fell on June 21 and the Allies continued to retreat. The Eighth Army, with yet another change of commander in chief, remained anxious. So did General Catroux, in command of the Free French troops drawn from around the Eastern Mediterranean, commenting on the day after Bir Hakim, "My view of the general situation was that Rommel had won through sheer attrition, thanks to the quality and number of his medium-sized tanks and his skilful use of motorized artillery. In a difficult situation he could bring up divisions from Gazala."[27] That said, fully cognizant of the danger, Catroux wanted to pursue the fight to the frontline. At the beginning of July de Gaulle agreed with

Fig 5.4 General de Gaulle, met by General Giraud, commander in chief of French forces in North Africa. Lengthy talks resulted in their appointment as joint heads of the French Committee of National Liberation, January 17, 1943. (IWM NA 3209)

Fig 5.5 Meeting of the French Committee of National Liberation, including M. Henri Bonnet, M. Jean Monnet, General de Gaulle, and General Giraud. (IWM TA 2022)

his general, but as a statesman and not simply a soldier, he responded, "I entirely approve your desire not to retire our forces from battle if the security of the Nile Valley is in question. But it remains absolutely essential that our troops not be engaged around El Alamein until they are properly armed and equipped. We cannot afford to diminish our forces."[28]

The Second Brigade of the Light Division (the second to be formed from French with contingents from the east) had left the Levant between April 21 and 23 to join the western forces, Force L, but contingents of troops from tank units left ten days or so earlier to begin the collection of heavy British matériel. It was assumed they would be used later in Cyrenaica, but the constant movement the brigade would be subjected to over several months testified to the difficulties British staff experienced in organizing the defense of the Nile Delta.

While still recouping their strength, the Second Brigade were ordered to relieve two brigades of the Fifth Indian Division,[29] and then install themselves between May 7 and 8 on the Halfaya plateau. The Brigade was then moved further along the coast, so that by May 15 and 16 it had become responsible for the Bardia sector. Then, with no change of mission, the Brigade spent the last of that month under orders from the Fourth Indian Division, then reattached to the Tenth Indian Division at the beginning of June. On June 17, with the first German motorized units beginning to harass them, the British units retreated, and the Second Free French withdrew to Halfaya, which they had left only the month before. Next they moved to al-Dab'a, then al-Kanayis where the army was digging in from June 23. On June 27 the brigade arrived at El Alamein, and the following day turned south with instructions to hold the position of Gebel Sambur. Scarcely had they arrived than they were sent off again, this time toward Helwan, roughly forty-eight kilometers outside Cairo, where they regrouped around July 2. On July 6 they were rejoined by Commandant Bavières' contingent, then transferred to Wadi Natrun where their units were deployed in work parties preparing the defense of the Delta; and then on August 23 to the crossroads of Alexandria and Amriya.

This constant shunting about suggests two ultimately complementary conclusions: either the British command (given the means at its disposal and Rommel's assumed intentions) was too busy preparing the defense of the Nile and/or it believed the Free French reinforcements could make only a marginal difference. Moreover, the flow of discussions between British and French generals at HQ through the summer months of June, July, and August testifies to the intensity of activity that dominated preparations for the defense of Egypt, but equally to the prevailing level of uncertainty.

The time for reengagement approached. During his regional tour of inspection General de Gaulle addressed his troops, emphasizing the connection between Free French operations abroad and the activities of the Resistance at home. "I know that each of you truly longs to have the opportunity to engage our common enemy, and your wish will soon be fulfilled, that I promise you. . . . Day by day reliable sources tell us that French resistance continues to grow."[30]

Rommel continued attacking up to the beginning of September, but his already thin supply lines were stretched even further and he had lost much of his transport, particularly tanks, while the Allies had their supply lines behind them, in depots based along the Nile just a few score kilometers away. The Front held for several weeks. Then the Allies attacked on the evening of October 23, the date chosen because Rommel was in Germany at that time and knew nothing of the evolving situation until the following day. He was unable to resume his North African command post

Fig 5.6 Long Range Desert Group (LRDG) in a Chevrolet in the Western Desert, May 25, 1942. (IWM E 12384)

until the morning of October 26, which consequently left a gap of forty-eight hours in the leadership of the Axis forces, allowing Montgomery to seize the initiative in Operation Lightfoot. In the meantime, the French Legionaries began a diversionary maneuver on the Naqb Rala plateau and the observation point at Humaymat. Close fighting with the Italian Folgere Division was notably marred by the death of Lieut. Col. Amilakvari, a figure of great significance for the Thirteenth, bringing the French to a halt. There followed for several months a period of difficult Anglo–French relations, the former debating the capabilities of the Free French.

On November 4, despite formal orders to the contrary from Hitler and Mussolini, Rommel ordered his troops to retreat. The Battle of El Alamein was over, and the Free French had played only a marginal part.

The Desert Commandos

It was in that same spring and summer of 1942 that the Free French set up autonomous commando action groups, acting with the Special Operations Executive (SOE) under the British High Command in Tripolitania,

Fig 5.7 LRDG crew sheltering in the lee of the Chevrolet truck during a sand-storm. They were part of a group travelling from Cairo to Siwa. (IWM E HU 24964)

behind the German–Italian lines. Embedded at the very heart of the Long Range Desert Group, they set about destroying the enemy's transport infrastructure.[31] Throughout the month of July, they targeted enemy communication and supply lines leading to El Alamein. In all, several trains and hundreds of trucks and planes were destroyed, severely hampering Rommel's preparations for the attack on the Delta.[32] In the last days of August and through September, having outflanked the Germans and Italians from the south around Kufra and Gialo, the SOE hassled the enemy in the area round Tobruk and Benghazi to sow disorder at the rearguard of the Afrika Korps, obliging Rommel to pull back his front-line troops believing there might be a fierce and overwhelming attack from the direction of Tobruk.[33]

Fig 5.8 Corporal Sillito, a member of a four-man Special Air Service (SAS) patrol, tasked to blow up the rail line in the enemy's rear. He became separated from his group and walked back a hundred miles to base without food or water. (IWM E 19781)

This 'secret' Desert War continued after El Alamein, particularly late in December 1942, when units of Capt. Jourdan and Lt. Martin participated in many attacks against enemy columns, and in sabotage operations against buildings and airdromes between Misrata, Tripoli, Sfax, and Gabès. Also worth remembering, though not strictly speaking in our geographic zone, are the feats of Capt. Bergé in Crete, who before being taken prisoner in mid-June had destroyed twenty-one planes and fifteen trucks on the airdrome at Candia.

To sum up, the participation of the Free French Forces in the overall struggle of the Allied forces in Egypt and the Western Desert remains indisputably small, and it is also true that at certain moments the British seemed unconvinced by their input or the missions that they attributed to them. Yet their contribution, if not crucial, was nonetheless important.

Birth of a Key Myth

What has to be emphasized is the importance of the psychological impact that the men who fought at Bir Hakim had on the Free France movement: France was in the war, even though her actual contribution remained modest. On June 10, de Gaulle sent the following message to General Koenig, "Know and tell your men that all France salutes you, and that you are her pride."[34] The following day, even while troops were still regrouping, the Free French leader delivered his now-celebrated speech: "On learning what the French accomplished at Bir Hakeim the whole nation experienced a wave of pride." On June 12, General Auchinleck declared, "The United Nations are filled with admiration and respect for these French troops and their valiant leader."[35] The next day, June 13, the western press, too, was full of praise for the resistance of the First Battalion of the Free French at Bir Hakim, a heroic feat putting them on a par with the *poilus* of Verdun in 1916, and describing the battle as the 'Desert Verdun.'[36]

All Allied leaders sent glowing congratulatory telegrams. That same day General Catroux, commander of the French in the Middle East, issued the order of the day, "Soldiers of Bir Hakeim, with these memorable actions you have reopened the book of national pride, closed since the armistice of 1939. . . . Let the whole world see there inscribed the hitherto unknown name of Bir Hakeim, and read of those whose valor made it famous. . . . All honor to you in whom the spirit of Verdun lives again to the glory of France and the instruction of the world."[37]

Churchill set the tone of the British view of the part played by the soldiers of the First Free French Brigade in the operational structure when Rommel launched his attack on May 26, 1942

> It is not yet possible for me to give any final account of the battle. . . . Rommel had expected to take Tobruk in the first few days, but the reception which he got deranged his plan. Very heavy losses in armour were sustained by both sides. However he held tenaciously to the inroads he had made, and we were so mauled in the struggle that no effective counter-stroke could be delivered. On 4th June an

attempt was made, but was repulsed by a counter-attack with heavy loss by artillery. The battle then centred upon Bir Hakeim, where the Free French resisted with the utmost gallantry.[38]

But it was without doubt in occupied mainland France that the impact of this was most deeply felt. During the weeks that followed, the *maquis* in Languedoc renamed itself Bir Hakim and the network and journal adopted the same name.

The draft report of the First Brigade of the Free French, dated June 14, 1942—the day following the retreat from Bir Hakim—began with this significant preliminary note: "All the archives of the Brigade Command were burned during the exodus of 11 June. Omissions and errors may have crept into the present document."[39] However, the essence does not lie in the detail of the battle. It lies rather in the symbolism of a free France, resuming her rightful place in the struggle that the Allies fought together, and is forever emblazoned in the memorable words of de Gaulle, "*le monde a reconnu la France quand, à Bir Hakim, un rayon de sa gloire renaissante est venu caresser le front sanglant de ses soldats.*"[40]

Notes

1 Chapter translated by Jill Edwards.

2 "When France's glory was seen once more to glimmer on the bloodied brows of her soldiers at Bir Hakim, the world saluted France," General de Gaulle speech in London, June 18, 1942.

3 In 1917, at the age of nineteen, Pierre-Marie Koenig volunteered and later served with the Foreign Legion in Morocco before joining de Gaulle on June 19, 1940. He participated in many operations in Africa and the Middle East and was swiftly promoted, first to the rank of colonel and then general.

4 The Free French Division (DFF) was roughly the equivalent of a 'Brigade Group.' The regular French equivalent would be a 'Division légère.'

5 Bir Hakim, the 'Well of Wisdom.' The Romanized spelling of this name varies.

6 The example most often cited is that of the men who together sailed to Britain from Isle de Sain on June 26, 1940.

7 They included the Thirteenth Demi-Brigade of the Foreign Legion with 2,300 officers, NCOs, and legionaries who had fought in the Narvik campaign in May, but of whom only 1,700 remained when they regrouped in Britain between June 19 and 20. Of these, 930 elected to stay on in England, and around 800 asked to be repatriated to Morocco.

8   Among the most celebrated of these are Captain Folliot, who traveled from French Syria into British Palestine with 126 men on June 27, 1940; Lieutenant Colonel Laurent-Champrosay, who reached the Gold Coast on July 6; similarly, the 'Bretagne' unit of the Free French Air Force, which later regrouped to become part of the permanent detachment of Chad's modest air forces.

9   From September 1940, the Free French had been engaged in combat with Italian troops under Marshal Graziani in the area around Sidi Barrani. After that, the Free French took part in Operation Compass, General Wavell's counteroffensive toward Bardia, Tobruk, and al-Agheila. At roughly the same time, in February 1941, Col. Leclerc left Chad for southern Libya. On March 1, Kufra surrendered.

10   "The Italian empire is collapsing under the attacks of our British allies aided by our French troops," BBC broadcast, January 31, 1941.

11   More precisely 4,070, of whom 973 were French (128 officers), 1,031 were legionaries, and 2,064 were indigenous—and of these, 750 were Africans. With these numbers it was possible for General Catroux to put together a provisional group of two light divisions with 261 officers, 167 NCOs, and 9,098 men.

12   Small mixed-service units, very mobile and endowed with tremendous firepower capable of hassling the Italian–German forces in the desert.

13   In fact the German–Italian forces to the west and the Allied forces to the east were not confronting each other except in the Gazala zone. As they stretched out to the south, the Axis lines became elongated in the direction of Mechili, and the same was true for the Allied lines toward Bir Hakim. Thus 'no man's land' extended to something like 150 kilometers.

14   In minefields, the devices were placed in ten rows, twenty-five to every ten square meters. Contrariwise in a mine 'ocean,' the mines were placed in a broader, more haphazard manner, with narrow passages which could be quickly seeded if threatened, but allowing entrance and exit to friendly vehicles. Altogether the French laid something in the order of 120,000 mines to the 200,000 laid by the Allies.

15   On May 21, 1942, the Commander of the Fourth Battalion issued Order no. 2047/4 which, for example, foresaw that vehicles needed to be stationed minimally 150 m apart; and that it was 'obligatory' for groups of men to stay close by each truck. See *Bataillon de Marche* (BM, Motorized Battalion), Private Collection no. 1K289; Service Historique de la Défense, Vincennes, Paris (hereafter SHD Vincennes).

16   RAS, most likely short for *Rien à signaler* (What can I say?). Idem BM in SHD/DITEEX, Vincennes, private collection no. 1K289.

17   One battalion of marine infantry, the Second Foot Battalion from Ubangi, and one battalion from the Pacific.

18 See Général Catroux, *Dans la bataille de Méditerranée, Témoignages et com-mentaries*, J. Juilliard, Paris, 1949; Colonel Paul Morlon, *Souvenirs d'un officier d'artillerie colonial, 1938-1976*, edition Bookpole, 2001; Maréchal Alexander, *D'El Alamein à Tunis et à la Sicile (1942-1943)*, Ch. Lavauzelle, 1949; W.B. Kennedy Shaw, *Patrouilles du désert, Opérations en Libye de 1940 à 1943*, Paris, Editions Berger-Levrault, 1948; Paul Carrel, *Afrika Corps*, Lausanne, 1948.

19 Order of the Day, no. 75, June 8, 1942.

20 In one day alone, June 10, at around 1300h, there was a massive raid of 130 German bombers. That in itself testifies to the importance Rommel placed on taking Bir Hakim.

21 The original telegram was not kept, owing to the final destruction of documents before leaving the fort, but its translation has been kept in the archives of the Seventh Armoured Division.

22 Gravier attacked Koenig's account, in André Gravier, *La Verité sur Bir Hakeim, à compte d'auteur* (Librairie Christmann, Essey-les-Nancy, 1990), 65.

23 *Journal of Modus Operandi* (JMO) (restored), SHD-Vincennes, 11P250.

24 *Journal of Modus Operandi* (JMO) (restored), SHD-Vincennes, 11P250.

25 Notably, the French destroyed a total of fifty-one enemy tanks and thirty-one armored cars.

26 From June on, General Koenig's Light Division stood up to 37,000 Ger-man–Italian troops, and to 1,400 enemy flights recorded over Bir Hakim during the battle, the position suffering a bombardment of something in the order of 1,400 tons of bombs and 45,000 medium- and large-caliber shells.

27 Telegram from General Catroux to General de Gaulle (London), sent June 16, 1942 from Beirut.

28 Telegram from General de Gaulle (London) to General Catroux in Beirut, July 6, 1942.

29 The Second Light Division was integrated in this division under the com-mand of General Briggs.

30 Reported in many logbook entries for August 8, 1942. See, for example, Twenty-First North African Company or 102 Transport Company.

31 The group attack was led by Cadet Officer Zirneld during the night of June 14 against a military airfield near Benghazi, and then an attack on the station at al-Rejima on June 18; attacks were carried out by Lt. Jacquier's group against the airfields of Derna and Martuba in the same period.

32 Zirneld was mortally wounded on July 24 after the attack on Fuka, and was quickly buried beside the Fuka–Qara road.

33 The two French groups consisted of twenty-two men, in comparison with the one hundred Allied combatants, something on the order of a fifth of the total engaged in that work.

34 All General de Gaulle's quotations are from his *Mémoires de Guerre: L'Appel*, vol. 1, part 2: *Documents*.

35 The Atlantic Charter of August 1941 signed by Churchill and Roosevelt defining war aims was extended to all Allied nations on January 1, 1942 when they became and called themselves thereafter the 'United Nations.' The organization UNO itself was not set up until 1945. The French press of June 12 repeated General Auchinleck's words echoing international praise of the Bir Hakim troops.

36 General Sir Alan Brooke, Chief of the Imperial Staff, wrote to assure de Gaulle that it was with great regret that after the long days of prolonged battling it had been necessary to give the order for evacuation, but that he was glad that at last two thousand of that valiant brigade were able to rejoin their units. He believed that exploits such as theirs continued the most noble of French traditions, echoing in the hearts of Frenchmen, and indeed of people everywhere. Alex Danchev and Daniel Todman, eds., *War Diaries, 1935–45: Field Marshal Lord Alanbrooke*, University of California Press, 2001.

37 Order of the Day, no. 23, June 13, 1942.

38 Winston Churchill's speech, July 2, 1942, *House of Commons Debates*, vol. 381, cols 527–611.

39 SHD-Vincennes, 11P250.

40 De Gaulle, *Mémoires de Guerre*, vol. 1, part 2: *Documents*.

6

Between History and Geography
The El Alamein Project: Research, Findings, and Results

Aldino Bondesan

The El Alamein project began in 2008 as a research project promoted by the University of Padova (Italy) and the Italian Society of Military Geography and Geology, in order to study and preserve the El Alamein battlefield.[1]

Several national and foreign institutions quickly expressed interest in the project and offered patronage when the Italian Senate and the House of Representatives signed memorandums of understanding between the University of Padova and the Italian Graves Commission (Ministry of Defense, Commissariato Generale Onoranze ai Caduti in Guerra), various research institutes, museums, and the Egyptian National Authority for Remote Sensing and Space Sciences.

Even today, access to the desert between El Alamein and the al-Qattara Depression is restricted to the military. The area has been adversely affected in recent years by rapid development of international resorts along the El Alamein coastal areas, and an ever-increasing tourist presence. At the same time the activities of oil-prospecting companies, creating new desert tracks, quarries, and workings across the area, have modified the most significant sites of the El Alamein battlefield: Ruweisat, Mitiriya, Deir al-Munassib, Naqb Rala, Qarat al-Humaymat, Menaquir, and al-Dab'a. The rate of construction around the El Alamein area, the sites along the coast, and the damage caused to the historical site underline the importance of pushing ahead with the project to record what remains.

Surveying and documenting these areas, before the site is transformed to an extent that results in the disappearance of such remarkable and unique historic war remains, is now clearly essential. The El Alamein project has two goals. The first is to establish a complete, detailed database of military archeological remains, and to publish the associated findings. Second, to create from those findings a framework of guidelines for the development of a well-designed historical, cultural tourist site on the old battlefield.

Accordingly, the project concentrates on the geological–historical analysis of the reciprocal relationships between the terrain and the development of military operations. Documentary and field research are based and carried out through a multidisciplinary approach, in close collaboration with researchers with expertise varying from military history to archaeology, from geophysics to topography, from geopolitics to sociology, and so on.

The main activities within the framework of the project can be summarized as follows: the discovery and tracing of several thousands of military emplacements and trenches by means of satellite and field missions, and the surveying of the geological and geomorphological map of the battlefield. The study is based on research in national and foreign historical archives of documents and original papers, including official reports, war journals, maps and sketches, combatants' accounts, books, pictures, and videos; the recovery of more than two hundred aerial photographs from Italian reconnaissance flights before the Alam al-Halfa battle, August 24, 1942; the implementation of a Geographical Information System to collect and analyze data obtained by remote sensing; geological–geomorphological analysis and military digging and emplacement mapping; around twenty field missions for surveying, cleaning, and restoration of emplacements (over three hundred were restored); and ultimately, the creation of the El Alamein Battlefield Historical Park.

From the first, the El Alamein project was oriented toward a military geoscience approach. Military geography is generally recognized in the broadest sense as the application of geographic principles to military affairs or military problems.[2] Military geology is the discipline of studying the interaction of earth sciences with military concerns such as terrain analysis, water supply, and the foundations and construction of military emplacements and buildings, roads, and airfields. Over time, this academic field has broadened into historical analysis and forensic work, opening new perspectives for military history studies.[3]

On the academic side, particular attention has recently been devoted to the reconstruction of battlefield areas, and to military operations in battles that occurred not only in the twentieth century but earlier, from prehistory to modern warfare. Historical data related to their geological setting

Fig 6.1 Defensive positions at El Alamein. All images in this chapter reproduced with kind permission of Aldino Bondesan.
a. Two foxholes dug by Italian paratroops at Hill 105. A foxhole is a vertical hole that allows one or two soldiers to stand and fight with head and shoulders exposed.
b. Antitank gun stronghold of the First Battalion of the 185th Regiment Folgore.
c. Italian machine-gun emplacement at Naqb Rala.
d. Artillery emplacement, probably 88 mm.
e. British trench at Camel Pass.
f. Trenches at Kaponga Box (Qarat al-'Abd) reinforced with grainstone blocks.

Fig 6.2 Items found in desert.

a. Wooden ammunition box.
b. Italian shorts.
c. Pack of 'Macedonia' Italian cigarettes.
d. British boots used by Italians after the fall of Tobruk.
e. Deactivated antitank mines.
f. Ceramic isolators along the palisade (a telegraphic line connecting the coast to al-Moghra).
g. The 'flimsy' was the standard four-gallon can used by the British. They leaked, were easily damaged, quickly corroded, and rarely used twice before being discarded.
h. Letter from an Italian soldier beginning 'VINCEREMO!!!!'—'WE SHALL WIN!!!!,' one of many paper documents found in the holes.

have significantly improved the understanding of military events, command decisions, and operational results; they have also been applied to the dissemination of knowledge through museums, expositions, and historical parks.

Geomorphological Outlines

The first exploratory missions to El Alamein in this framework were devoted to the geological and geomorphological investigations carried out in the Western Desert, south of El Alamein, mainly from Deir al-Munassib to al-Taqa Plateau. Freely available digital elevation data derived from the Shuttle Radar Topography Mission (SRTM-3) and images of the Advanced Spaceborne Thermal Emission and Reflection Radiometer (ASTER), accompanied by field surveys, have led to the production of geomorphological and geological maps, both at a scale of 1:40,000.[4] The maps outline the main rocky and sedimentary outcrops in the area, and the geomorphological processes and related landforms. The Western Desert, far from being flat and monotonous, is in fact the result of the complex interplay of structural, gravitational, and fluvial processes. Concentrated in the southern sector are reliefs lower than three hundred meters.

El Alamein's battlefield is characterized by an arid to hyperarid climate that develops typical desert morphologies: hamada, serir, and wadi-fan systems and so on. In the El Alamein area the climate is arid subtropical, and is characterized by mild, dry winters and dry, very hot summers. The hottest months are July and August, with temperatures ranging from 0°C to 40°C. Rainfalls decrease toward the south, while in the same direction mean temperatures and evaporation increase—so much so that the southernmost sector of the Western Desert is considered one of the driest regions of the world.[5] Mean rainfall is 200 mm a year along the coast and decreases significantly in the Naqb Rala area (50 mm a year). The prevailing winds blow from the northwest.

In the area located along the Mediterranean coast east of the Nile's delta, coastal forms and paleocoastal features develop up to some tens of kilometers inland. Active sebkhas are present in the northern sector of the study area, along the Mediterranean coast, where a number of touristic resorts have already dramatically changed the natural environment. A series of eight ridges, locally called *kurkar*s, run parallel to the present coast.[6] They are the remnants of ancient emerged coastlines. Their elevations range from tens to hundreds of meters and represent the paleostructure of the Nile delta.

Going southward, more typical arid environment morphologies are found. Four main Aeolian depressions are present at Deir al-Qattara, Deir Alinda, Deir al-Munassib, and Deir al-Munafid, together with some minor ones. They developed in an east–west direction and deepen to around thirty meters. They are formed on nearly horizontal structural surfaces and are carved mainly in limestone rocks. To the south, a flat rocky surface is marked by random wadis, while a continuous wadi-fan system generates a belt of soft deposits at the foot of the al-Taqa plateau in the southernmost sector of the study area. This area is characterized by mesas and cuestas forming a step-like morphology toward the great Qattara Depression, whose maximum depth is 165 m below sea level.[7]

The geological background of the area is demonstrated in the geological map of Egypt, sheet no. 20 (1:250,000).[8] The stratigraphic sequence time span is from Early Miocene to Pleistocene. The *kurkars* area is characterized by Pliocene–Pleistocene limestones: the al-Hagif and Alessandria Formations.[9] In the central part is a Pliocene dolomitic carbonate sequence outcrop, the Marmarica Formation, while the southern sector at the border with al-Qattara Depression is characterized by Early Miocene clastic sequence with alternating layers of sandstones, marlstones, and limestone rocks[10] of Moghra Formation, Middle Miocene in age.

Military Remains

Traces of the three battles of El Alamein preserved in the desert are revealed in a huge complex of fortifications, trenches, and diggings, numbering tens of thousands. The traces of cross-connecting tracks built during the war, and the edges of minefields, are also evident. Although many areas have been reclaimed during oil exploration and exploitation activities, there are still many landmines and unexploded ordnance (UXOs) under the desert surface.

The British line of defense set up in 1941 was formed by four fortified sites known as 'boxes': the main entrenched camp of El Alamein, and the three fortified strongholds of Deir al-Shein, Qarat al-'Abd—called 'Kaponga Box' by the British, and 'Fort Menton' by the Axis forces—and finally the 'Camel Pass Box' at Naqb Abu Dweiss.

Urban expansion erased the strongholds belonging to the entrenched belt of El Alamein, and despite research, the site of Deir al-Shein remains undiscovered. The underground structures of Kaponga Box and Camel Pass are in a rather good state of preservation. There are still intact under-

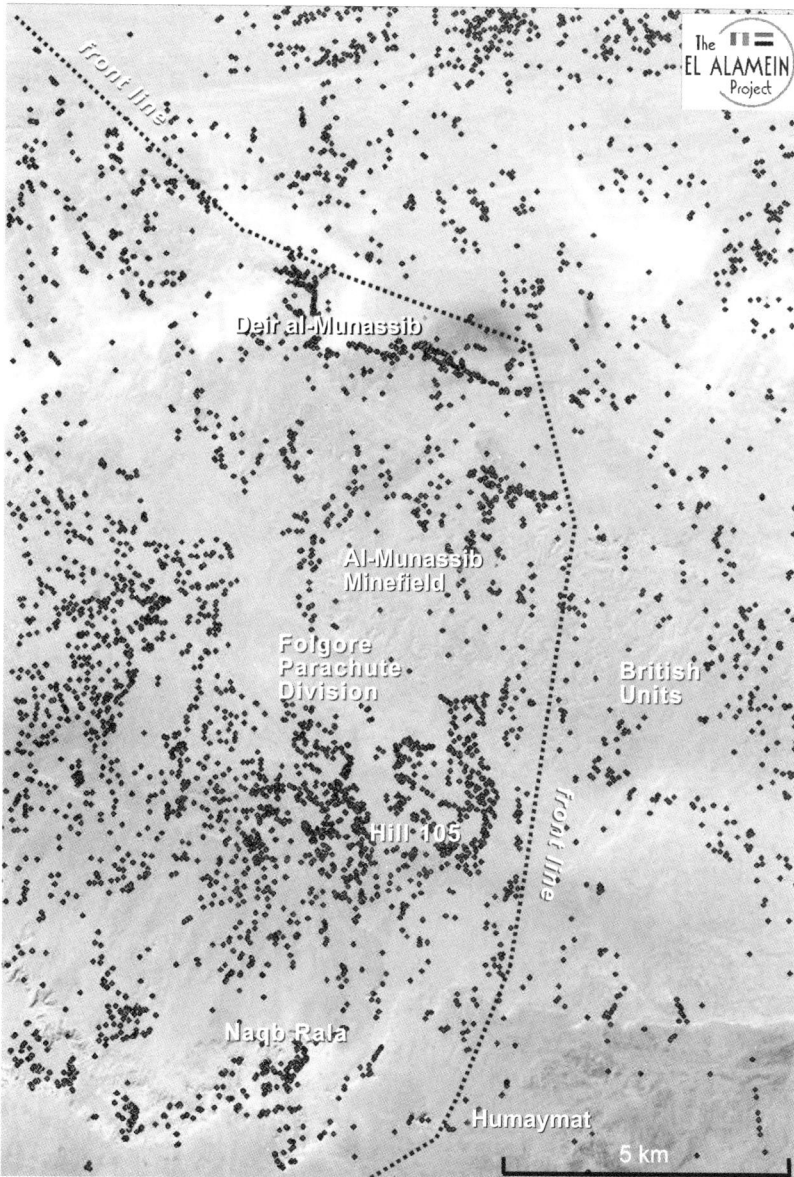

The EL ALAMEIN Project

front line

Deir al-Munassib

Al-Munassib Minefield

Folgore Parachute Division

British Units

Hill 105

front line

Naqb Rala

Humaymat

5 km

Fig 6.3 Distribution of defensive positions and strongholds of the Folgore Division in the southern sector of El Alamein. There are about five thousand holes and diggings.

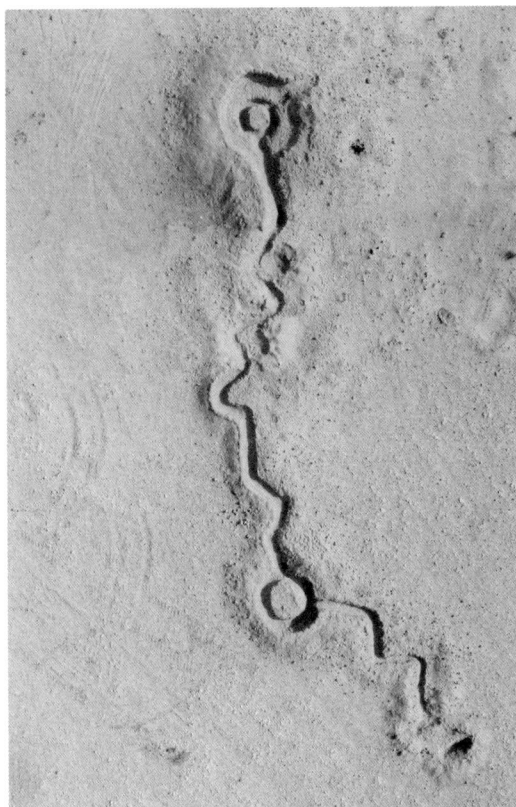

Fig 6.4 Example of aerial photography taken with the KAP system. Emplacement of the 47/32 antitank gun battery commanded by Second Lieutenant Massoni along the line of security to the northeast of Hill 105.

ground masonry shelters here, some partly buried by sand, and remains whose roofs have collapsed. Then there are complex positions, isolated or in groups of dozens or hundreds, that have been occupied by various military units of the opposing armies during the battle. The function of the holes is identified today from their geometry, shape, depth, disposition, and from items preserved inside or around the site. We identified different kinds of defensive positions such as light and heavy artillery emplacements, machine-gun nests, emplacements for fusiliers, command posts, ammunition or equipment depots, motor vehicle shelters, observation posts, foxholes, resting-holes, firing positions, radio or telephone posts, camp kitchens, field hospitals, and so on. Many are individual resting-holes where soldiers would sleep, eat, and leave their own belongings. The vehicles were spaced not less than a hundred meters apart to minimize damage from air strikes or artillery bombing.

The Italian lines in the southern front have been particularly studied. The defensive organization included the minefield first laid by the British in 1941, and later conquered and reinforced by the Italians after the battle of Alam al-Halfa. The minefield was garrisoned by a line of platoon and company strongholds, reinforced by 47/32 antitank guns, light mortars, and Breda machine guns. Given the scarcity of men, materials, and weapons, and with fewer than five thousand soldiers along a fifteen-kilometer front, the line was discontinuous, with large gaps between one combat post and the next, and with no reserve troops at the rear. This first belt was the 'line of security.' In the rear was the 'line of resistance' formed by a second minefield, and a second set of strongholds and firing posts.

In the immediate rear lines, set anything from a few hundred meters to three kilometers back, was the Folgore Artillery Tactical Group, with around eighty pieces of artillery. The pieces were heterogeneous, with artillery groups provided by other divisions in line, and of variable calibers (mostly 75/27, 88/56, 90/53, 100/17, 100/23, 105/28, and 152/45)—many dating from the First World War.

The minefields were bordered by hedges of barbed wire. Their rim is still visible on the ground, from the holes and the piles of stones used to hold the poles of the barbed wires. Today, in the area defended by the Folgore Division, mines are very rarely found; they are generally fragments of casing badly deteriorated by erosion. Nevertheless the region is not yet completely safe and there remains the chance of finding unknown mined areas and UXOs. The mines laid during the war were mainly Italian, German, British, and French. Many tracts of the frontline were defended by antipersonnel mines, often linked to antitank mines and functioning as booby traps. In many cases, the combatants used remote-control artillery shells and aerial bombs, ignited by long wire.

The emplacements were generally shallow because of the hardness of the bedrock (about 50–80 cm), reinforced by stone walls and sandbags. When dug on rocky surface, they are quite well preserved, while in areas covered by flashflood or Aeolian sediments, they have almost all been erased by runoff erosion. The impact craters of the bombs are not easily recognizable. When exploding on soft sands they excavated large craters, soon filled with sand; when falling on a hard rocky surface, they left little but smooth traces of impact.

Fig 6.5 Memorial stone laid at the El Alamein command post of the Fifth Battalion, 186th Regiment Folgore Parachute Division on the Naqb Rala hills in front of Qarat al-Humaymat.

Hundreds of wrecks abandoned after the battle have been removed, and for years fed Egypt's steel industry. All the objects scattered in the desert were collected over time, while many buried metallic materials have been excavated, recovered, and lately destroyed during the Egyptian Army's de-mining operations. Today very little evidence of the battle remains at the surface, apart from some rare fragments of military equipment or tin cans. The excavations for the restoration of the holes brought to light some interesting items for the historical reconstruction. For example, the objects you can still find may be letters, newspapers, or paper documents, cartridge cases, bullets, remains of helmets, pieces of fabric or accoutrements, tent clothes, buttons, wooden boards, tin cans, remnants of gas masks, bottles, boxes, and personal items. Such objects have little value to collectors, but are essential for the reconstruction of historical sites. Although much equipment was shared between the two armies, some findings have made it possible to assign a location to one or another of the opposing forces.

The various sectors of the frontline were connected by the main tracks and a dense network of secondary routes. All the tracks developing on bedrock with little or no sedimentary cover have been preserved over time and are still passable. Some, like the Rommel Track and the Red Track, are still used by vehicles heading to the oilfields of al-Qattara. The routes built by the British have gravelly macadam surfaces, where a local pink dolomite was used as ballast. The macadam preserved the base from soil erosion; and the routes, thanks to a reverse effect of erosion, are now slightly elevated over the desert surface. Stumps of the telegraph poles, and the ceramic insulators of the famous palisade that enabled the telegraph to connect the coast with the Oasis of Moghra, are still visible across the desert.

The 'Cleaning Missions' in the Battlefield

At the end of 2009 a special protocol signed with the Italian Society of Military Geography and Geology (SIGGMI), the National Association of Paratroopers of Italy (ANPd'I), and the web magazine www.conge datifolgore.com gave a boost to the project. Thanks to the work of about two hundred volunteers, a series of missions in the desert, called 'cleaning missions,' were organized to detect and restore the Italian positions in the southern section of the battlefield.

To date, more than five hundred emplacements have been detected, measured, photographed, and surveyed on the ground; and from the satellite, about three thousand were identified and georeferenced. More than one hundred holes have been excavated and restored to their original condition, and some interesting objects found during the excavations have been collected and cataloged; today the desert returns only the few that escaped the meticulous collection by Bedouin, the corrosive action of the hostile climate, and unfortunately also the predations of collectors.

The cleaning missions were interested in the front held by the Folgore Parachute Division and the Pavia Infantry Division, where the main battles in the southern front were fought. Camel Pass, Qarat al-Humaymat, Naqb Rala, Hill 105, Deir al-Munassib, and Deir Alinda evoke the highlights of the Second and Third Battles of El Alamein.

Volunteers, some in military service with the Italian paratroopers, have dug up the holes where the Folgore paratroopers defended the retreat of the Axis at the end of the battle of Alam al-Halfa, fighting against Brigadier G.H. Clifton at Deir Alinda. They found and surveyed the observation post of Lt. Marco Gola, awarded the Gold Medal of Military Valor. He was among the first to face the Foreign Legion on the ramp at Naqb Rala, where the paratroopers of Col. Izzo during the night of October 23, 1942 repelled the troops of Lieutenant Colonel Dimitri Amilakvari.

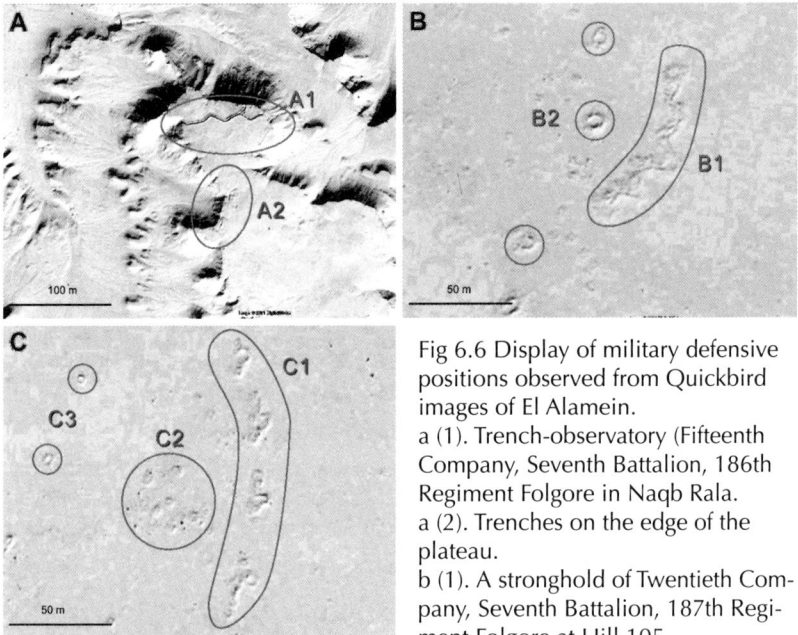

Fig 6.6 Display of military defensive positions observed from Quickbird images of El Alamein.
a (1). Trench-observatory (Fifteenth Company, Seventh Battalion, 186th Regiment Folgore in Naqb Rala.
a (2). Trenches on the edge of the plateau.
b (1). A stronghold of Twentieth Company, Seventh Battalion, 187th Regiment Folgore at Hill 105.
b (2). Rear command/artillery/support emplacements.
c. (1). Battery belonging to the Trieste Division embedded in the Folgore Artillery tactical group on the back lines of Hill 105.
c. (2). Resting hole for the gun crew.
c (3). Shelters for vehicles and support materials.

We located the long trench used as headquarters of the Eleventh Company of the Folgore on the southern flank of Deir al-Munassib, where Capt. Costantino Ruspoli (also awarded the Gold Medal of Military Valor) fell while holding the British attack during the great battle. Many other places and names were identified during reconnaissance in the desert.

Sites were surveyed to create an image database with Geographic Positioning System (GPS) surveys and to study geomorphological and geological observations, in addition to the processes of sedimentation and prospecting that may identify any artifacts and burial places. Survey and reconnaissance are still performed during the field missions.

The Geographic Information System

In recent years, the use of software for storing and processing a variety of geographic information makes it possible to study even complex problems using georeferenced data, that is, data sharing the same geographical coordinates. The combination of all this information into a single geo-graphic database is the Geographic Information System (GIS) described as "a powerful set of tools for collecting, storing, retrieving at will, trans-forming and displaying spatial data from the real world for a particular set of purposes."[11]

GIS is increasingly used for the study and management of historical and military information in different geographical areas and for different issues, for example, the study of the Italian military campaign in Rus-sia.[12] Also, interesting applications of digital terrain models in the study of problems related to military geography have been investigated by Frank-lin and Guth,[13] Guth,[14] and Obrock and Guth.[15]

The GIS implemented in the El Alamein project[16] provides an inte-grated base that can quickly manage a complex set of information. The system was developed primarily using ArcGIS™; many intermediate steps, however, made use of different software that has proved very useful, particularly in the field surveys, such as Google Earth and its georeferenc-ing tools for the distinguishing of trenches and holes, AutoCAD Map™ for digitization, and ENVI™ for the processing of remote sensing data. Field data were archived into Access™.

Initially, the problems to be solved were mainly related to scale and georeferencing. Particularly complex was the georeferencing of sketches of the battlefield drawn by veterans, or found in monographs dealing with historical reconstruction, more for the poor topographic accuracy than for their general unreliability. In these cases, the topo-graphical data have been linked to morphological elements, ensuring rather good georeferencing. In any case, the tools used have made it easier to identify objects with different spatial resolutions, such as maps or sketches at different scales, or the detection of natural or manmade forms of different sizes.

Satellite imagery. The geological–military study of the El Alamein area made use of satellite images from various sources, particularly Quickbird, Landsat, and ASTER images. The Quickbird images were used for the detection of artifacts of war, such as trenches, pits, and tracks still preserved on the battlefield. Quickbird is an artificial satellite for commercial remote sensing at high spatial resolution, the property of DigitalGlobe, able to record images in panchromatic mode with a resolution of 60–70 cm, and in multispectral mode with a resolution of approximately 2.4 to 2.8 m.

ASTER images were used for the interpretation of geological and geomorphological areas and the creation of a digital terrain model (DTM) of the area of El Alamein. The Advanced Spaceborne Thermal Emission and Reflection Radiometer (ASTER) is one of five remote sensors located onboard the satellite Terra (EOS AM-1). The satellite is part of the Earth Observing System (EOS) and was placed in a geostationary orbit by NASA in 1999. In particular, the sensor ASTER has been active since February 2000. ASTER provides high-resolution images of the earth in fourteen different wavelengths, ranging from the electromagnetic spectrum of visible light to infrared. The angular resolution of the images is between 15 and 90 m.[17] The sensor data allow the creation of detailed maps of temperature, emissivity, reflectance, and elevation of the land surface.

The Landsat images were used mainly for the general definition of the battlefield. Landsat is a constellation of satellites for remote sensing. We used data from Landsat-4 and Landsat-5, equipped with a sensor called Thematic Mapper (TM); Landsat-6, which is equipped with an Enhanced Thematic Mapper (ETM); and Landsat-7, with a spatial resolution of 15 m in panchromatic.

Digital elevation models. Digital elevation models (DEMs) derived from ASTER (30 m/pixel resolution) and SRTM (90 m/pixel resolution)[18] have been used to place contour lines. These were compared with the less-detailed information of the 1:100,000 topographic map (1942) previously georeferenced. Processing the DEMs, we obtained the slope map, the exposure map, and the hill shading map of the battlefield. These thematic maps have been proved to be particularly useful to highlight the main geomorphological features of the study area, such as, for example, the presence of *kurkar*s, escarpments, and *deir*s.

Aerial photographs. The GIS contains numerous black-and-white aerial photographs from some surveys performed during certain phases of the battle. Particularly significant are the 210 aerial photographs collected during Italian reconnaissance just before the battle of Alam al-Halfa, in which the dislocation and amount of vehicles, weapons, and troops deployed on the British side of the front may be clearly discerned. This is a shot made by the Italian Royal Air Force on August 24, 1942 with a specially equipped aircraft Cant Z 1007bis. All frames were georeferenced on the base of control points recognized by comparison with current satellite images.

Aerial photographs of the time are integrated by Corona and Soyuz images, whose low resolution, however, makes them less useful to the reconstruction of the battlefield. For the first time, in the eleventh mission of the El Alamein project, which was held in November 2011, detailed pictures of strongholds were made by use of a kite aerial photograph (KAP) system. This technique, first proposed in 1886 by Arthur Batut and also used by the military until the advent of aviation, consists of taking photographs from heights ranging from a few to several hundred meters, holding up a camera in zenithal position with a lifter kite. The device consists of a rotating rig equipped with an automatic shutter (System BEAK-AuRiCo with gentLED intervalometer) for repeatedly triggering on a 13-megapixel digital camera). From a height of two hundred meters, in the experiment carried out in the desert, the KAP has allowed the recognition of the defensive positions and of certain forms and craters generated by bomb explosions and traces of the borders of minefields, undetectable by satellite photos. This technique, extended to other areas of the battlefield and combined with measurements on the ground, made possible a detailed analysis of both the location of units down to the level of platoon, and recognition of defensive structures.

Topographic maps, military maps, sketches, and drawings. All the maps dating to wartime were found and used. They were based on former British surveys and maps and edited by the Italian Geographic Military Institute. In particular, we made use of the following 1:100,000 scale sheets: El Alamein, al-Hammam, Moghra, Qarat Somara, and al-Dab'a, covering the whole area of study.

As previously indicated, in the GIS we included various sketches and drawings made in the field during the battles, such as some sketch maps stored in the military archives of the Italian Army General Staff in Rome, or sketches of the battlefield reconstructed retrospectively by veterans.

We used maps showing the locations of German minefields, reproductions of original maps (including the Rommel maps found at the National Archives),[19] tables published in the volume edited by the Italian Historical Office of the Army General Staff, and the relevant official historical publications.[20]

Database of Military Artifacts

Data obtained from field surveys of trenches and holes were included in an Access™ database. The software tags contain all the information from the forms filled during field surveys. In particular, the form contains for each hole an identification code, the date of issue, the mission number, and the name of the compiler. It also reports the geographic coordinates, WGS84, the location, and a set of information concerning the characteristics and use of the trenches, including the shape, type, and probable use, dimensional characteristics, the geological–geomorphological outlines, the army and unit occupying the site (on the basis of its geographical location), and any artifacts found within the structure. It also provides a brief description of each artifact and its relationship to any nearby objects, as well as a record of any restoration work carried out. On the forms are also listed the reference numbers of any photographs or field sketches of the trench.

The measurements were carried out in accordance with standardized protocols, in particular regarding acquisition of the photographic material. The protocol provides that every surveyed defensive element, trench, emplacement, foxhole, and so on, is photographed from the four cardinal directions, so that both the structure and the horizon will be shown. In this way it is possible to depict in detail both the digging and the surrounding environment. The database also contains scans of the sketches of the trenches made by the surveyors.

Historical Photographs

As part of the research project, many historic photographs were collected for both their military and geographical aspects. The scanned images were included in the GIS whenever possible, indicating the probable sites of gun positions.

The Geological Map of the Southern Front

On the basis of the 1:500,000 map developed by Conoco Coral and Egyptian General Petroleum Corporation (1986–87), and other previous geological bibliography for this area,[21] spectral data from the ASTER sensor have been processed, allowing us to obtain a geological map of the area at scale 1:40,000. The identification of several rocky outcrops and surface deposits in the area was made possible through the processing of satellite imagery. Several false-color compositions and transformations of the original bands were performed through mathematical and statistical operations, such as relationships between bands and principal components analysis (PCA).

The Geomorphological Map of the Southern Front
For the editing of the geomorphological map of the southern front at 1:40,000 scale, a literature search was performed to allow not only the identification of forms and processes that are characteristic of desert environments, but also to get information on those specific morphologies in this area, such as *deir*s and *kurkar*s.[22] The identification of these forms was based primarily on the use of remote sensing data, on DEM analysis, and the results obtained from the survey of ground control points (GCPs).

The Ground Control Points
The interpretation of remotely sensed data was supported by the choice of thirty-six GCPs. The analysis of the control points led to the verification of the lithological composition of the surface through precise analyses of the spectral signatures derived from ASTER images, and to the ground verification of the correct interpretation of satellite data and acquisition of additional information through photographic study.

The analysis was developed through the following phases: a) determination of sampling points by calculating the spatial coordinates; b) photographic field survey according to a protocol especially developed for this purpose; c) spectral signature analysis by calculation of the indices Band Ratio (BR) and Relative Band Depth (RBD);[23] d) statistical analysis applied to the indices BR and RBD obtained through measures of central tendency and variability, calculation of frequencies, and bivariate analyses between different indices.

The El Alamein Battlefield Historical Park
As part of the work of protection of the places of the battle, it was decided to promote the creation of the El Alamein Battlefield Historical Park. The park will be created by placing a series of memorial stones with low environmental and landscape impact in the places of the main flow of the battle, and will be implemented in two distinct phases for the southern and northern sector.[24] About one hundred memorial stones will be placed by the end of the project inside the entire battlefield;

each stone will be part of a single itinerary dedicated to the fighting that occurred, or to the units present, in the area. There is a close connection between the battle sites and the geological and geomorphological features of the battlefield, so that the description of each visiting path is intimately connected with the morphological characteristics, location of defenses, and military events. The park is therefore a good example of the application of military geology in a critical area to the history of the Second World War.

About fifty stones have been laid in the southern sector of the battlefield where Italian Folgore and Pavia Divisions were deployed and were subject to repeated attacks by the Eighth Army; this happened after the Second Battle of El Alamein (Deir al-Munassib, September 30, 1942), and in the Third Battle, mainly during Operation Lightfoot. Northern itineraries will be created and placed during 2012 and 2013.

In the initial phase (March 2011) some iron signs were laid in imitation of a sundial which, in 1942, served to facilitate orientation in an area almost totally devoid of topographical references. The damage to some of them by vandals corrupted the signs, leaving only crumbling concrete.

Each stone shows the coat of arms of the division that fought there in 1942, in addition to indications of geographical location, identification number, and the names of those who have contributed to it, with dedications.

Each site installation coincides with a site that was of particular importance during the armed clashes. Using specific publications in progress, or free software like Google Earth™ and GPS technology, visitors can start virtual tours or directly visit the sites of military actions. Moreover, the stones represent tangible points for the remembrance of the fallen.

The memorial stones have also been designed to be produced in pairs and, at the request of the donor, to be located one in the desert and the other in Italy, to create a sense of direct link to the El Alamein battlefield. These Italian memorial stones, the counterpart of the desert ones, have been installed in city parks, barracks, and other sites.

The park has no government funding and is entirely sponsored by the subscriptions of individual donors. The installation takes place through the work of self-financing volunteers. The financial costs of construction are partly supported by private sponsors, and that allows us to limit the cost of production and transport to the benefit of supporters of the El Alamein Battlefield Historical Park.

The Itineraries

Five distinct routes are allotted to the southern sector of the front, each designated a letter of the alphabet and color. Each itinerary refers to a geographic area over which the Italian troops were deployed, and which was affected by the conflict.

Itinerary A: The fighting at Naqb Rala. This is the southernmost sector of the Italian defensive line occupied by the Fifth Battalion of the 186th Regiment, Folgore Division. The mesas hills, ranging about two hundred meters above sea level, form a natural bulwark on which Colonel Izzo, commander of the battalion, carefully deployed about 350 paratroopers. Here on the night of October 23, 1942, two battalions of the Free French Brigade, supported by British soldiers and heavy weapons, were repelled by paratroopers, at the cost of heavy losses.[25] The battle took place at Naqb Rala (*naqb* in Arabic means pass) that cuts the low mountains of the eastern plateau of al-Taqa. The defense was favored by the conformation of the ground, which forced the French and British units to be channeled into a wide corridor, known as 'the Ramp,' where the paratroopers, separated in small groups, could counterattack, hiding behind the small bumps and rocks that form outcrops on this sector. The ten memorial stones that were placed show the arrangement of the companies (Thirteenth, Fourteenth, and Fifteenth, Folgore Division) and the command posts located there.

Itinerary B: Hill 105: The Raggruppamento Ruspoli. Hill 105 is a wide and uniformly rocky plateau that develops in correspondence with a structural surface of calcareous rock of the Pliocene Age. The eastern side, facing the British deployment, and the northern and southern margins, are marked by a low escarpment that has a vertical drop of several meters, incised by wadis that radiate in a centrifugal direction toward the neighboring areas. The Raggruppamento Ruspoli (Ruspoli Group) was formed by the Seventh Battalion, the Eighth Sappers Battalion, a company of Second Battalion, the Thirty-First Sappers Battalion of Col. Paolo Caccia Dominioni, and some batteries of the Folgore Artillery Tactical Group, reinforced, during the Third Battle, with Pavia elements.[26] The concentration of the defensive line at this point was conditioned by specific geological–geomorphological elements, determined mainly by the presence of a rocky surface that allowed for high trafficability (mobility: volume and speed) of motorized vehicles and armored personnel carriers—hence its choice as the main line of attack by the British—and the slightly higher elevation than adjacent areas, to guarantee the defenders even a small position of advantage. To the north, the surface of the desert was more articulate in low relief and sandy plains, less easily passable, and defended by the largest minefield in the front of El Alamein: the al-Munassib Minefield, almost five kilometers wide. Here Montgomery exerted his maximum pressure to implement the breaching of the southern front during the third battle. After two days and nights of heavy fighting, from October 23 to 25, 1942, the British attack shattered the 'line of resistance' and broke through the 'line of security,' leading to the annihilation of several companies of the Folgore. The British units retreated, moving north to the main attack during Operation Supercharge.

The tour is organized along three main lines that refer to commands and artillery positioned on the immediate rear lines—the line of resistance—set back from the second mined strip, and finally to the line of security on the frontline, facing the minefields placed along the British front.

Itinerary C: The Folgore Division resists at Deir al-Munassib. The Deir al-Munassib depression is the main Aeolian depression across the front, and, along with Deir Alinda and Deir al-Qattara, forms a corridor with an east–southeast/west–northwest axis. It was a salient in the British lines, representing a threat to Montgomery, who repeatedly tried to conquer it. After failed attacks in the more southern positions, on October 26 the Fourth Battalion Folgore deployed on the southern flank of the depression, facing north and east, came under increased British pressure. Here, repeated attacks of British armored and infantry units led to heavy losses among the paratroopers and still more among the attackers. The paratroopers, reduced to a handful of men, managed to fight and repel the British offensive. Here too, the geomorphology very strongly influenced Italian defensive frame. The southern flank of the depression made it possible to maintain a dominant position over the attackers, and the rocky outcrops provided even a modest protection. On the east, defended by the Twelfth and some of the Eleventh Company, the emplacements were aligned on the edge of the relief, which rises very gradually from a few meters to ten meters over the minefields that separated the Italians from the Eighth Army.

The itinerary includes emplacements of the Twenty-Sixth Company that guarded the al-Munassib Minefield at the rear, the commands and artillery support of the Trieste and Pavia Divisions, the positions of the

Second Battalion Folgore deployed west of Deir al-Munassib, and the lines garrisoned by the Tenth, Eleventh, and Twelfth Companies.

Itinerary D: al-Taqa Plateau: The southern front. The al-Taqa Plateau covers about twenty kilometers from the well-known hill of Qarat al-Humaymat up to the Camel Pass and Pass for Cars. It is a plateau composed of terraces at different altitudes and bounded on the south by systems of very steep slopes, interrupted only by the passage of Naqb al-Khadim. Here came the first units of the Folgore in August 1942. The area was conquered during the Battle of Alam al-Halfa in late August and early September, and then occupied by the infantrymen of Pavia Division, who presided until the withdrawal in November. Due to the steep escarpments, the plateau formed an impenetrable natural barrier to both light and armored vehicles and in fact, no fighting occurred during the third battle.

The tour is limited to the eastern side of the al-Taqa Plateau, where the Pavia Division was settled on the higher rocky terrace facing the great al-Qattara Depression to the south. To the west, a memorial stone indicates the pass from which the palisade crossed the relief going to Moghra Oasis.

Itinerary E: Operation Beresford. The scenario of Operation Beresford belongs to the final stages of the Battle of Alam al-Halfa when, in an attempt to close the retreating Italo–German columns, Montgomery tried to occupy Deir al-Munassib with an attack from the north by the Fifth New Zealand Brigade, 132nd British, and Forty-Sixth and Fiftieth Royal Tanks. The Folgore (Italy) and Ramke (Germany) Parachute Divisions were deployed on the northern edge of Deir al-Munassib, in Deir Alinda and Deir al-Anqar. They repelled the attack at the cost of the annihilation of the Tenth Battalion Folgore, which was never reconstituted. Even here, the morphology of the Aeolian depressions strongly influenced the development of the defensive organization of Axis troops along the margins of depressions.

This route is dedicated to the different units who fought in this area in the early days of September 1942.

Notes

1   The author gratefully acknowledges: Lamberto Fabbrucci, Nicola Petrella, Walter Amatobene, Mauricio Nicolas Vergara, Laura Bortolami, Roberto Francese, Ludovico Slongo, Matteo Massironi, Stefano Furlani, and many

other colleagues and students. The author is indebted to over two hundred volunteers who came to work and survey in the desert of El Alamein, and to over a hundred donors who sponsored the memorial stones of the historical park.

The El Alamein project is the result of the collective work of many authors and organizations. Among these we acknowledge and thank the Egyptian National Authority for Remote Sensing and Space Sciences (NARSS); Franco Coren and Roberto Francese of the Italian National Institute of Oceanography and Applied Geophysics (OGS); Gen. Vittorio Barbato, Commissioner of the Italian Grave Commission (Ministry of Defense—Commissariato Generale Onoranze ai Caduti in Guerra); Franco Porcelli, Scientific Attaché of the Italian Embassy in Cairo; and Gen. Giovanni Fantini, President of the National Association of Paratroopers of Italy.

The El Alamein Battlefield Historical Park is managed by an informal organizing committee: the general coordination was conducted by the University of Padova, Department of Geography, SIGGMi, www.congedatifolgore.com and ANPd'I. The working group includes Aldino Bondesan, Walter Amatobene, Lamberto Fabbrucci, Nicola Petrella, Antonio Cardinali, and Flavia Breda. The design phase was carried out in collaboration with the Ente Scuola Edile in Piacenza (Italy), and the Piacenza ANPd'I Section. The execution of the first signals was sponsored by Claudio Paggiola and Giovanni Furlani. Transport was organized and partly funded by www.congedatifolgore.com, Tarros, and ECL. The memorial stones were laid during the 'cleaning missions,' with the help of Folgore paratroopers, veterans, and other volunteers. The donors of the memorial stones are cited in the journal *Folgore!* and institutional web sites (www.siggmi.it; www.congedatifolgore.com). Gotica Toscana Onlus collaborated in the field research.

2   J.M. Collins, "Military Geography for Professionals and the Public," *Association of the United States Army*, 1998; see also E.J. Palka and F.A. Galgano, *Military Geography: From Peace to War* (Boston: McGraw Hill, 2005).

3   D.R. Caldwell, J. Ehlen, and R.S. Harmon, *Studies in Military Geography and Geology* (Berlin: Springer, 2006); P. Doyle and M.R. Bennet, "Fields of Battle, Terrain in Military History," *Geojournal Library*, 64 (2002); J. Ehlen and R.S. Harmon, "The Environmental Legacy of Military Operations," in *Reviews in Engineering Geology* 16 (2005), 51–66 ; J.R. Underwood and Peter L. Guth, "Military Geology in War and Peace" (Boulder, CO: *The Geological Society of America* 13 (1998): 245; E.P. Rose and C.P. Nathanial, *Geology and Warfare: Examples of the Influence of Terrain and Geologists on Military Operations* (Boulder, CO: *The Geological Society of America* 13 (2000): 498.

4   Aldino Bondesan, S. Furlani, M.N. Vergara, L. Fabbrucci, R. Francese, and N. Petrella, "Il GIS per la ricostruzione del campo di battaglia di El Alamein (Egitto, 1942) attraverso remote sensing e l'analisi della cartografia storica militare." Supplemento di *Geologia dell'Ambiente*, Numero Speciale "Geografia e Geologia Militare" (April, 2011): 17–22.

5   H. Kehl and X. Bornkamm, "Landscape Ecology and Vegetation Units of the Western Desert of Egypt," in *Geopolitical Ecology: Analysis of a Desert Region*, ed. by B. Meisser and P. Wycisk, "Catena Supplement," 26, 407–38.

6   N.S. Embabi, *The Geomorphology of Egypt: Landforms and Evolution*, vol. 1, *The Nile Valley and the Western Desert* (Cairo: The Egyptian Geographical Society Special Publication, 2004).

7   Embabi, *Geomorphology of Egypt*.

8   R. Said, *The Geology of Egypt* (Amsterdam: Elsevier Publishing Co., 1962); and R. Said, *The Geology of Egypt* (Rotterdam: Balkema, 1990): 734.

9   R. Said, *The Geology of Egypt* (Amsterdam: Elsevier Publishing Co., 1962); and R. Said, *The Geology of Egypt* (Rotterdam: Balkema, 1990): 734.

10 A. El-Barkooky, M. Hamdan, S.M. Hassan, N. Christie-Blick, S. Goldstein, and Y. Cai, "Sequence Stratigraphy of the Lower Miocene Moghra Formation in the Qattara Depression, Northwestern Desert, Egypt," paper presented at the AAPG Annual Convention, Denver, Colorado, June 7–10, 2009.

11 P.A. Burrough, *Principles of Geographical Information Systems for Land Resource Assessment* (Oxford: Clarendon Press), 1986.

12 P. Plini, S. Di Franco, V. De Santis, and R. Salvatori, "Un sistema informativo geografico sulle operazione dell esercito italiano durante la campagna di Russia (1941–1943)," *Supplemento di Geologia dell'Ambiente, Numero Speciale: Geografia e Geologia Militare* 4 (2011): 17–24.

13 K.B. Franklin, and L. Guth, "Effects of DEM Re-interpolation on *Viewshared* Computation," in *Military Geography and Geology: History and Technology*, ed. by C.P. Nathanail, R.J. Abrahart, and R.P. Bradshaw (Nottingham, UK: Land Quality Press, 2008), 295–301.

14 L. Guth, "Challenges for Military Application of High Resolution Digital Elevation Models (DEMs)," in *Military Geography and Geology*, 303–12.

15 K. Obrock, and L. Guth, "Filling Holes in SRTM DEMs Using ASTER DEMs," in *Military Geography and Geology*, 313–22.

16 Bondesan et al. "Il GIS per la ricostruzione del campo di battaglia."

17 Y. Yamaguchi, A.B. Kahle, H. Tsu, T. Kawakami, and M. Pniel, "Overview of Advanced Spaceborne Thermal Emission and Reflection Radiometer (ASTER)," *IEEE Transactions on Geoscience and Remote Sensing* 36 (1998): 1062–71.

18 T.G. Farr, et al., "The Shuttle Radar Topography Mission," *Review of Geophysics* 45 (2004), doi:10.1029/2005, RG000183, 2007.

19 http://www.nationalarchives.gov.uk/

20   Official national documents: United Kingdom Military Series, Australia, Australian War Memorial publications; and New Zealand, The Official Story of New Zealand in Second World volume series, N.Z., etc.

21   El Barkooky et al., "Sequence Stratigraphy"; R. Said, cited in *The Geology of Egypt* (1990).

22   Embabi, *Geomorphology of Egypt*.

23   M.A. Gomarasca, ed., *Elementi di Geomatica* (Galliate Lombardo, Varese: Associazione Italiana di Telerilevamento, 2004); L.C. Rowan and J.C. Mars, "Lithological Mapping in the Mountain Pass, California Area, Using Advanced Spaceborne Thermal Emission and Reflection Radiometer (ASTER) Data," *Remote Sensing of Environment*, 84 (2003): 350–66.

24   A. Bondesan, S. Furlani, M.N. Vergara, and M. Massironi, *Geomorphology of the Southern Sector of the El Alamein Battlefield* (Egypt) (extended abstract), IV Giornata dei giovani geomorfologi, Como, settembre 2011, 28–30.

25   P. Caccia Dominioni and G. Izzo, *Takfir* (Milano: Longanesi e C., 1972).

26   M. Montanari, *Le operazioni in Africa Settentrionale*, vol. 3: *gennaio–novembre 1942* (Roma: Uff. Storico, SME, 1993).

7

Silent Service

The Royal Navy and the Desert Victory

Nick Hewitt

T he Second Battle of El Alamein has been justifiably identified as
the key turning point in the Western Desert campaign and, arguably, even of the war in the west. Winston Churchill wrote of the
battle that "it marked . . . the turning of the 'Hinge of Fate.' It may almost
be said, 'Before Alamein we never had a victory. After Alamein we never
had a defeat.'"[1] He went on to give the fourth volume of his *History of the
Second World War* the subtitle *The Hinge of Fate*.

But without losing sight of what was achieved on land, it is important
to remember one of the most important reasons for Montgomery's victory. By the end of 1942, the Royal Navy had secured almost total control
of the Mediterranean despite being at times outnumbered, outgunned,
and faced with perhaps the most intransigent enemy of all: geography.
Without this control of the sea, it is probably not an exaggeration to
argue that Operation Supercharge might never have taken place at all.

Before the Second World War, British naval strategy in the Mediterranean had been founded on one vital premise: cooperation with a powerful
and modern French fleet, which controlled the Western Mediterranean
from bases scattered around the south of France and the coastline of
France's North African colonies. The British Mediterranean Fleet, commanded by Admiral Sir Andrew Cunningham and based at Alexandria
and Malta, had responsibility for the Eastern Mediterranean. With no
significant German naval forces in the Mediterranean in September 1939,
the Allied navies dominated the theater of operations, even after the entry
of Italy into the war on June 10, 1940.

Fig 7.1 The sinking of the *Bartolemo Colleoni* after her encounter with HMAS *Sydney*, July 19, 1940. (IWM A 219)

The Franco–German Armistice of June 22 changed the strategic balance at a stroke. Cunningham's fleet, consisting of four old battleships, one obsolete aircraft carrier capable of operating just twelve aircraft, nine cruisers, twenty-five destroyers, and twelve submarines, was now outnumbered by the Italians alone, whose fleet numbered six battleships (two brand new), nineteen cruisers, around seventy-five destroyers and smaller escorts, and 113 submarines. The Italians also enjoyed overwhelming superiority in the air, with over two thousand aircraft operating short distances from home bases. Cunningham also faced the very real possibility of French warships being used against him by the Italians or the Germans. Just as importantly, the geographic balance had now altered. The Mediterranean was now almost entirely ringed by hostile or potentially hostile coastline, should the Germans decide to occupy the collaborationist Vichy French state and its North African colonies. What remained was neutral. British power now depended on the key bases of Gibraltar in the west and Alexandria in the east, along with the vulnerable islands of Malta and Cyprus, the former uncomfortably situated just ninety-six kilometers away from Italian air bases in Sicily.

The British Admiralty contemplated withdrawal from the Mediterranean altogether, but this was vetoed by Churchill, who would not contemplate abandoning either the vital supply route to the Far East via the Suez Canal, or—more importantly—the only theater of war in which the British could directly engage an Axis power. A new force was hastily put together and dispatched to Gibraltar to fill the vacuum left by the French in the west; this was the famous 'Force H,' under the command of Admiral Sir James Somerville.

The British were then faced with a difficult decision: how best to deal with the potential threat posed by the French fleet, still largely intact and much of it based in Mediterranean ports. Under the terms of the Franco–German Armistice, the French fleet was supposed to remain under French control and demilitarized, but nobody had much faith in Hitler keeping his word. On July 3, 1940, French ships in British ports were seized, generally peacefully; although at Devonport, blood was shed on board the giant submarine *Surcouf*: the first fatalities in what one author has christened 'England's last war with France.'[2] On the same day, Somerville's Force H was dispatched to the Algerian port of Mers-el-Kebir, where the new French battle cruisers *Dunkerque* and *Strasbourg* were based, along with two older battleships and a number of smaller vessels. Somerville's task, codenamed Operation Catapult and personally ordered by Winston Churchill, by now Britain's new prime minister, was to do whatever it took to neutralize the French warships. The French commander, Admiral Marcel-Bruno Gensoul, was given an ultimatum: either join forces with the British, sail to a British port and be impounded, sail to a port in the French West Indies and be immobilized, or scuttle within six hours. If he refused any of these options, Somerville had orders to fire on the French fleet. When Gensoul contacted Paris for instructions, he reported that the only option he had been given was to scuttle within six hours. This 'offer' was unsurprisingly rejected and he was instructed to resist. At 1754h Somerville's ships opened fire. The old battleship *Bretagne* blew up almost immediately, and sank with heavy loss of life when a shell penetrated one of her magazines. Her sister ship *Provence* was damaged, along with the battle cruiser *Dunkerque* and several smaller warships. The incomplete battle cruiser *Strasbourg* made a dramatic bid for freedom, escaping the British blockade and fending off an air attack, before nightfall ensured her safety; she reached Toulon the following day. On July 6, Somerville's Swordfish torpedo bombers returned to Mers-el-Kebir, inflicting further damage on the remaining French ships. Another attack at Dakar crippled the brand-new battleship *Richelieu*. A French force marooned at Alexandria, directly under the guns of Cunningham's fleet, wisely decided to disarm.

The attack on Mers-el-Kebir was a gamble. The loss of life was truly dreadful; 1,297 Frenchmen died, and another 350 were wounded, most aboard the *Bretagne*. Many Frenchmen never forgave the British for what they saw as an appalling betrayal, and the attack came close to bringing the collaborationist Vichy French regime, which governed the unoccupied zone of France, back into the war on the Axis side. It led directly to Vichy air raids on Gibraltar, and Vichy agreement to Axis use of bases in Syria and Bizerta. But Churchill's ruthless decision ended the alarming possibility of modern French warships with Italian or German crews roaming the Mediterranean, as well as sending a clear signal to neutrals, notably in the United States, that his government was prepared to do whatever it took to win the war.

This still left the Italians, who, emboldened by the French defeat, began to operate with increased confidence. In particular, they began to run heavily escorted supply convoys across the Mediterranean to their armies in Libya. Admiral Sir Andrew Cunningham has been compared to Nelson, notably by his biographer, and when faced with an enemy who outnumbered him he acted in the finest Nelsonian tradition and went on the offensive. He began by using his smaller ships and aircraft to harry Italian coastal shipping running along the Libyan coast, a tactic which he was able to maintain for much of the next two years with notable success. Then in early July, he received reports that a strong Italian force was at sea, returning from Benghazi in Libya after escorting a convoy. On July 9, Cunningham managed to locate and engage the Italians. Although the engagement was little more than an inconclusive skirmish, later grandly entitled the Battle of Calabria, Cunningham pursued the Italians to within sight of their own coast, and his flagship, the elderly battleship HMS *Warspite*, scored a hit on the battleship *Julio Cesare* at a range of twenty-four kilometers. Ten days later the Australian cruiser HMAS *Sydney* kept up the pressure by sinking the Italian cruiser *Bartolomeo Colleoni* in a running fight off Crete.

Italian strategy is often characterized as faintheartedness, sometimes willfully as a result of lazy stereotyping. The Italians had no incentive to seek out a fleet action. Although Cunningham's action had startled them, the vital convoy had already been safely delivered by the time his force found the Italian fleet, and he had required a considerable degree of luck to make the interception. Essentially, the British base at Alexandria was too far away to mount an effective challenge for control of the central Mediterranean. Only forces based at Malta could effectively interdict the Italian supply traffic to the North African battlefields. But Malta was marooned just a few minutes' flying time from the Italian coast, and a naval striking force could not operate from the island without the support of far more modern fighter aircraft than Churchill was willing or able to send out from the UK in 1940, when Britain was fighting for its life against the full weight of the German Air Force. A stalemate existed, one which the Italians could have exploited by attempting to seize Malta when it was at its most vulnerable, had any senior Italian commander realized its importance and taken advantage of its vulnerability at this time.

Fortunately for British strategy in the Mediterranean, however, none did so, although the idea of seizing the island was discussed by both Italian and later German planners several times over the next two years. Instead, toward the end of the year it was Cunningham who was able to break the deadlock in a single, daring blow. On the night of November 21, 1940, twenty-one obsolescent Swordfish torpedo bombers launched from the aircraft carrier HMS *Illustrious* attacked the Italian fleet at anchor in its main base at Taranto, in southern Italy. Achieving complete surprise and dropping flares to illuminate their targets, they sank the battleships *Littorio*, *Conte di Cavour*, and *Caio Duilio* at their moorings for the loss of only two aircraft. The results of the raid were immediate and decisive; as Churchill later wrote, "By this single stroke the balance of naval power in the Mediterranean was decisively altered."[3] The Italians moved all their remaining seaworthy warships to safer harbors in the far north of the country, and the British were able to move about the Mediterranean almost unmolested. One key result of this was the availability of warships to support the advance of General Richard O'Connor's Western Desert Force along the Libyan coast road to Tobruk in December. Conversely, for the first time his Italian opponents found their supply ships being intercepted and sunk by submarines and strike aircraft based at Malta. The Taranto raid was the first seaborne air strike carried out against a defended base and was studied with great interest by, among others, the Japanese, who used it as a model for the subsequent attack on the American fleet at Pearl Harbor.

In January 1941, the Germans were forced to step in to assist their hard-pressed Italian ally. On land, General Erwin Rommel's Deutsches Afrikakorps was dispatched to stabilize the situation and save Mussolini's North African empire. Rommel's arrival coincided with the transfer of most of O'Connor's troops to Greece, which had been attacked by Italy on October 28, and consequently the DAK was able to sweep back across the desert, besieging Tobruk and capturing O'Connor and thousands of British and Commonwealth troops. At the same time, to support Rommel by winning back control of the Mediterranean and neutralizing Malta, the Luftwaffe's X. Fliegerkorps, a specialist antishipping formation, was transferred to Sicily and immediately made its presence felt by badly damaging HMS *Illustrious* and sinking the cruiser HMS *Southampton*. Cunningham's offensive was put on hold until a replacement carrier, HMS *Formidable*, arrived in theater. For the next two years, the ebb and flow of the North African campaign would be directly linked to the shifting balance of power at sea and, in particular, the availability of Malta as a knife held to the throat of Rommel's supply lines.

On March 25, 1941, Ultra intelligence revealed that the Germans were pressuring the Italian Navy into attacking British convoys transporting troops to Greece. Realizing that major Italian surface units would be at sea for the first time since Taranto, Cunningham diverted the convoys and took his fleet to sea on the night of March 27, to ambush the Italian fleet off Cape Matapan. The following day, torpedo bombers from the aircraft carrier HMS *Formidable* damaged the Italian battleship *Vittorio Veneto* and cruiser *Pola*. Cunningham decided to risk a night action to achieve a more convincing victory. With the advantages of radar, superior gunnery, and sheer weight of firepower, his battleships found and sank not only *Pola* but the cruisers *Zara* and *Fiume* and two destroyers that had been sent to assist her. The Italians were hopelessly unprepared for night fighting, Cunningham later writing that "They were no further advanced than we had been at Jutland twenty-five years earlier."[4] After the war, he also reflected that what had become known as the Battle of Matapan had been "more like murder than anything else."[5]

Taranto and Matapan gave the Mediterranean Fleet a moral ascendancy over the Italian Navy from which it never truly recovered. One immediate consequence was that Cunningham's ships could carry out the high-risk evacuation of Greece without interference by Italian warships, when that disastrous campaign collapsed in April. It then allowed him to first sustain the defense of his incomplete forward operating base on Crete, and then manage yet another evacuation once it was clear that the island was lost. All of these operations, Cunningham wrote at the time, "may be said to have been carried out under the cover of the Battle of Matapan."[6]

Despite the absence of opposing warships, however, Crete was by far the hardest battle that the Mediterranean Fleet had to fight. By May 1941, German air power in the Mediterranean had been temporarily enhanced by the arrival of VIII. Fliegerkorps in southern Greece, and Cunningham's fleet faced well over a thousand German combat aircraft. Against this, the British could deploy just twenty worn-out, obsolete fighters on Crete, and the four Fulmar fighters remaining on board Cunningham's battered carrier *Formidable*. The 'naval' battle of Crete was thus fought between a navy and an air force. As such, it was a battle that the Mediterranean Fleet could not hope to win—simply surviving would be an achievement.

Tactically, Crete was a disaster for the Royal Navy. Although Cunningham's ships mauled a German invasion convoy during the battle's defensive phase, and carried some fifteen thousand battle-weary soldiers to safety during the evacuation that followed, three cruisers and six destroyers were sunk, and another seventeen ships were damaged. Of the hard-worked cruisers, only HMS *Phoebe* escaped unscathed, and 2,261 men were killed. The battle compared to a major fleet action, yet the only enemy warships sighted were a few Italian destroyers escorting the invasion convoys. However, the fact that the Mediterranean Fleet continued to operate in these conditions and never relinquished its control of the sea was a pyrrhic victory of sorts. And there was another, arguably more important, aspect. When asked to continue the evacuation on the night of May 31, Cunningham famously declared: "It takes the Navy three years to build a new ship. It will take three hundred years to build a new tradition. The evacuation will continue." The Navy could come out of the battle with its head held high, secure in the knowledge that it had not let the Army down, as reflected by a toast which was supposedly popular in Mediterranean Fleet wardrooms at the time: "To the three services, the Royal Navy, the Royal Advertising Federation, and the Evacuees." The Army could continue to rely on the fact that, when the chips were down, the Navy would be there. That continued faith was hard to put a price on.

Further opportunities for the Axis to wrest control of the Mediterranean presented themselves as autumn turned into a disastrous winter for

Fig 7.2 Field Marshal Erwin Rommel with Field Marshal Albrecht Kesselring in desert camp, October 31, 1942. (IWM HU 5622)

the Royal Navy. In November, German submarines sank first the aircraft carrier *Ark Royal* and then the veteran battleship *Barham*. The following month, the battleships *Valiant* and *Queen Elizabeth* were crippled at anchor in Alexandria harbor, in an extraordinarily daring operation by Italian *maiale* (human torpedo operators). The ships sank upright in shallow water, and the British managed to create a convincing impression that they were still seaworthy; but in reality, the Italians had command of the sea within their grasp, had they but known it. Still paralyzed by Taranto and Matapan, the battleships of the Regia Marina remained in port.

Wartime propaganda and popular mythology, particularly in Great Britain, has created a stereotypical image of Italians at war that is not fully deserved. At sea, Italian light forces and submarines remained active. However, the battle fleet was the victim of a cumbersome command structure that took all semblance of individual initiative away from the commanders at sea. Moreover, Italian ships were modern and fast but lightly armored; they lacked radar and were inadequately provided with antiaircraft armament. The Italian Navy was also a political tool, with one arm tied behind its back by Mussolini's desire to have a powerful fleet behind him at any peace conference.

Hindsight shows how failure to exploit the opportunities provided by Crete and the disasters of November and December effectively ended any possibility of the Italians achieving a strategic victory at sea. Reinforced by new ships, the Royal Navy would continue to operate in the Mediterranean. But it had yet to win the most important battle of all: the battle to block Axis supply routes to North Africa in the face of overwhelming German and Italian air power, and correspondingly open the Mediterranean to friendly shipping. The fall of France closed the Mediterranean to most merchant ships, and convoys to Egypt had to steam around South Africa. This increased the distance for an Egypt-bound convoy from 4,800 km to 20,800 km, keeping valuable hulls at sea for weeks and stretching shipping resources to the limit. Sometimes fast convoys through the Mediterranean simply had to be risked, notably Operation Tiger in early 1941, which was dispatched on Churchill's personal order to bring urgently needed tanks to the Middle East. Thanks to excellent security only one ship from Tiger was lost, but losses in the Mediterranean were generally three times as high as the Atlantic, and the direct route was only used in emergencies. In contrast, Axis convoys had only to make a very quick, direct crossing from Italy.

The linchpin of the Mediterranean convoy war was Malta, the only British outpost in the central Mediterranean, lying astride Rommel's lines of communication. Malta was a vital weapon. Despite the island's vulnerability at the start of the war, the initial Italian aerial bombardment between June and December 1940 had proved ineffective, although it famously gave rise to the legend of three lone Gladiator biplanes, which were supposedly all that stood between Malta and defeat in the summer of 1940.[7] The situation worsened following the arrival of the Luftwaffe in January 1941. Initially the Germans concentrated on trying to sink the damaged carrier *Illustrious*, which aim they failed to achieve, but over the next six months they widened the scope of their operations to a full-scale blitz of the island, dropping some 2,500 tons of high explosives and leveling more than two thousand civilian homes.

Malta's first torment only came to an end when the German bombers were withdrawn, first to take part in operations over Greece and Crete, and then to join in the German invasion of the Soviet Union, Operation Barbarossa, on June 22, 1941. After weathering this initial storm, the British were able to gradually reinforce the island with stronger naval and air forces, and then take the offensive, using Malta as an advance striking base. Malta-based submarines sank three hundred thousand tons of Axis shipping between July and September 1941. Foremost among these underwater marauders was HMS *Upholder*, commanded by Lieutenant Commander David Wanklyn, the most successful Allied submariner of the Second World War, who was awarded the Victoria Cross for his service in the Mediterranean before being killed in action in April 1942. The success of the submarine campaign, supported by strike aircraft and increased operations by surface ships, led the German naval liaison staff in Rome to describe the situation as catastrophic; the Italian merchant shipping losses during the period are described in the Italian official history as "the worst losses of the whole struggle."[8] These successes at sea directly helped the British desert army to build up the overwhelming superiority in tanks and aircraft it enjoyed at the start of Operation Crusader in November 1941.

Keeping Malta in the fight required huge resources. As Malta threatened Axis convoy routes to North Africa, so the island was in turn dependent on its own convoys to sustain it. The Malta convoys were among the most heavily escorted of the Second World War, involving quite extraordinary numbers of warships—Operation Substance, run from Gibraltar in September 1941 during a comparatively quiet period, involved three capital ships, an aircraft carrier, five cruisers, and a staggering eighteen destroyers, as well as a corvette and nine submarines. This fleet-sized force was charged with the protection of just twelve merchant ships, one of which was sunk.

In December 1941, Malta's lull ended with a vengeance. Strong Luftwaffe air units returned to the Mediterranean and began to relentlessly pound Malta's airfields and the capital, Valletta. Between January 1 and July 24, 1942 there was only one 24-hour period without an air raid on

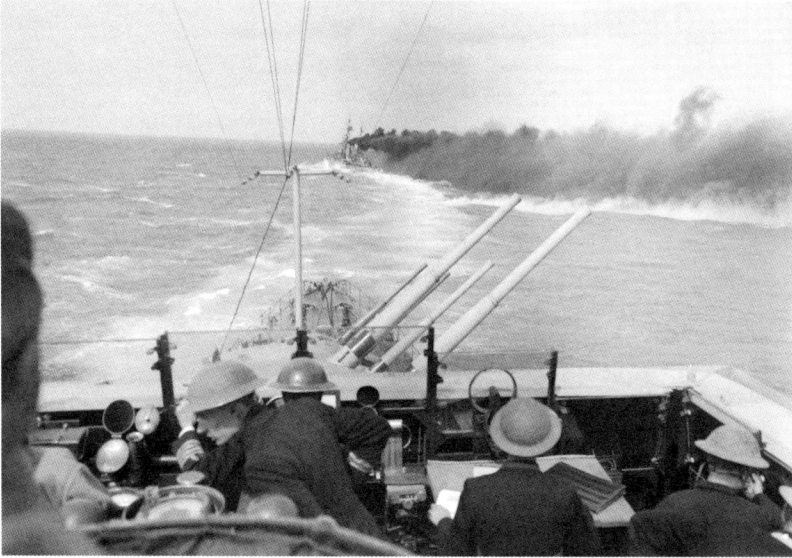

Fig 7.3 HMS *Cleopatra* throwing out smoke signals to cloak convoy ships from attack. (IWM A 8166)

Malta. During March and April, twice the tonnage of bombs that fell on London during the Blitz was dropped on the island. The civilian population began to lead an almost troglodyte existence, eking out their lives underground, suffering from malnutrition, scabies, and at one point, typhoid. There were 1,493 deaths among the islanders, and 3,764 were wounded, including many children.[9] It was Malta's perseverance in the face of such terrible adversity that prompted King George VI to award the entire island the George Cross in April 1941, "to bear witness to a heroism and devotion that will long be famous in history."[10]

Gradually, the Germans and Italians also began to lay an almost impenetrable belt of mines around the island. On December 19, Force K, the striking force of destroyers and light cruisers permanently based at Malta, ran into an uncharted minefield, losing the cruiser *Neptune* with catastrophic loss of life, and the destroyer *Kandahar*. A second cruiser, HMS *Aurora*, was damaged and Force K was effectively finished as a fighting unit. Unacceptably high losses to mines then forced the withdrawal of Malta's last offensive naval unit, its submarine flotilla, and with the airfields too battered to sustain strike aircraft, the island was essentially toothless. It was also becoming increasingly hard to sustain resistance;

Fig. 7.4 On the horizon, HMS *Airedale* seen blowing up after a direct hit from enemy bombers during a convoy from Alexandria to Malta. (IWM A 10473)

casualties among the inbound supply convoys were dreadfully high and Malta was starting to run desperately short of food, fuel, and ammunition. In Convoy MW10 in March, just three ships were delivered, and all were sunk soon after arrival; the convoy was also subjected to a rare intervention by the Italian battle fleet, resulting in what became known later as the Second Battle of Sirte. Malta's torment once more had a direct impact on the Desert War. With the island impotent, the Axis supply lines were again more secure, allowing Rommel to strike west, pushing toward Egypt in a dramatic offensive that secured first Benghazi and then Tobruk before stalling at an obscure railway halt called El Alamein.

It was thus perhaps unsurprising that the German commander in chief, Feldmarschal Albert Kesselring, felt secure enough to report that Malta had been neutralized on May 10, 1942. Two days before, Churchill had telegraphed his commander in chief in the Middle East, General Claude Auchinleck, emphasizing that the loss of Malta "would be a disaster of the first magnitude to the British Empire, and probably fatal in the long run to the defence of the Nile Valley."[11] But Kesselring's overconfidence was to be Malta's salvation. It almost immediately resulted in the premature withdrawal of key Luftwaffe units, which were desperately needed elsewhere, creating a vital lull during which new Spitfire fighters were flown into Malta—some, famously, from the US aircraft carrier *Wasp* following Churchill's personal request to Roosevelt. Axis mines were cleared, allowing the return of the submarines. However, the situation was still desperate for the civilian population. In June, simultaneous attempts were made to resupply the island from both the east and west, but Operation Harpoon, the western convoy, resulted in the arrival of just two ships. None at all made it from the east in Operation Vigorous.

Finally, in August the decision was taken to lift the siege whatever the cost. Operation Pedestal was the biggest convoy battle of the Second World War. On August 10, fourteen fast merchant ships set sail for Malta escorted by two battleships, three aircraft carriers, seven cruisers, and twenty destroyers. Three days later, five surviving merchant ships limped into Valletta harbor, among them the famous tanker *Ohio* lashed between two destroyers to stay afloat. The aircraft carrier HMS *Eagle* and two cruisers of the escort had also been sunk. Pedestal did not in itself mean the end of the siege, but it bought Malta time, allowing the island to build up its defenses, operate offensively against Rommel's supply lines, and stave off starvation. Kesselring tried again to subdue Malta from the air in October 1942, desperately aware that the survival of Rommel's desert army was in the balance, but he failed, leaving the Afrika Korps and its Italian allies desperately short of supplies at El Alamein in November, and prompting Rommel to write later that "Malta has the lives of many thousands of German and Italian soldiers on its conscience."[12] The island's situation gradually eased as the Axis armies were driven westward, and the siege finally ended with the Axis collapse in North Africa and the reopening of normal shipping routes between Gibraltar and Alexandria. By mid-1943, Allied navies completely dominated the Mediterranean.

This chapter was intended to illustrate two principal points. The first is how the Royal Navy seized control of the Mediterranean by facing up to three consecutive threats. The ruthless destruction of the French fleet eliminated the first, and bold and imaginative tactics against the Italians eliminated the second. But naval forces alone could never defeat the third, the Luftwaffe. However, the Royal Navy's warships were never designed to be political tools, kept neatly polished in harbor, which was arguably at least part of the raison d'être of Mussolini's Regia Marina. As a genuine sea power, the British understood that warships were 'assets,' in the modern parlance; weapons to be used and possibly lost, although preferably not needlessly. The Royal Navy could have withdrawn from the Mediterranean after the arrival of the Luftwaffe's dive bombers and kept its ships intact, but surrendered control of the sea. Instead, like a punch-drunk boxer refusing to go down, the Mediterranean Fleet, Force H, and the forces based on the island fortress of Malta continued to put to sea (and take off) in the face of appalling casualties.

The second principal point is how the ebb and flow of the struggle at sea dictated the rhythm of the land battle. When the Royal Navy had the upper hand, Malta exerted a stranglehold on Rommel's supply lines, leaving him starved of the resources he needed to succeed. Only during those periods when the Royal Navy, battered and bruised, was forced onto the defensive, and Malta knocked out of the fight, was Rommel able to fight at full strength. The Royal Navy's success in retaining at least partial control of the Mediterranean, sometimes against impossible odds, between 1940 and 1942, ensured that what could have been Rommel's most decisive advantage, his short maritime supply lines, was negated. This allowed the British armies to fight on equal or even superior terms throughout the desert campaign, despite their aircraft, tanks, fuel, ammunition, and men generally having so much farther to travel before they could go into action. Kesselring's hubris in declaring Malta beaten in May 1942 meant that, at the key moment, the maritime pendulum swung in Britain's favor, giving Montgomery the overwhelming advantage in men and matériel he needed to secure a crushing victory at El Alamein.

It can, therefore, legitimately be argued that, like so many other British land campaigns over the centuries, El Alamein owed its success in no small part to the unseen work of the 'far distant, storm-tossed' ships of the Royal Navy.

Notes

1   Winston S. Churchill, *The Second World War*, vol. 4: *The Hinge of Fate* (London: Cassell, 1955), 541.

2   Colin Smith, *England's Last War with France* (London: Phoenix, 2010).

3   Winston S. Churchill, *The Second World War*, vol. 2: *Their Finest Hour* (London: Cassell, 1949), 481.

4   Viscount Cunningham of Hyndhope, Admiral of the Fleet, *A Sailor's Odyssey* (London: Hutchinson, 1951), 337.

5   Michael Simpson, ed., *The Cunningham Papers*, vol. 1: *The Mediterranean Fleet 1939–1942* (Aldershot: Ashgate/Navy Records Society, 1999), 239.

6   Simpson, *Cunningham Papers*, vol. 1, 313.
7   The aircraft were nicknamed *Faith*, *Hope*, and *Charity*. It seems likely that there were always more than three Gladiators, and they were certainly soon joined by more modern Hurricane aircraft, which did most of the damage to the incoming Italian raiders.
8   Donald Macintyre, *The Battle for the Mediterranean* (London: Pan, 1964), 94.
9   I.C.B. Dear, ed., *The Oxford Companion to World War II* (Oxford: Oxford University Press, 2001), 558.
10   The George Cross is Great Britain's highest award for gallantry in circumstances for which military gallantry awards are not normally given. This is commonly described as for actions which did not take place 'in the face of the enemy.' Malta's was one of only two collective awards of the George Cross in history, the other going to the Royal Ulster Constabulary in 2000.
11   Churchill, *The Hinge of Fate*, 275.
12   B.H. Liddell Hart, ed., *The Rommel Papers* (London: Collins, 1953), 289.

8

Feeding the Fortress
Malta, Summer 1942

Thomas Scheben

At Each Other's Throats

For more than a century, Malta had been Britain's main base in the Mediterranean, and its importance to this day lies in its strategic position midway between Gibraltar and Alexandria, roughly 3,700 kilometers east to west, with the Tunisian coast 297 kilometers to the southeast, and Sicily ninety-six kilometers to the north.[1] A small and rocky island, even in peacetime Malta was heavily dependent on imports; in wartime it had also to support, maintain, and keep operative modern mechanized military forces. Caught up in the war by virtue of their geographic position, the outlook for the Maltese people was grim. When Italy declared war on May 10, 1940, Malta was potentially in a position to cut Italy off from its North African possessions, but was equally vulnerable to Italian attacks or blockade. This pivotal position placed it in the struggle between Axis convoys endeavoring to supply their forces in North Africa, and Allied ships supplying the garrison and people of Malta.

Malta is an archipelago of three inhabited islands—Malta, Gozo, Comino—and several small, uninhabited rocks. Malta, with its capital Valletta, is the largest of the islands, at 246 square kilometers. Malta's most valuable naval assets are its bays and harbors. The Grand Harbor on the east coast is one of the world's greatest natural harbors: 3.7 kilometers from breakwater to shore and 1.6 kilometers at its greatest width, allowing then almost six square kilometers of anchorage for capital ships.[2] For naval powers with regional interests, Malta held the key Mediterranean position.[3] With Tunis under Vichy control after the Fall of France in 1940, it was the last Allied position remaining.

Harbor-related naval and commercial activities provided most non-agricultural employment for the Maltese. Of these, His Majesty's (H.M.) Royal Naval Dockyard was very much the most important industrial installation. Inaugurated in 1848, it operated under supervision of the vice admiral, Malta. Employee numbers fluctuated in relation to economic cycles, and to the diplomatic, military, and naval situation in the Mediterranean. In 1939 the dockyard employed around ten thousand workers, reaching its wartime peak of twelve thousand in 1945.[4] H.M. Dockyard School[5] provided the only formal vocational training facility for the various skilled labor trades supporting the navy and the other services.

An Island 'Blitzed'

With a relatively small garrison in Malta, Britain held an almost impregnable position there as long as her fleet controlled the surrounding sea. The emergence of airplanes able to target bomb-loads precisely enough to sink powerful capital ships in striking distance from Sicily reduced Malta's importance as a base for surface ships. The British Mediterranean battle fleet shifted base to Alexandria. Submarines and a small strike force of two light cruisers and some destroyers, operating from Malta from October 1941 against Italian convoys, were responsible for most of the mounting Axis ship losses,[6] compared with the RAF. When the Luftwaffe returned in force, the fleet quit—as did submarines from May 1942, when heavy losses meant they dared surface in Grand Harbor only during darkness.

However, whatever importance Malta lost as a naval base, it gained as an airbase menacing Axis supply lines between Naples, Palermo, and Tripoli on the Libyan coast, a hub for Allied air traffic through the theater of operation, and later for aerial reconnaissance and support of offensive operations against Tunisia and Sicily. Thus Malta became Churchill's proverbial "unsinkable aircraft carrier."[7] Whenever circumstances allowed, the RAF bombed Italian harbors and airbases, mostly at night. Given the fighter and bomber ranges of the period, it was particularly the control of the airdromes in Cyrenaica that had a direct impact on the situation around Malta, because Axis control meant protection for Tripoli and Benghazi and the closure of the Central Mediterranean straits to Allied shipping, while the RAF presence there brought relief for the RAF on Malta, menaced Axis supplies to Africa, and at least reduced the Axis threat to naval transport through the straits. In a sense, Mediterranean campaigns were to some extent battles for airfields.[8]

Fig 8.1 Troops disembark from ships in Grand Harbor, Malta, January 21, 1942. (IWM GM 344)

These simple geographical basics were only operable if there was any air force available to make use of them. Neither the RAF nor the Luftwaffe had enough aircraft in the Mediterranean theater (or elsewhere) to do everything at once. Often supreme commands confronted difficult choices: whether to support land or naval operations, or to go for a strategic air campaign and select the proper local set of targets. It was only after the American industrial weight was put behind the Allied effort, and the overstretched Luftwaffe began to be bled white in late 1943, that the RAF and the United States Army Air Force (USAAF) finally gained the upper hand in that theater.

The Luftwaffe made three concentrated efforts against Malta. In January 1941, the Royal Navy set up a double convoy codenamed Operation Excess to ship supplies to Malta and Greece.[9] A preliminary airstrike of Wellington bombers from Malta against Naples damaged some Italian

Fig 8.2 Kingsway, the heavily bomb-damaged principal street in Valletta, Malta, being cleared of debris by service personnel and civilians, May 1942. (IWM A 8701)

ships, keeping their battle fleet in harbor. Italian high-altitude bombing attacks were repulsed, so that both convoys reached their targets safely. But on January 9 the Luftwaffe made their first appearance in the Mediterranean theater with a furious attack against the Royal Navy. Two cruisers were sunk, and the aircraft carrier HMS *Illustrious*, whose planes provided the aerial umbrella for the operation, was severely damaged. Undetected, she limped into Grand Harbor, where the dockyard worked frantically to get the ship ready for a dash to Alexandria. It took the Luftwaffe five more days to relocate its prey and send the Stukas out again to finish her off. Headlined 'The Illustrious Blitz,' the story of how crew and workers succeeded under constant airstrikes and made the carrier sneak out to finally reach safety is one of the great Maltese legends of the Second World War.[10]

But almost every miss on the *Illustrious* scored hits on the densely populated residential areas close to the dockyard. Their inhabitants suffered heavily with loss of home and life, but were spared worse when a bomb hit the yet unloaded freighter *Essex*. Her four thousand tons of ammunition were sufficient to blow the whole harbor area to smithereens, but miraculously the explosion of the bomb was contained by the heavy bulkheads of the engine room. The Luftwaffe then shifted their attention to the airfields in order to suppress the RAF. Their relentless pounding, though again wreaking havoc on the surrounding villages, paid off, and the first German units of what entered history as Deutsches Afrikakorps (DAK) reached Tripoli with minimal losses. When Rommel started his first offensive toward Egypt, Malta got some respite, with the Luftwaffe redeployed toward North Africa and the Eastern Mediterranean, where it was kept busy for the rest of the year. The epic siege of Tobruk proved to be as much a contest in the air as it was on the ground and at sea.

Then in spring 1941, Stukas and Messerschmidts appeared in the Eastern Mediterranean, conquering Crete by air, while the Royal Navy suffered crippling losses evacuating the British expeditionary corps. Pearl Harbor, in December 1941, meant the withdrawal of capital units to the Far East, leaving the British Mediterranean fleet a mere shadow of its once proud self by the end of 1941. Combined with the catastrophic spring of 1941, the British position in the Mediterranean and the Middle East appeared so fragile that it might crumble under just one more energetic German push. It never came. Crete's potential against Alexandria and the Suez Canal was never really exploited, because from July 1941 the war against Russia drew most of the Luftwaffe into what was, from Hitler's point of view, the primary theater of operation. Rommel's advance toward Egypt became bogged down at Tobruk, while all possible reinforcements fueled Barbarossa. However, the heavy losses suffered by the German elite parachutists there had a beneficial impact on the fate of Malta, convincing the Führer to abandon Operation Herkules and never to try an air assault of that dimension again. Now he was only too ready to grant priority to Rommel's advance into Egypt in summer 1942.[11]

By then, everybody had learned the lesson about air superiority being the foremost precondition for naval operations. When Malta was granted the breathing space to recover, it soon found its teeth against Axis shipping, as well as Italian harbors and Sicilian airdromes. The Regia Aeronautica was forced to resort to high-altitude raids with small numbers of planes, which usually hit everything except their proposed targets. For the civilian population, this meant some relief after the incessant German waves of dive bombers. On the other hand, the erratic Italian bombing, usually by night, made many people stay in the open and watch the thrilling air battles, even though these caused heavy casualties if a bomb accidentally fell into such a crowd of spectators or on a family around the dinner table.

Italian admirals were often reluctant to risk a major encounter at sea, even with odds in their favor. On several occasions this cautious attitude saved the Royal Navy from disaster. Poorly designed Italian submarines and gallantly led smaller surface units could not overcome the shortcomings of the main battle fleet and the inability of the Regia Aeronautica to deliver targeted low-altitude attacks against Allied ships. Yet even without the British battle fleet, Malta gradually regained striking power high up in the air and in the deep blue. Axis losses mounted steadily, reaching unacceptable dimensions by the end of the year. Each side was faced with the problem of running supply convoys, which, though not seriously threatened by the enemy's surface forces, were in extreme peril from attack from above and below the surface.[12] The breaking of the German Enigma code[13] meant that few Axis convoys escaped unscathed. When the Russian winter grounded II. Fliegerkorps on the eastern front, Hitler decided to divert them to reinforce the Luftwaffe in Sicily. Together with the X. Fliegerkorps they formed Luftflotte II under the command of Field Marshal Albert Kesselring. The Maltese realized something was up when the Italians intensified their attacks. Even in daytime, people ran for shelter when the alarm was sounded. And in December, they knew things were going from bad to worse when Stukas screamed out of the sky once more. Their target was not just to bomb Malta into silence and soften it up for an eventual invasion, but also to kick the Royal Navy out of the game. For that, Hitler increased the number of German U-boats, and Italian commandos attacked the harbor defense of Alexandria. Success came almost immediately. In a couple of weeks, the navy lost several capital ships. Axis losses decreased almost instantly, so that Rommel received enough supplies to switch seamlessly from retreat to counteroffensive.

By February 1942, the Desert Fox had reconquered Cyrenaica and had stopped in front of the Gazala–Bir Hakim line to regroup. The original Axis plan, Operation Herkules, called for Rommel to continue his final push into Egypt and toward the Suez Canal, but only after taking Malta in a joint German–Italian airborne and amphibious operation. The date for Operation Herkules was set for July 10. Hitler, however, backed the Desert Fox. He wanted an immediate operation of about three weeks to take Tobruk and forestall a pending British offensive, and only then to concentrate all available airpower on the postponed assault on Malta. The Italian Supreme Command being deeply divided about the invasion, Mussolini, too, backed Rommel's plan. With the Eighth Army defeated, the Tobruk garrison surrendered on June 21 and 35,000 prisoners of war, mainly South Africans, were marched into captivity. Thousands of tons of conquered provisions and fuel kept the panzers rolling. Rommel now saw the road to Alexandria open, and believed that a completely isolated Malta would simply fall without further effort, like a ripe apple. Again the two dictators agreed, thus sparing Malta from invasion that year. This decision was arguably the greatest gamble of the Mediterranean campaign.

The strategy had the full support of Albert Kesselring. Indeed, the five-month air campaign had been the most concentrated effort against Malta during the Second World War, April marking its peak. The Axis had established almost undisputed air–sea control over the Central Mediterranean, and on Malta their air crews hardly found any military targets and infrastructure left worth bombing. In early May, II. Fliegerkorps had reported to Berlin that, "from March 20 until April 28, Malta has been completely eliminated as a naval and air base . . . 6,557,231 kilograms of bombs [have] been dropped." That was more than the amount of bombs dropped on Great Britain during the peak of the Battle of Britain in September 1940.[14]

Kesselring considered the Royal Air Force on Malta beyond recovery,[15] a grave misjudgment as it soon turned out. But for the time being, Malta had ceased to endanger Axis supply convoys. Their shipping loss rate declined from 77 percent in November 1941 to less than 2 percent in April 1942. However, the almost constant raids of up to four hundred planes, additional escort duty for convoys, and the stubborn resistance of the RAF on Malta had taken its toll on the Luftwaffe as well. "Neither side knew how badly the other was doing, nor seemed able to correct proven errors,"[16] though in fact the Germans were faring worse. In June several German formations were diverted to France, Russia, and North Africa where, in early July, Rommel's advance had been checked at an obscure railway station named El Alamein. Raids on Malta continued, but when their frequency and intensity slackened, the RAF took every chance to rebuild first its defensive, and then its offensive capabilities. The Axis air offensive against Malta lost its continuous and strategic character. Instead, a few sharp raids were directed against air fields on Malta as prequels to Axis convoy operations that focused on protection of convoys against attacks from the east. But the sea blockade against Malta was maintained during the summer months, and every ship approaching the Central Mediterranean, if spotted, had to run its gauntlet.[17]

Malta: "We Had the Frontline at the Front Door"

The situation of the Maltese people during these months was described by Mabel Strickland, editor of the *Times of Malta*, in a 1943 BBC interview.[18] By the end of the war, ninety-two soldiers of the King's Own Malta Regiment (KOMR) and the Royal Malta Artillery (RMA) and 1,597 civilians had been killed due to enemy action, and 1,818 severely injured, some maimed for life.[19] Undernourishment, miserable sanitary conditions due to overcrowding and living in shelters, and lack of medical treatment had contributed to this list. In addition to loss of life, both Malta and Gozo had suffered severe material damage. Official sources calculate that by December 1944, nearly 28,000 houses had been destroyed or damaged: 5,316 destroyed, 5,019 severely damaged, 17,618 partially damaged, with an additional 2,922 already repaired by July 1944.[20] Compared with other civilian targets in Europe or Japan, worse was averted partly by the rock shelters. Unlike traditional German or British city centers, or Japanese wooden cities, little timber was used in building, even for roofs; and there was less wooden furniture inside. Italians and Germans usually targeted ships and military infrastructure with high explosives. They never resorted to the sophisticated combinations of explosives, incendiary bombs, and anti-personnel bombs that were later perfected by the Allies against German and Japanese cities.[21] Thus Malta was spared the devastating conflagrations that virtually wiped out whole cities elsewhere, claiming more victims than the actual bombs themselves.

Fear of air raids, the tediousness of taking shelter several times a day under intensive attack, and loss of homes, meant spending at least a whole night in air-raid shelters for many families, sometimes throughout the war. There was little basic defense in 1939,[22] but the Maltese were skilled in mining and stonemasonry. Maltese limestone, easily quarried and cut, was itself a strategic asset used for civilian and military buildings and subterranean structures. In 1942, existing underground cisterns or tunnels, some dating back to the Knights Hospitaller, were turned into public shelters, while affluent families had private shelters dug. Workshops, supply dumps, and so on, also went below. By summer 1942, about two-thirds of the population had this kind of shelter. Not all proved bombproof against direct hits of the Luftwaffe's 500-kg bombs, but they provided adequate protection against blasts, splinters, and direct hits of light bombs.[23]

Life in cramped, damp quarters was uncomfortable. The medical authorities registered a significant increase in epidemic sicknesses due to densely populated dwellings lacking sufficient air circulation. Lack of soap and fresh water spread infestations of scabies and other parasites caused by deteriorating sanitary conditions. But the loyalty of the Maltese population remained unshaken. Setting aside political issues, the majority of Maltese still saw their future as part of the British Empire. Some pro-Italian sympathizers were detained early in the war and the most prominent ones deported, spending the war involuntarily in comfortable exile in Uganda.[24] Whatever attraction fascist Italy might have held, the first Italian bombardment of Malta barely twelve hours after Italy's declaration of war on May 10, 1940, settled the issue. The Maltese rallied behind the Empire.

The church provided vital support. Ever pragmatic, British rule from 1800 guaranteed the protection of the Catholic faith, and in 1807 had supported the appointment of the first archbishop of Maltese nationality.[25] Despite occasional difficulties with Protestantism and secularism, which had politicized the clergy in the 1930s, during the war Archbishop Dom Mauro Caruana stood firmly in the British camp. Moreover, the church provided indispensable support to many social services; and parish priests, the undisputed community leaders in this most Catholic of societies, did everything to see their villages through this second siege.

Malta's colonial government was highly centralized. The governor, as commander of a fortress, was a general, while the lieutenant governor was a colonial official who ran the civil administration.[26] Its departments were headed by a mixture of British and Maltese directors, some of them heroes of the siege—like the Chief Medical Officer Professor Albert Victor Bernard or the Director of Education Albert Laferla[27] who died of exhaustion during the war. Together with some elected Maltese deputies, these formed the Government Council, usually presided over by the lieutenant governor and active in domestic affairs. There was no local or municipal administration. This left the parish priest, to whom people looked for guidance, the churches themselves becoming the most important communication centers.

On the outbreak of the war, Malta was divided into regions, each entrusted to a regional protection officer, who in turn officiated over protection for the villages and urban districts.[28] Frequently Maltese teachers, politicians, doctors, or some of the nobility became responsible for the daily war-related affairs of their communities. The work included organizing evacuation or shelter for refugees, registration and rationing procedures, issuing all sorts of permits, or enforcing restrictions. The government knew the defense of Malta depended on the wholehearted support and cooperation of the Maltese people. It was they who provided the labor for services, filled the ranks of military (the RMA and the KOMR),[29] tended the soil, drove vehicles, and repaired bomb damage on harbors, roads, buildings, and airfields—in other words, kept the fortress going.

"The Most Drastic and Early Measures Are Needed to Restore the Situation at Malta"[30]

In peacetime, Malta produced just about 30 percent of its food and about 5 percent of its needs in other commodities.[31] Its markets were mostly the Mediterranean—mainly Italian, until the boycott of Italian goods in the Abyssinian crisis.[32] Wartime trading with Britain was difficult and made worse by the need to economize on shipping space.[33] Most staples were not at first affected, and other goods were beyond the means of most Maltese families anyway. But as long as most basic goods were available, families barely felt a change.

Imports from Sicily were cut, and most merchant shipping ceased except under convoy. The government had used the grace period from September 1939 to stockpile up five to eight months' supply of crucial commodities like wheat, flour, sugar, edible oil and fats, and coffee, as well as soap, kerosene, and coal.[34] The Food Control Board of the First World War had been revitalized in 1935 to control prices.[35] From September 1939, the Board's authority was expanded[36] and then replaced by a food and commerce control officer with wide powers,[37] and the government dealt with profiteering[38] by withdrawing the licenses of offending retailers.[39]

Fuel was crucial for conducting military operations, but also for agriculture and for electricity in urban zones.[40] Drinking water had first to be pumped hydraulically. Normal water consumption was about 2.7 million gallons per day, 2.5 million of which had to be pumped from subterranean aquifers, the rest from other sources. These usually dried up in summer and had to be replaced by water from artificial reservoirs, drawing on accumulated reserves.[41] Public transport was cut, putting additional stress on workers evacuated from homes around the Grand Harbor to the countryside, and now expected somehow to commute to work.

In peacetime, Malta imported about 78 million tons of oil annually and had storage capacity for about 1.5 million tons, roughly ten weeks' supply.[42] So additional reserves of fuel were stored in metal canisters distributed in camouflaged dumps countrywide to avoid loss and catastrophic explosions in case of a direct hit—though only after the authorities learned the hard way. Domestic kerosene for cooking and lighting was scarce. The distributors' carts were often accompanied by police to control the crowds. Throughout the war, even after the introduction of rationing, disorganized distribution was a constant complaint. Only a small percentage of the houses could draw on electricity, and bomb damage and coal shortage either completely cut or limited even that supply.

However, much of the initial nervousness calmed down after a while. At first glance, the Regia Marina had appeared superior to the Royal Navy ships in the Mediterranean, especially when their ally France was unexpectedly knocked out of the war after June 1940. However, initial encounters with the Italians, usually triggered by convoy operations, made it obvious that naval superiority was more than just tonnage, ships, and guns. And like the Regia Marina, the Regia Aeronautica's tactics of high-altitude bombing were even less efficient against ships than against targets on land. After the initial clashes in summer 1940, and the success of the Swordfish torpedo-bombers against Taranto, the Italians avoided surface battles even against inferior British forces. Consequently, British convoys reached Malta regularly and without losses.[43] It was estimated that Malta would need about 26,000 tons of supply per month, approximately the cargo of three large merchantmen.[44] Given the Italian disasters in North Africa, the loss of Italy's colonial empire in East Africa, and poor progress of the Italian invasion in Greece, from a Maltese perspective the outlook for 1941 looked quite optimistic, and whatever stress and inconvenience the war had caused so far might prove to be only temporary.

One year later, that perspective had changed. The German intervention in North Africa, the campaigns in Norway and the Balkans, the battle of the Atlantic, and finally the Pacific had cost the Royal Navy dearly, and put commercial shipping under heavy strain. In Malta, the Blitz had killed many, left more homeless, and had wrought havoc on the military and civilian infrastructure. But convoys kept sailing, and suffered only minor losses. From February to May, thirteen ships brought around a hundred thousand tons of supplies to Malta. In addition submarines were employed to take supplies on board, when they headed for their base on Malta. A typical load would consist of about two dozen persons, 147 bags of mail, two tons of medical stores, and roughly a hundred tons of kerosene and aviation fuel. Between June and December 1941, sixteen trips were run, continuing until December 1942.[45] Fast freighters and minelayers conducted solo runs into Valletta relying on speed, darkness, and sometimes luck. Small amounts of vital stocks and passengers were brought in by bombers and other Allied planes dispatched to Malta. Nevertheless, the depleted fleet found it increasingly difficult to muster the numbers necessary for complex convoy operations, usually involving several dozen ships and a substantial part of the available air strength.

By September that year, resupplying Malta had become urgent. The population had been increased by expanding British forces which, during the war, numbered between twenty and thirty thousand—some of whom were Maltese, increasingly drafted into combat activities—and caused mounting consumption of fuel and ammunition. Flying fighter aircraft to Malta from aircraft carriers also regularly required full fleet operations. In the convoy Operation Halberd, eight cargo ships reached Valletta with the loss of one freighter. With the exception of coal, fodder, and kerosene, Malta was now considered restocked with sufficient supplies to last until May, 1942.[46]

Not knowing if or when the Luftwaffe might return in strength, rationing was seriously considered only after the Blitz. At first, Governor Bonham-Carter[47] announced that rationing was not intended as long as no acute shortages occurred.[48] Instead, the government simply reduced the amount of various items released to wholesalers. This led to hoarding, price inflation, and ultimately fueled the black market. Illness forced Bonham-Carter's resignation. Following a rather chaotic period of experiments,[49] a general rationing scheme was introduced in April, 1941.[50] Criticized as too late, it was also too draconian, seeking to compensate for earlier lack of price control, insufficient stocks, overconsumption, and wastage.[51] Problems meant rationing and distribution had to be modified several times, but the system remained operative for the duration of the war.

Rationing began with sugar, coffee, matches, and soap, but by late summer extended to a dozen items. Every household had to register with a nearby grocery shop for its rations. Because the quantity of goods had been government-restricted from the beginning of the war, the additional effect of rationing was small, but ensured a more equal distribution. The fact that a commodity did not appear on the ration card did not mean there was no shortage. It often meant that stocks were insufficient to guarantee a share to every customer. Soaring prices and public outcry convinced the government that commodities and prices had to be systematized; and by the end of 1941, control price-lists were created for almost all items and services. The price control board was set up but was never a real success;[52] in fact, later in the war, the rising cost of living led to an open worker's strike in the dockyard.[53]

"It Is a Very Small Part of What We had Hoped For"[54]

When war broke out, Malta had about 24,000 acres under cultivation, almost equally distributed between the main island and the much smaller island of Gozo. About a third of this was dedicated to wheat and barley, the better remaining soil to grapes, citrus fruits, and a variety of vegetables. In 1940–41, beans, for example, yielded two pounds per person, while the 24,000-ton bumper potato harvest provided Malta's consumers with about two pounds a day each for three weeks, and had to be eaten fast since they could not be stored through the hot summer.[55] The three-week potato boom allowed the saving of more than a thousand tons of flour for later use. It was the last opportunity for the islanders to worry about eating up a surplus of anything.

Based on January, 1942 consumption, the authorities had estimated Malta's flour stocks would last until May, its coal to the end of March, benzene and kerosene to the end of April, and aviation fuel into the summer. But the return of the Luftwaffe changed that. Hundreds of tons of stores were destroyed in the air raids, bombed oil-storage tanks were blazing, and the reserves of fuel and ammunition were melting away in the continuous air battles. Enemy attacks on the harbor zone were met with three hundred antiaircraft guns spitting thirteen thousand rounds a day high over Valletta's Grand Harbor.[56]

On April 6, 1942, a Chiefs of Staff memorandum summarized the Maltese supply situation as: wheat and flour would be exhausted in early July, and several minor foodstuffs some weeks earlier. Animal fodder would be gone by the end of June, fuel for the power station, coal, and coke between end of May and mid-June. Heavy antiaircraft ammunition would be spent by the end of June, light antiaircraft artillery rounds a

Fig 8.3 Keith Park, air officer commanding, Mediterranean, visiting a bomb dump at Luqa, and talking to the crew of a Vickers Wellington operating out of Malta. (IWM CM 4530)

month later, aviation spirit by August.[57] Without renewed efforts to supply, the Maltese islands would be starving and almost defenseless by the end of June.

Most families, without homes or income, had to rely on some form of social assistance.[58] Often they were not able to afford even their rations, still less goods on the free (mostly black) market. For the poor, communal kitchens had been established in 1941.[59] They were allocated one cooked meal, either at noon or in the afternoon, from the kitchen where they were registered, in return for one half-ration allocation. Besides helping the homeless to make ends meet, this system saved working people from shopping and cooking after a hard day's work, and often a long commute. The advantage for the government was obvious. Communal feeding was the most efficient use of the scarce reserves of essential food and fuel, the latter now often wood from destroyed buildings.

The government tried to expand the system as quickly as possible. This meant commandeering available ovens and utensils. Additional equipment was created from dockyard scrap metal when there were no ships to work on in the harbor. Output was so efficient that the Communal Feeding Department was mostly able to keep up with the rapidly expanding number of kitchens.[60] Premises were to be found everywhere; staff were recruited from hotels and restaurants, now barred from serving meals, and some expert staff were detached from the army. Malta was divided into eight districts, with an area manager overseeing the town or village managers. Administrative staff might be storekeepers, sales assistants, or charwomen. Kitchens were sometimes run by nuns.[61] Horse owners readily agreed to sell or hire their horses to the department, so that at least the animals would be fed.[62] In the critical summer months of 1942, the government took steps to commandeer draft animals for harvest and food supply.[63]

The first of these 'Victory Kitchens' opened in March 1942 in Rabat.[64] From just 269 subscribers in January, the Communal Feeding Department registered two thousand in April, and four thousand in May. By June, forty-two kitchens catered for seven thousand clients in twenty-three locations, the average kitchen serving about two hundred people. By then there were enough seasonal vegetables, and also meat from animals slaughtered owing to lack of fodder. By the end of October, about 147,000 clients were served, though fresh vegetables were no longer available, and personnel hired from every corner were still inexperienced. Rapid expansion had required tremendous improvisation[65] and still more patience. Yet by the end of the year, the Victory Kitchens were feeding about two hundred thousand people—almost every Maltese who was not drafted into military service.[66]

But the Communal Feeding Department was blamed for emptying the markets of produce, leaving customers empty-handed or forced onto the black market. So in that sense the Victory Kitchens' wholesale purchases raised prices, contributing to profiteering.[67] Once the food situation eased, subscribers to the Victory Kitchens dropped. By spring 1943, around 18,600 customers were registered, but the government maintained a skeleton organization in case the situation worsened again.[68] With the fall of Sicily, the last kitchens finally closed in September 1943.[69] They had been much less popular with the public than with the government. Few had managed to serve decent meals,[70] indeed the food of most of them was described as somewhere between dreadful and uneatable.[71] One particular dish was thrown away by many people, even though near starving, because it was simply inedible.[72]

The last great convoy, with about fifty thousand tons of supplies, had reached Malta on September 24, 1941; a smaller one with three freighters in January, 1942. But the March convoy unloaded less than half of its sixteen-thousand-ton cargo. In April the Chiefs of Staff decided that in view of the situation no convoy could be sent to Malta in May.[73] Other convoys were hard hit. Operation Harpoon lost four out of six cargo ships, and all eleven freighters of Operation Vigorous were forced to abandon their mission, none of them reaching Malta. Out of seventeen merchantmen in two convoys only two had reached Malta, with about fifteen thousand tons of supply. Some fast ships, submarines, and air transport kept a trickle of special stores, aviation fuel, and ammunition flowing in, but not enough to replenish the dwindling stocks of staples and kerosene. Anticipating high loss rates, Governor Dobbie warned London in his last report from Malta on April 20, 1942, that "if five ships are run and only two or three arrive, it is vital to our survival to ensure that the whole or the major part of their cargo is unloaded. Otherwise we shall at the best be in the same critical position after the operation as we are now."[74] And that was what happened.

"The Ordinary Person was Getting Just Enough to Eat"[75]

Replacing the exhausted General Dobbie as Governor, Field-Marshal Lord Gort's first and foremost task was to save Malta from starvation and inevitable surrender. On May 7, shortly after arriving, he surveyed available stocks of essential commodities, and ordered cuts in sugar and rice rations.[76] Admiral Sir Guy Russell,[77] Gort's chief of staff, proposed the British nutritionist Professor (later Sir) Jack Drummond[78] be brought out to assess and advise on handling the food emergency. Drummond had been appointed chief scientific adviser to the Ministry of Food in 1940, shortly after the introduction of food rationing in Britain. His theories on sustainable healthy diets became the brains behind British food policy during the war. He increased self-sufficiency by expanding the acreage under cultivation with the slogan 'Dig for Victory,' and reduced food imports by concentrating on goods with high nutritive value. It was, said Lord Gort, thanks to Drummond's application of these ideas to Malta's problems that real starvation never took hold during the siege.[79] Drummond stayed on in Malta from June 7–21, writing his *Report on the Food Situation in Malta*,[80] later known as the *Drummond Report*. Returning to London, Drummond gave a first-hand account to the Chiefs of Staff, emphasizing that the British garrison suffered more from the effects of rationing than the local population, which was "believed to be eking out supplies from their hidden stocks of food."[81] Even so, stocks laid in the early days of the siege were now probably near exhaustion.[82]

Neither the investigations nor the report were secret,[83] but the full report was not disclosed even to Maltese members of the Government Council, for fear that the statistics would provide the enemy with valuable information on Malta's supply status.[84] Censors were ordered to erase everything related to rising prices.[85] People knew, of course, what happened to the convoys; and the Luftwaffe's command of Malta's air space was plain to see.

It was already plain enough. After only two freighters from Operation Harpoon reached Malta, Lieutenant Governor Jackson explained the situation on Rediffusion on June 20, 1942

> We received 15,000 tons of stores from the two ships which arrived. That is something and certainly a help, but it is a very small part of what we had hoped for. . . . I have said in examining our position, we first calculated the time for which our bread could be made to last. That calculation gave us a certain date, which I shall call the 'Target Date.' . . . Our next task was to see how we could make our other vital necessities last to the Target Date.[86]

Far away in Russia, the panzers approached the Volga, while the Japanese finally subdued the Philippines and battled at the gateway to Australia. In North Africa, the Afrika Korps reached for Tobruk, which fell on June 21. On Malta, the complete failure of one and partial failure of another convoy—they had witnessed the two survivors of Operation Harpoon limping into Grand Harbor—made it clear that "a desperate situation would arise by the middle or end of July unless every effort were made to utilize to the greatest possible extent for consumption supplies of home produced foods."[87] Gort broadcast his food strategy to the public: "We must stand on our own resources and everyone must do everything in his or her power to conserve our stocks and to ensure that best use is made of all the available resources that remain to us."[88] Even so, an import of about 36,000 tons annually would be necessary just to maintain the drastically reduced rations, and ten thousand tons more to raise them above starvation level.[89]

Although the basic purpose of the visit was the design of a long-range policy, Governor Gort asked them to prepare an emergency report in order to estimate the possible survival period and give some recommendations regarding the composition of further cargoes to be shipped by submarines or later convoys.[90]

In peacetime, the average intake amounted to about 2,500 calories per day, but by the time of the investigation, this had already shrunk to about 1,500 calories per day provided by the official rations. Back in London, Drummond spelled out the situation: "the conclusion of our officials was that in June the ordinary person in Malta was getting just enough to eat, but would feel the scarcity of sugar, coffee, edible oil, soap and fuel. The heavy workforce and the troops were not getting enough to eat."[91] Some stocks could just be stretched to the target date; tinned food, like fish, would last months longer. Rations of these could be increased, instead of items in shorter supply. Stocks of animal fodder were almost exhausted, and a schedule for slaughtering the animals was drawn up.[92] As an incentive to their owners, the government offered higher prices for their purchase, to balance out the effect of the (temporarily) increased meat supply on the market.[93]

The advisers supported the continuation of the slaughtering schedule and rapid reduction of the remaining livestock. They recommended importing at least 1,250 tons of milk powder per annum, representing about 0.15 liters per head per day for the entire population.[94] When the fortunes of war swung decisively toward the Allies, the massacre of the Maltese goats came to an end; a year later, the lieutenant governor stated that about half of the prewar number of goats were still alive.[95]

The most important staple food, however, was bread. Temporary and local shortages had already occurred in early 1942, when bakeries were destroyed (as well as road transport) by air raids. On such occasions, the government hastened to calm down the population, which tended to panic even at such limited emergencies or mere rumors of a bread shortage.[96]

Occasionally, people looted bread carts when their owners took cover during an alarm.[97] In a joint pastoral letter read in churches on April 12, the Sunday after Easter, the Bishops of Malta and Gozo prepared their flocks for further hardships and sacrifice, asking them to accept deeper rationing with faith.[98]

Among the non-food items, cuts in kerosene were particularly painful. The Maltese population consumed about 409,150 liters per week in summer, some 31,800 more in winter. By February, after four months without a shipload of kerosene and the destruction of several dumps by bombs and fire, the ration was reduced, bringing down monthly consumption to about 218,200 liters.[99] A further 50 percent fuel cut from July 20[100] inflicted grave hardship on the population,[101] making home cooking almost impossible, but creating a further incentive to subscribe to the Victory Kitchens. Further misery was caused by damaged water and sewage pipes. Some of the water reservoirs had been hit, the water reserves for the hot season had leaked out, and water restrictions were imposed in spring 1942.[102]

War Is a Disease

Drummond and Wall's proposals for emergency measures, as for a long-term strategy, passed their reality check. Malta would have reached the target date, and in the composition and quantity of the rations following the crisis of 1942, the influence of their report is clearly traceable. In the end, however, what kept Malta in the war was the success of Operation Pedestal, in Malta known also as Santa Marija Convoy, because the last ships reached Grand Harbor on August 15, the Feast of the Assumption. Operation Pedestal was a tactical disaster turned into a strategic victory. Nine out of fourteen merchantmen, together with one aircraft carrier, two cruisers, and a destroyer were sunk. However, the thirty thousand tons of cargo that reached Valletta, and the petrol, oil fuel, kerosene, and diesel fuel of the legendary tanker *Ohio*, pushed the target date ten weeks further into December, beyond the existing stocks of only a few weeks.[103] Starvation was indeed only averted by a very narrow margin. At that moment, nobody would have dared to predict that a new convoy would arrive at all—or at what cost.[104]

The Luftwaffe was still only a hundred kilometers away in Sicily and operating from bases along the North African coast. Kesselring initiated a new all-out air offensive against Malta in October to reopen Rommel's supply line for the pending Battle of El Alamein. This time, the Stukas and Messerschmidts were beaten back with heavy losses, Axis ship losses mounted, and finally the defeat of the Desert Fox in the dunes and sands of the Egyptian desert was enthusiastically celebrated by the Maltese population.

The government kept expectations of an immediate improvement of the supply situation low, warning that the favorable development and safer arrival of further convoys had not yet eased the supply situation decisively.[105] But now, kerosene and edible oil rations were again issued in every ration period, though the sugar ration remained low.[106] In December, as more ships reached Malta unopposed, the government allowed itself cautious optimism, and permitted some increases in rations for 1943.[107]

The year 1942, as the Chief Medical Officer later recalled, had been the worst for the Maltese people: 2,159 more people died than in the previous year, 1,092 through military operations. Similarly, 584 fewer children were born than in 1941—a figure already 1,456 down on the 1940 rate. Reviewing the impact on the population's health of epidemics, wounds, and lack of medicaments or proper treatment, "War," Professor Bernard declared, "is a disease."[108]

Food stocks and consumption in Malta 1942

1. Civil stocks of principal foodstuffs (in tons)[109]
   (Wheat/flour= civilian and military stocks)

Commodity	Dec. 1, 1941	June 1, 1942
Wheat and flour (as flour) [1]	16,600	5,435 [1]
Edible oil	470	164
Lard/margarine	602	198
Butter	130	115
Milk	1,080	223
Canned meat	1,220	777
Canned fish	353	593
Sugar	2,780	621
Coffee	272	35
Tea	133	129
Rice	453	42
Cheese	258	147
Fodder	11,000	nil

[1] Including maize.

2. Civilian consumption of principal imported foodstuffs
   per month in tons if not otherwise stated.

Commodity	Normal	Before convoy	Reduced [1]
Flour	3,000	2,000	2,350
Edible oil	165	135	45
Lard/margarine	119	93	93 [2]
Butter	36	15	
(Canned) milk	7,800 cases	6,000 cases	6,000 cases
Canned meat and fish	Unknown	150	180
Sugar	750	240	180
Coffee	64	51	Very small
Tea	15	14	14
Rice	63	72	18
Cheese	60	37.5	20
Fodder	2,800	small	Nil

[1] Reduced level reached by target date, under the assumption that all grain could be requisitioned from the farms and all stocks were exhausted completely by mid-October.
[2] Including the remaining stock of butter.

3. Biweekly rations of rationed foodstuff as per July 5, 1942
   (Example: family of 5–6 persons)[110]

Commodity	Quantity [1]
Bread	800 grams per person per day
Edible oil	1.28 liters
Kerosene	4.6 liters per week
Fats (lard, margarine, butter)	1,200 grams
Cheese	400 grams
Rice	400 grams
Coffee	400 grams
Tinned meat	3 tins of 396 grams each
Preserved or tinned fish	1 large tin
Tinned milk	Only for pregnant women and babies
Pasteurized milk	Only for hospitals, and children between 2 and 9 years of age

[1] Traditional Maltese weights are converted into the metric system.

Notes

1   A full appreciation of Malta's geography and geostrategic position is given by Dennis Castillo, *The Maltese Cross: A Strategic History of Malta* (Westport: Praeger Security International, 2006), 2–9.

2   Castillo, *The Maltese Cross*, 2–9.

3   Fernand Braudel, *Das Mittelmeer und die mediterrane Welt im Zeitalter Philipps II.*, vol. 1 (Frankfurt: Suhrkamp, 1994), 153.

4   Figures from Edward Zammit, *A Colonial Inheritance: Maltese Perceptions of Work, Power and Class Structure with Reference to the Labour Movement* (Malta: Malta University Press, 1984).

5   Christopher Pollaco, *An Outline of Socio-Economic Development in Post-War Malta* (Malta: Mireva Publications, 2003), 136–43.

6   The statistical basis for analyzing Axis ship losses in the Mediterranean was established in 1955 by the Air Historical Branch of the British Air Ministry and has been used with only few adjustments ever since in most publications on the topic; see Douglas Austin, *Malta and British Strategic Policy 1925–43* (London/New York: Frank Cass, 2004), 191f. A full list can be found in Reinhard Stumpf, "Probleme der Logistik im Afrikafeldzug 1941–1943" in *Vorträge zur Militärgeschichte*, vol. 7: *Die Bedeutung der Logistik für die militärische Führung von der Antike bis in die neueste Zeit*, ed. by Horst Boog et al. (Bonn: E.S. Mittler & Sohn, 1986), 218.

7   A map plotting the radius from aircraft in relation to the Axis shipping routes is depicted in I.S.O. Playfair, *The Mediterranean and the Middle East*, vol. 2 (London, HMSO, 1956). Refer to the Naval and Military Press reprint (2004), map 25 (following p. 278).

8   Philip Guedala, *Middle East 1940–1942: A Study in Airpower* (London: Hodder and Stoughton, 1944), 181.

9   There are quite a few monographs on the Mediterranean convoy operations to be consulted for details, for example, David A. Thomas, *Malta Convoys* (Barnsley: Pen&Sword, 1999); Richard Woodman, *Malta Convoys 1940–1943* (London: John Murray, 2000). An excellent single-volume account of the whole naval war is given by Jack Greene and Allessandro Massignani, *The Naval War in the Mediterranean 1940–1943* (London, Chatham Publishing, 1998), which also takes a close look on the Italian side of the hill—or better: of the wave.

10 See for instance Charles J. Boffa, *The 'Illustrious Blitz': Malta in Wartime 1940–1942* (Malta: Progress Press, 1995) with lots of anecdotal evidence, or Kenneth Poolman, *HMS Illustrious: The Fight for Life* (Bristol: Cerberus Publishing, 2004), 56–66.

11 German code name for the planned invasion of Malta; the Italian one was C3. The decision-making process is traced in all detail by Ralf-Georg

Reuth, *Entscheidung im Mittelmeer* (Koblenz: Bernard und Graefe, 1985). For the planning, see John D. Burtt and David Pastore, "The Planning for the Invasion of Malta, 1942," *World at War* 16 (February–March, 2011): 28–37, worldatwarmagazine.com/wp-content/uploads/2012/04/WW16-TOC.pdf. A summary based exclusively on literature in English is given by Stephen Kavanaugh, *Hitler's Malta Option: A Comparison of the Invasion of Crete (Operation Merkur) and the Proposed Invasion of Malta (Operation Hercules)* (Ann Arbor: Nimble Books, 2010).

12   Donald MacIntyre, *The Battle for the Mediterranean* (London: Pan Books, 1964), 99.

13   For the role of deciphering/intelligence operations in the Mediterranean, see Ronald Lewin, *Entschied Ultra den Krieg?* (Koblenz: E.S. Mittler & Sohn, 1981); Alberto Santoni, *Ultra siegt im Mittelmeer* (Koblenz: Mittler & Sohn, 1985). "Ultra" was the code name of the deciphering system and respective machine, variations of which were used in a couple of countries throughout the war.

14   Cajus Bekker, *Angriffshöhe 4,000: Ein Kriegstagebuch der deutschen Luftwaffe* (München: Wilhelm Heyne Verlag, 1973), 263; Erhard Jähnert, *Als Sturzkampfpilot an allen Fronten: Mal oben–mal unten*, vol. 1: *1935–1943* (Würzburg: Flechsig-Verlag, 2010), 171; Karl Gundelach, *Die deutsche Luftwaffe im Mittelmeer, 1940–1945*, 2 parts (Frankfurt/Bern/Cirencester: Peter Lang, 1981), part 1, 357.

15   Gundelach, *Die deutsche Luftwaffe*, 400.

16   Stewart Perowne, *The Siege within the Walls: Malta 1940–1943* (London: Hodder & Stoughton, 1970), 113.

17   Gundelach, *Die deutsche Luftwaffe*, part 1, 402–406.

18   *Times of Malta*, henceforth abbreviated *ToM*, with dates given in day/month/year order. Recorded at full length in Perowne, *The Siege within the Walls*, 139–43.

19   Joseph M. Wismayer, *The History of the King's Own Malta Regiment* (Malta: Said International, 1989), 196–209, 262; Joseph Attard, *Britain and Malta: The Story of an Era* (Malta: PEG Ltd., 1995), 167. Figures differ slightly in various publications. I have been unable to figure out the number of Maltese casualties in the Royal Navy and the merchant navy.

20   Joseph M. Pirotta, *Fortress Colony: The Final Act 1945–1964*, vol. 1: *1945–1954* (Malta: Studia Editions, 1987), 9.

21   Illustratively described by Jörg Friedrich, *Der Brand: Deutschland im Bombenkrieg 1940–1945* (Berlin, List Verlag, 2004), 21–28.

22   Charles A. Jellison, *Besieged: The World War II Ordeal of Malta 1940–1942* (Hanover: University Press of New England, 1984), 25ff, 109f, with some figures. On the history of shelter construction, with lots of eyewitness

accounts, see Anthony Zarb-Dimech, *Taking Cover: A History of Air-raid Shelters. Malta: 1940–1943*, ed. by Charles J. Boffa (Malta: 2001).

23   Austin, *Malta and British Strategic Policy*, 74f; Jellison, *Besieged*, 110; Zarb-Dimech, *Taking Cover*, 153–63, with facsimiles of official lists showing exact location and capacities.

24   The full story is told in Carmel Farrugia, *Polluted Politics: Background to the Deportation of Maltese Nationals to Uganda in 1942* (Malta: Midsea Books, 1995).

25   Beforehand, most clerics of the upper echelons were ethnic Italians.

26   For a list of these persons, with photographs, see John A. Mizzi and Mark Anthony Vella, *Malta at War*, vol. 1 (Rabat: Wise Owl Publications, 2001), 240f.

27   Their biographies are yet to be written. Some biographical data of Maltese personalities can be found in Michael J. Schiavone, *Dictionary of Maltese Personalities*, 2 vols. (Pietà: Pubblikazzjonet Indipendenza, 2009).

28   A full list of the districts and their initial office holders was published in *The Government Gazette*, May 16, 1941; see also *ToM* 15.5.1941. During the war, the districts were readjusted here and there, as were their office holders.

29   For a history see Wismayer, *King's Own Malta Regiment*, and Dennis Rollo, *The Guns and Gunners of Malta* (Malta: Mondial Publishers, 1999).

30   Cunningham to Pound, March 17, 1941, in Michael Simpson, ed., *The Cunningham Papers*, vol. 1 (Ashgate: The Navy Records Society, 1999), 303.

31   Jellison, *Besieged*, 23.

32   *ToM* 13.11.1935.

33   *ToM* 20.11.1939.

34   Austin, *Malta and British Strategic Policy*, 88.

35   *ToM* 22.09.1935; *ToM* 29.10.1935. It had already existed in the First World War.

36   *ToM* 25.08.1939.

37   *ToM* 19.09.1939; *ToM* 20.09.1939.

38   *ToM* 13.09.1939; *ToM* 14.09.1939; *ToM* 16.09.1939.

39   *ToM* 14.09.1939; *ToM* 18.09.1339.

40   For some details on water and electricity consumption and means of economizing, see *ToM* 6.3.1941.

41   *ToM* 20.08.1936.

42   *ToM* 13.09.1936.

43   A list of convoys to and from Malta is provided by Thomas, *Malta Convoys*, 197f, and in greater detail for 1941–42, by I.S.O. Playfair, *The Mediterranean and the Middle East*, 324.

44   Warren G. Berg, *Historical Dictionary of Malta* (London: The Scarecrow Press, 1995), 94.

45 MacIntyre, *The Battle for the Mediterranean*, 100; Castillo, *The Maltese Cross*, 180; John Wingate, *The Fighting Tenth* (London: Leo Cooper, 1991), 181f; Mizzi and Vella, *Malta at War*, vol. 5, 1497, 1509 with some examples of shiploads.

46 MacIntyre, *The Battle for the Mediterranean*, 104f.

47 Sir Charles Bonham-Carter, GCB, CMC, DSO, 1876–1955, Governor and Commander in Chief, Malta, March 1936–October 1940. He was followed by General Sir William Dobbie, April 1940–42; Field Marshal the Right Honourable Lord Gort, 1942–September 1944; then Lt. Gen. Sir Edmond Schreiber, September, 1944–July 1946.

48 *ToM* 30.1.1939.

49 For some shortcomings see *ToM* 14.12.1940. Some vivid descriptions are found in Joseph Micallef, *When Malta Stood Alone* (Malta: Imprint Ltd., 1981) 33ff, and the letter columns of *ToM* are full of complaints and anecdotes.

50 Regulations published in *The Government Gazette*, 01.04.1941, summarized in *ToM* 02.04.1941.

51 *ToM* 4.12.1941; ToM 21.10.1943.

52 In Jellison, *Besieged*, 222, the author has compiled a list of black market prices as opposed to the official maximum prices.

53 For some figures on salaries and purchasing power see David Wragg, *Malta: The Last Great Siege 1940–1943* (Barnsley: Pen & Sword, 2003), 191f. Figures for 1941 were discussed in the Government Council as summarized in *ToM* 16.12.1941.

54 Address of Lieutenant Governor Sir Edward Jackson after the failure of Operation Harpoon; *ToM* 21.6.1942.

55 Potatoes were Malta's only export crop worth mentioning, but the average 10,000 tons sent abroad annually could not leave the islands due to war conditions.

56 Jellison, *Besieged*, 159–62.

57 "Malta Supply Situation," memorandum by the Chiefs of the Imperial General Staff, reprinted in Mizzi and Vella, *Malta at War*, vol. 5, 1522f.

58 Social insurance, retirement or pension schemes, and so on were almost nonexistent or only rudimentary.

59 For some details see Sunday *ToM* 7.12.1941.

60 R. Leslie Oliver, *Malta Besieged* (London: Hutchinson, 1944), 124.

61 *ToM* 30.7.1942.

62 *ToM* 1.7.1942.

63 *ToM* 12.7.1942; ToM 20.7.1942.

64 The Government Council, Protocol of 3.3.1942/*ToM* 6.3.1942; ToM 11.3.1942.

65 *ToM* 30.10.1942; ToM 31.10.1942.

66 Micallef, *When Malta Stood Alone*, 172f; Jellison, *Besieged* 170, 229; Per-owne, *The Siege within the Walls*, 119; Wragg, *Malta*, 194ff.

67 *ToM* 10.9.1942; ToM 25.9.1942.

68 *ToM* 10.3.1943; ToM 17.3.1943; ToM 31.7.1943.

69 *ToM* 30.8.1943.

70 *ToM* 16.9.1942.

71 Jellison, *Besieged*, 229 with some dramatic quotations. Again the letter columns of *ToM* are full of comments and complaints.

72 *ToM* 2.9.1942; ToM 3.9.1942.

73 Playfair, *The Mediterranean and the Middle East*, vol. 3, 183.

74 Dobbie to Admiralty, April 20, 1942, reprinted in Mizzi and Vella, *Malta at War*, vol. 6, 1810.

75 Woolton to Churchill, September 5, 1942, PRO CO 852/493/1. The Earl of Woolton was Minister of Food between April 4, 1940 and November 11, 1943.

76 *ToM* 14.5.1942.

77 J.R. Colville, *Man of Valor: The Life of Field-Marshal The Viscount Gort* (London: Collins, 1972), 249.

78 Prof. (Sir) Jack Drummond, D.Sc., FRIC, FRS, 1891–1952. For a short appreciation, see Alice M. Copping, "Sir Jack Cecil Drummond, F.R.S., a Biographical Sketch," *Journal of Nutrition* 82 no. 1 (1964): 1–9. Scattered information about his biography and his scientific approaches and ideas can be found in James Fergusson, *The Vitamin Murders—Who Killed Healthy Eating in Britain?* (London: Portobello Books, 2007).

79 Fergusson, *The Vitamin Murders*, 39.

80 Public Record Office ref. CO 852/493/1, quoted as D/W and number of the paragraph in which the paper is organized. Accompanying correspondence under the same reference is identified by sender, receiver, and date. The report was frequently mentioned in contemporary papers like *ToM*, in debates of the Government Council, and in later publications, but it was never extensively published. Only Micallef gives a short summary and uses some figures (he does not provide any archival references of his primary sources, only the type of files he was using) in *When Malta Stood Alone*, 164ff.

81 Drummond, D.Sc., FRIC, FRS, 1891–1952.

82 Douglas Austin, *Churchill and Malta's War 1939–1945* (Stroud: Amberley Publishing, 2010), 207.

83 No wonder, in view of the long list of interviewees; see D/W Appendix I. Secrets were not easily kept on such a small island, where Maltese civil and military personnel were closely interrelated with the ordinary population by neighborhood and family bonds. Information and opinions that were gossiped about openly in British Malta, and frankly discussed in the newspapers, would have brought their authors directly into a concentration

camp—if not to the scaffold—in Hitler's Germany or Stalin's USSR. On the other hand, the isolated situation of the fortress island made spying, as well as any transfer of intelligence gathered by espionage, rather difficult. Neither the Germans nor the Italians had any intelligence network on Malta, and they lacked detailed information about the situation there.

84   *ToM* 3.7.1942.
85   *ToM* 24.7.1942, for example by shooting down an airplane or seizing a submarine, by which means most mail was shipped between Malta and Great Britain.
86   *ToM* 21.6.1942.
87   D/W para. 4.
88   *ToM* 17.6.1942.
89   D/W para. 275.
90   D/W para. 9–11.
91   Woolton to Churchill, September 5, 1942, PRO CO 852/493/1.
92   D/W para. 62, Appendix 3, 2–5.
93   *ToM* 18.6.1942.
94   D/W para. 105.
95   *ToM* 31.7.1943.
96   *ToM* 8.4.1942; Dobbie to Secretary of the Colonies, reprinted in Mizzi and Vella, *Malta at War*, vol. 5, 1738; Micallef, *When Malta Stood Alone*, 161f.
97   *ToM* 27.3.1942.
98   Mizzi and Vella, *Malta at War*, vol. 5, 1753.
99   *ToM* 24.1.1942; Mizzi and Vella, *Malta at War*, vol. 4, 1141; vol. 6, 1799; figures in D/W para. 225.
100   *ToM* 13.7.1942.
101   D/W para. 226.
102   *ToM* 23.4.1942; ToM 14.5.1942; ToM 15.5.1942; Mizzi and Vella, *Malta at War*, vol. 5, p. 1786.
103   The dramatic convoy operation that saved Malta is the climax of every work on Malta in the Second World War and forms the entire subject of some monographs as well. Most recently, Woodman, *Malta Convoys 1940–1943*, 433–54 has the story, as well as an extensive bibliography of earlier works.
104   Wragg, *Malta*, 198.
105   *ToM* 15.8.1942; ToM 29.8.1942; ToM 13.11.1942.
106   *ToM* 2.10.1942.
107   *ToM* 23.12.1942; ToM 24.12.1942.
108   The Government Council, Protocol 27.3.1943, cf. also the official 1942 Health Report as printed in *ToM* 8.2.1944.
109   Compiled from D/W para. 92f, Appendices 2 and 7.
110   Sunday *ToM* 5.7.1942.

9

"The Highest Rule"
Rommel as Military Genius

Antulio J. Echevarria II

"What genius does is the highest rule."

— *Carl von Clausewitz, 1831*

Erwin Johannes Eugen Rommel (1891–1944) is probably both the most and least well-known of Hitler's generals. The name Rommel is more familiar to the public than any of the other generals who served the Third Reich. Yet, much of what the public knows about history's famous 'Desert Fox' is shrouded in myth. It is a myth, moreover, that was deliberately fashioned and aggressively nurtured by Rommel himself and, as the war progressed, by the extensive resources of the Nazi propaganda machine. It is also a myth that has on the whole endured, despite the collective efforts of military historians and biographers to portray the 'real' Rommel. Indeed, the decades since the end of the Second World War have seen historians and other writers both add to and clear away substantial portions of the Rommel myth.[1] What remains, however, seems enough to qualify Rommel as one of history's great, if controversial, captains—perhaps even a military genius.[2] He did, after all, defeat a number of able British commanders before the run was broken by Montgomery at El Alamein.

The problem with attempting to describe any exceptional skill or talent as genius is that the term has become highly romanticized.[3] It is as rare as beauty, and just as difficult to define. For this reason, genius was not examined in any depth by Enlightenment thinkers, who considered it more of an exception than a rule, and thus not suitable for scientific study.

Military genius is still a popular topic today among the general public, but scientific study has instead gravitated toward understanding military expertise, which is a different and clearly much broader phenomenon.[4]

In contrast, the Prussian military theorist Carl von Clausewitz (1780–1831) did treat the topic in some depth, and he did so partly in response to the opinion emerging at the time that Napoleon Bonaparte was a military genius. Clausewitz, in fact, dedicated an entire chapter of his masterwork, *On War*, to laying out some basic attributes which, in his view, ought to form the starting point for any discussion of military genius. This chapter has not received the scholarly attention given to other parts of *On War*, and it is thus less well-known; however, it does offer an objective and resilient framework for analyzing the phenomenon of military genius systematically. Moreover, it has the added benefit of having been developed by a renowned military theorist and practitioner who, like Rommel, was part of the military tradition that historians have come to refer to as the German way of war.[5] Applying Clausewitz's framework to the famed Desert Fox reveals that the very qualities that made Rommel an exceptional military commander, if not exactly a military genius, were also the ones that ultimately caused him to fail.

Clasusewitz's Concept of Military Genius

Clausewitz defined military genius as the harmonious balance of the principal qualities comprising reason *(Verstand)* and passion *(Gemüt)*. These included intelligence, energy, steadfastness, resolve, strength of temperament, and strength of character.[6] For Clausewitz, intelligence was the ability to reason clearly. It went hand in hand with the capacity to exercise sound judgment, which in turn required a special coup d'oeil, or the ability to grasp a military situation quickly.[7] Energy was necessary to overcome the resistance of one's enemy as well as the inertia of one's own military machine. Examples might include a commander's personal quest for glory, or his desire to satisfy his own honor, motives often regarded as negative but each of which had a positive side. Steadfastness and resolve went hand in hand: the former was the ability to stay focused when confronted with unexpected adversities; the latter was the determination to persevere over the long haul. Strength of temperament was much like what today is described as self-discipline: the ability to resist the influence of emotion and remain rational. Strength of character, a term widely used in military organizations throughout the nineteenth and most of the twentieth century, meant self-confidence, which was not to be confused with obstinacy. Physical courage meant the ability to function despite the debilitating influence of danger and the physical privations of war; psychological courage was the willingness to accept responsibility, to be decisive in a crisis.

True genius was only possible when these traits were in balance.[8] Together, they served as something of a counterweight to the elements of danger, physical exertion, uncertainty, and chance, which collectively made up the atmosphere of war. However, too much of one quality, such as energy, would lead to an imbalance, a character flaw, that would likely affect a commander's judgment in an adverse way. Interestingly, Clausewitz did not consider Napoleon a military genius, though some military writers did, because the Corsican's ambition was simply too great. He could not refrain from overextending himself and his army.

Yet, for Clausewitz, genius was also something more than this ideal balance of character traits. It was the innate force or ability that gave form and substance to art: genius is the innate aptitude *(ingenium)*, by which nature gives the rule to art.[9] By definition, then, a genius does not copy existing rules or models. Rather, his achievements provide the models, or rules, that others imitate. Rules were defined as fundamental cause-and-effect relationships, and conduct of war was thought to have them just as economics and other activities. Napoleon, though Clausewitz did not consider him a military genius, is an example of a commander who used the rules of warfare differently from his predecessors, and with revolutionary effect on the battlefield.

Military genius, thus, requires a mastery of the fundamental cause-and-effect relationships of warfare. Yet, as Clausewitz stressed: "What genius does must at once be the perfect rule, and theory can do nothing better than to show how and why this is so."[10] Genius can, in other words, make its own rules, or use old ones in different ways: "A true quality of genius belongs to every level of command, from lowest to highest, though history and posterity reserve the title of genius only for those who have served at the highest position—that of Commander in Chief—for here the demands on understanding and psychological makeup are much greater."[11]

Rommel as Military Genius
Nothing in Rommel's youth and social background suggested that he might have the innate ability to rise to high-level military command,

Fig 9.1 Rommel, commander of the German forces in North Africa, with his aides during the desert campaign. (IWM HU 5625)

let alone become one of history's great captains. His time as an officer candidate then as a cadet in the 124th (Sixth Württemberger) Infantry Regiment demonstrated that he was above average at drill and leadership, and of solid character, but hardly exceptional.[12] When war broke out in 1914, however, that all changed. His service as a junior officer in the First World War showed him to be intelligent, brave, bold, and resourceful. To be sure, tens of thousands of other young men possessed similar qualities, and demonstrated them prolifically in the trenches, often in appalling conditions and against overwhelming odds. However, only a few were lucky enough to have their exploits recognized with the highly coveted awards of the Iron Cross, first and second classes, as well as the Pour le Mérite. Rommel, thus, quickly entered a class of his own as a junior officer, which was likely the reason he would obtain one of the rare officer billets in the postwar Reichswehr. He also was clever enough to cultivate his image as a battlefield leader among his subordinates and superiors, both during the war and afterward. His book, *Infantry Attacks* (1937), was as much about self-promotion as it was about distilling combat lessons for company-grade officers.[13] On one level it was little more than a collection of war stories; but on another it was an unusual intellectual accomplishment, which also lacked the stigma of being bookish.

Rommel was also lucky enough to experience more than the static 'war of position' that the German Army was forced by circumstances to carry out on the western front. On the Italian and Romanian fronts, he practiced first-hand, albeit on a small scale, exactly the kind of 'war of movement' the Kaiserheer wished to follow overall. He later identified the following differences between the two

> In a mobile action, what counts is material, as the essential complement to the soldier. The finest fighting man has no value in mobile warfare without tanks, guns, and vehicles. Thus a mobile force can be rendered unfit for action by the destruction of its tanks, without having suffered any serious casualties in man-power. This is not the case with position warfare, where the infantryman with rifle and hand grenade has lost little of his value, provided, of course, he is protected by antitank guns or obstacles against the enemy's armor. . . . Hence position warfare is always a struggle for the destruction of men—in contrast to mobile warfare, where everything turns on the destruction of enemy material.[14]

By all accounts, Rommel also possessed exceptional energy, steadfastness, resolve, self-discipline, self-confidence, as well as physical and psychological courage. On September 14, 1914, for instance, he was wounded in the leg after charging half a dozen French infantrymen with a bayonet.[15] The wound was nearly fatal, but he survived, and was awarded the Iron Cross, second class. He later received the Iron Cross, first class, for an action on January 29, 1915, in which, nearly encircled, he led his company on an attack through French positions in order to return to German lines. He demonstrated his bravery again when he continued to remain in command of his company after being seriously wounded on August 9, 1917, during the assault on Monte Cosna.[16] He was awarded the Pour le Mérite for his successful assault on Mount Mataiur, though an usually high number of these seem to have been given out during this

Fig 9.2 Major General O'Connor (center), architect of the early Italian defeat, and other British soldiers (Brigadier John Combe, left; Major General Gambier-Parry, right) having been captured at Derna, Libya, April 1942. (IWM MH 5554)

stage of the Alpine campaign.[17] He continued to show the same courage as he rose in rank, consistently placing himself at the point of attack.

Yet, Rommel also proved himself to be an adroit political soldier. He is sometimes portrayed as the archetypical 'good German,' whose affinities with Adolph Hitler and the Nazi party were more a matter of professional necessity than personal choice. However, his sympathies were decidedly pro-Hitler and he took aggressive steps to ingratiate himself with the Fuhrer, or high-ranking party officials.[18] Rommel's book, *Infantry Attacks*, became a bestseller and a popular gift among the Hitler Youth.[19] In essence, he became a willing poster child for a Nazi agenda that touted German military prowess and glorified war.

Whether lieutenant or field marshal, Rommel's signature trademark was exerting his personal influence at the decisive point. However, this trademark revealed that he was what today would be called a micromanager, a leader who was not willing to trust his subordinates with important tasks. He often intervened in military operations to run his subordinates' units for them, which was contrary to the accepted German tradition. One notable example is the Seventh Panzer Division's attempt to cross the Meuse River on May 13, 1940, during the campaign in France. The attempt failed despite Rommel's personal intervention because, in his view, his subordinate officers "were appalled by their heavy losses and unwilling to press forward."[20] Ironically, while he typically expected nothing short of instant obedience from his own officers and men, he frequently disregarded his superiors' orders, or creatively reinterpreted them so that they were less restrictive.

Rommel's tendency to intervene dovetailed with his penchant for shifting blame to others—superiors, peers, or even subordinates—for operational mistakes or failures, while taking credit for success. After a failed attempt to take Tobruk in May 1941, for instance, he put the onus for failure on his subordinates' inexperience and lack of training: the troops had employed improper tactics, which resulted in high casualties (1,200 men killed, wounded, and missing).[21] Indeed, inexperience and lack of training are usually prominent factors in any military failure. In this case, however, Rommel's habit of asking too much of his men, of overestimating their capabilities while underestimating those of his foes, was also to blame. Too often he disregarded the physical and psychological limitations of the personnel under his command. It is worth mentioning that his inclination to shift blame also kept him from turning an objective eye toward, and perhaps addressing, his own shortcomings so as to improve his method of command and increase his organization's chances for success in the long term. The words of his erstwhile commander, General Hermann Hoth, during the campaign in France, namely, that Rommel should not be allowed to command a corps until he had acquired "greater experience and a better sense of judgment," were prophetic.[22]

Certainly, Rommel's habit of avoiding or redirecting blame partly reflected his personal insecurities, some of which likely derived from his common background and lack of elite social status. He did not belong to the military aristocracy, and had no martial tradition associated with his family name. He was thus at a decided disadvantage—so he believed, and

Fig 9.3 Rommel with his Chief of Staff, Fritz Bayerlein, in the North African desert. (IWM HU 5628)

with some justification—when it came to competing with his peers and gaining recognition for his exploits. In other words, it is at least possible that he felt the need to advertise, even exaggerate, his achievements so as to stay competitive with his peers. However, it is even more likely that his self-promotion was fueled principally by what Clausewitz once described as a commander's lust for glory; this desire, in turn, was fed by Rommel's growing image as an extraordinary military commander, which had to be nurtured. As Clausewitz pointed out, such desire is not always negative, and can be a positive force; however, it essentially went unchecked, and made Rommel a high-risk subordinate.

Rommel's skills seem to have peaked at the battle of Gazala in June of 1942, about one week before the First Battle of El Alamein.[23] Here, he followed a bold but somewhat predictable scheme of maneuver. His plan called for a wide envelopment of the British left flank, followed by a sharp turn across the British rear toward Tobruk. It was bold because it pushed the Afrika Korps' logistics to its extreme limit, and a bit beyond. The entire plan nearly failed because of that. Yet, it was also entirely in keeping with Rommel's desired pattern of operations, which were in turn based loosely on his 'rules' of desert warfare. These rules required fighting battles of attrition aimed at "wearing down [the opponents'] material and breaking their cohesion" through the concentration of one's own forces and the "highest possible degree of mobility."[24] He believed that, in the desert, encirclement alone was not sufficient to destroy another mobile force, since it could always find a way to "break out at will through an improvised defensive ring," as long as its "organizational structure remains intact."[25]

Rommel's style of leading from the front proved effective time and again, and in the case of Gazala, likely saved him from defeat. He was always able to issue orders, and counterorders, faster than his opponents. He was inside their 'decision cycles,' to use one of today's popular military expressions. However, most of the successes he enjoyed during that battle and the subsequent victorious assault on Tobruk were also the result of his foe's ineptitude. During the encounters that took place in and around the 'Cauldron' or 'Sausage Pot' (May 30 to June 1, 1942), for example, Rommel had rashly maneuvered himself between the proverbial rock and a hard place. The master enveloper had found himself enveloped: to his west he had a series of extensive minefields with a half dozen fortified 'boxes,' or strong points, occupied by infantry brigades, dug in and reinforced with tanks and artillery; while to his east he faced several British armored formations, some of which were armed with the new American Grant tanks with their very effective 75-mm guns.[26] A vigorous, concentrated attack by Lieutenant General Neil Ritchie's armored formations would have crushed the Afrika Korps, which had lost a third of its tanks and was desperately low on fuel. Indeed, it may well have ended the Rommel legend, and eventually the North African campaign. However, that did not happen. Instead, Ritchie launched several brigade and smaller attacks in piecemeal fashion, which the Axis forces were able to defeat one at a time. It was little more than the devil's luck to have such an obliging opponent.

Fig 9.4 'War without Hate': three aircrew of no. 39 Squadron, RAF, buried by Germans, lie in graves in front of the wreckage of their Martin Maryland Mk II, southwest of Gazala. (IWM E 7297)

During the pursuit and exploitation that followed the fall of Tobruk in the summer of 1942, Rommel needed to leapfrog his air cover forward, if he were to have any real hope of taking Cairo. However, this he did not do. His operations were obviously hampered logistically, and that situation needed to be remedied as well. Axis forces required roughly one hundred thousand tons of supplies per month during the late summer and early autumn of 1942, but were only receiving half that on average.[27] However, the issue of air coverage had to be dealt with first. Rommel's ground operations and the movement of his logistics were severely affected by the limited operational range of Axis air cover, which could not prevent his forces or the ports in Libya from being bombed.

To illustrate the point: as the Allies advanced in Italy in 1943, their air cover also leapfrogged to new bases and airfields so as to ensure coverage would be in place for the next series of ground operations. This task was, obviously, made easier by the fact that more of the Luftwaffe's planes were being diverted to defend the German homeland from Allied bombing offensives. Nonetheless, the fact is that forward movement of ground forces was often driven by the need to capture another airfield, rather than to destroy another enemy mechanized unit, so that air cover could be extended. In other words, fire and movement, always mutually reinforcing on a tactical level, had by the Second World War become interdependent on an operational one as well. Yet, Rommel appreciated this fact far too late in the North African campaign (though he appears to have learned it by the battle for Normandy), and never took effective action to ensure his formations had adequate protection from the Allied air forces.

By July 1, 1942, as the First Battle of El Alamein began, Rommel was unavoidably moving from a war of movement—where his tight decision cycle and his penchant for aggressive action and pushing his forces to their limits gave him the advantage—to a war of position, where numbers and firepower would win the day. Admittedly, he attempted to avoid that by trying to get ahead of the retreating British but he was unable to do so. He was also mentally and physically drained, notwithstanding the emotional boost that undoubtedly resulted from his promotion to Generalfeldmarschall in late June. His troops were also clearly exhausted, having fought almost nonstop across some eight hundred kilometers of desert, and his tanks were low in fuel and ammunition, and badly in need of refitting.[28] He and what was left of the Afrika Korps may also have been suffering from an acute case of overconfidence, after having inflicted a humiliating defeat on the British Eighth Army earlier. Either way, Rommel once again overestimated the capabilities of his troops, while at the same time underestimating those of his foes. This recklessness was his chief character flaw. While it was, on the whole, less evident during the summer battles of Gazala and the subsequent capture of Tobruk, by July 1942 it had returned in spades. By July 21, 1942, Rommel's forces had lost 70 percent of their manpower, 85 percent of their armor, 65 percent of their antitank weapons, and 50 percent of their heavy antiaircraft guns.[29]

Time and again he had gotten himself out of desperate situations, predicaments that, to be sure, were largely his own fault. However, the uniqueness of the terrain around El Alamein and the rapidity with which British strength would be able to grow meant that he would henceforth be deprived of room to maneuver, and thus, of the ability to create chaos for his adversary. These advantages, coupled with the intelligence edge that the Allies enjoyed through Ultra, Rommel's renewal of the Axis offensive on August 30, 1942, known as the Second Battle of El Alamein or Alam al-Halfa, was doomed from the start. Even though he allegedly scaled back his objectives, he apparently retained high hopes for this desperate battle. As he confided in his wife, Lucie: "I have worried so much about this day, but I am taking the risk because I will not have another chance, in terms of the moonlight and ratio of forces. So much is at stake. If I succeed, this may have a decisive effect on the course of the war."[30] Indeed, so much was at stake. Yet, Rommel's plan of attack was very reminiscent of Gazala, too much so, in fact, and that alone would have been reason enough for the British to have been prepared for it, even without Ultra. And so they were. The Italian infantry were to launch a pinning attack to the front, while the Afrika Korps were to punch through a perceived twenty-one-kilometer gap between the southern positions of the British forces and the Qattara Depression, and then turn north toward the Alam al-Halfa ridge and the coastal roads leading west into El Alamein. However, the Allies' advantages in the areas mentioned above, as well as insufficient reconnaissance on the part of Rommel's troops, began to tell almost immediately. The attack bogged down, and Rommel called it off on September 4, 1942. Montgomery received the credit for stopping Rommel; and, in truth, it was his battle to lose—which was a remote, but real, possibility had he counterattacked prematurely. Yet, his plan was essentially the same as that of his predecessor, Auchinleck. The fact that it required little imagination on the part of the British, or much adjustment after Ultra essentially delivered Rommel's plan, is a further strike against the genius of the Desert Fox.

When Montgomery launched the final battle of El Alamein on October 23, 1942, Rommel was in Germany on much-needed sick leave. He returned to North Africa on the evening of the 25th; but it would not matter. The material superiority of the British Eighth Army and its supporting organizations would prove decisive. Montgomery enjoyed a 2:1 superiority in manpower, a 3:1 superiority in aircraft, and more than a 4:1 superiority in medium tanks.[31] It was nothing more than a First World War-style battle of attrition; but it was one Montgomery could win with his preponderance of force, and one that Rommel could not. There were several moments of crisis when Montgomery had to exert his will over subordinate commanders not used to grinding forward into a hailstorm of enemy fire. But overall, it was a matter of military science, the mathematics of attrition, and military art would have no say. The Clausewitzian realm of chance, "wherein creative genius is free to roam," had been greatly, and wisely, restricted by Montgomery's decision to build overwhelming material superiority.[32] It was also significantly reduced by the interdiction efforts of Allied air power, which had severely limited Rommel's flow of supplies. He attempted to launch a few counterattacks, but the lack of fuel and ammunition was crippling. His army was simply overextended and, essentially, exposed, and had been since the First Battle of El Alamein, though he and many of those around him failed to realize it. There was no way to deflect blame in this case.

On balance, Rommel's style of command, while often praised by military historians, was actually ill-suited to the conditions in which he found himself. It resembled the leadership style in vogue in the nineteenth century, where the timely appearance of the commander at the decisive point on the battlefield might tip the scales toward victory. However, in the twentieth century, command at higher levels was relentlessly expanding to encompass more dimensions, such as operational-level air support and theater-level intelligence. It also required expanding control over broader areas geographically. Rommel did not incorporate those dimensions into his method of command quickly enough. To borrow a chess analogy, Rommel was the equivalent of a chess player who succumbed to the temptation of fixing his attention on one piece, even if it is the most powerful one, while neglecting to move his other pieces into positions of advantage.

This is not an error a true grandmaster would make. Yet, Rommel's conduct of the campaign in North Africa followed this pattern consistently. He repeatedly went on the offensive with his armor and, though enjoying several brilliant tactical successes, overextended himself logistically, and with respect to his air cover. For his part, Hitler, rightly or wrongly, only wanted the campaign in North Africa to have a secondary, or even tertiary, priority. For the Fuhrer, the war in the east was what mattered, and it had literally become a life-and-death struggle for Nazism. Ultimately, Rommel was unwilling or unable to function within such political and strategic restrictions. He achieved great victories with limited resources; but those successes were not what he had been asked to do initially. Had the war against Russia gone as Hitler had expected, perhaps the North African campaign would have received a higher priority. But it did not. Rommel's habit of making reckless, perhaps even ruthless, decisions and putting extraordinary demands on his troops consistently overcommitted his Panzerarmee. As a result, it was exposed time and again to high risks, and eventually maneuvered into a position where it could hardly avoid being crushed.

Rommel's particular type of military genius, if indeed it qualifies as that, was unbalanced. It did not fit the Clausewitzian ideal because Rommel's lust for glory was too great, and impaired his ability to see how modern war had changed and to develop ways to integrate its new dimensions into his style of command. Perhaps no real military commander ever will fit the ideal; but at least the analytical framework that Clausewitz left us also helps us understand why.

Notes

1   Classic examples are: Desmond Young, *Rommel: The Desert Fox* (New York: Harper & Row, 1950); Paul Carell, *The Foxes of the Desert*, tr. Mervyn Savitt (New York: E.P. Dutton, 1960); David Irving, *The Trail of the Fox: The Search for the True Field Marshal Rommel* (New York: E.P. Dutton, 1977).

2   Liddell Hart wrote that Manstein, whom he believed to be Germany's ablest commander of the war, certainly possessed 'military genius.' See Erich von Manstein, *Lost Victories*, tr. Anthony Powell, introduction by Martin Blumenson, foreword by Capt. B.H. Liddell Hart (Novato, Ca.: Presidio, 1982), 13.

3   Penelope Murray, ed., *Genius: The History of an Idea* (Oxford: Blackwell, 1989); examples are: Col. (Ret.) T.N. Dupuy, *A Genius for War: The German Army and the General Staff, 1807–1945* (Englewood Cliffs, N.J.: Prentice Hall, 1977); David Downing, *The Devil's Virtuosos: German Generals at War 1940–5* (New York: St. Martin's Press, 1977).

4   For an example of genius in popular literature see Harold Bloom, *Genius: A Mosaic of One Hundred Exemplary Creative Minds* (New York: Warner, 2002), 11, which defines genius as "a transcendental awareness capable of broadening the consciousness of others through exemplary works." One reason for the decline in scholarly interest was the emergence of so-called scientific measures, such as the Intelligence Quotient (IQ), to restrict entry into elite academic institutions: Catherine Morris Cox, *Genetic Studies of Genius*, vol. 2: *The Early Mental Traits of Three Hundred Geniuses* (Stanford: Stanford University, 1926 repr. 1969). Thomas H. Killion, "Clausewitz and Military Genius," *Military Review* 75, no. 4 (1995): 97–100, explains genius in terms of 'expert' theory.

5   Robert M. Citino, *The German Way of War: From the Thirty Years' War to the Third Reich* (Lawrence: University Press of Kansas, 2005).

6   Carl von Clausewitz, *Vom Kriege. Hinterlassenes Werk des Generals Carl von Clausewitz*, 19th ed., ed. Werner Hahlweg (Bonn: Ferd. Dümmlers Verlag,

1991), Book 1, ch. 3, 246, 238. Compare the English translation: Carl von Clausewitz, *On War*, ed. and tr. Michael Howard and Peter Paret (Princeton: Princeton University Press, 1976), 104, 110.

7   Clausewitz, *Vom Kriege*, Book 1, ch. 3, 234–35; *On War*, 102.

8   Clausewitz's model for military genius was his mentor Scharnhorst, who possessed the proper balance of intellect and temperament. Clausewitz, "On the Life and Character of Scharnhorst," *Historical and Political Writings*, 85–109.

9   Compare Immanuel Kant, *Kritik der Urteilskraft*, ed. Wilhelm Weischedel (Frankfurt: Suhrkamp, 1974), sec. 46, 241–42, sec. 49, 253, 255; Immanuel Kant, *Philosophical Writings*, ed. Ernst Behler (New York: Continuum, 1986), 224, 233, 235; and Clausewitz, *On War*, ed. and tr. M. Howard and P. Paret, 161.

10   Clausewitz, *Vom Kriege*, Book 2, ch. 2, 284; *On War*, 136.

11   Clausewitz, *Vom Kriege*, Book 1, ch. 3, 250–51; *On War*, 111–12.

12   Dennis Showalter, *Patton and Rommel: Men of War in the Twentieth Century* (New York: Berkley Caliber, 2006), 31.

13   Oberstleutnant Rommel, *Infanterie Greift an: Erlebnis und Erfahrung* (Potsdam: Ludwig Voggenreiter, 1937).

14   B.H. Liddell Hart, ed., *The Rommel Papers*, tr. Paul Findlay (New York: Da Capo, 1953), 133.

15   Terry Brighton, *Patton, Montgomery, Rommel: Masters of War* (New York: Crown Publishers, 2008), 25.

16   Showalter, *Patton and Rommel*, 45, 55–62.

17   David Irving, *The Trail of the Fox* (New York: Avon, 1977), 18–23.

18   Showalter, *Patton and Rommel*, 25–35.

19   Brighton, *Patton, Montgomery, Rommel*, 51–52.

20   Pier Paolo Battistelli, *Erwin Rommel: Leadership, Strategy, Conflict* (Oxford: Osprey, 2010), 20.

21   Liddell Hart, *Rommel Papers*, 133; Irving, *Trail of the Fox*, 112.

22   Irving, *Trail of the Fox*, 68.

23   For purposes of this chapter, the events around El Alamein between July 1, 1942 and November 4, 1942, are treated as three distinct battles; see Niall Barr, *Pendulum of War: The Three Battles of El Alamein* (New York: Overlook Press, 2005), xxxix–xl.

24   Liddell Hart, *Rommel Papers*, 199.

25   Liddell Hart, *Rommel Papers*, 199.

26   Martin Kitchen, *Rommel's Desert War: Waging World War II in North Africa 1941–43* (New York: Cambridge University Press, 2009), 218–38; see also http://www.youtube.com/watch?v=QdmXhnjyn6I.

27   Barr, *Pendulum of War*, 218–24.

28   Kitchen, *Rommel's Desert War*, 262–64.

29 Kitchen, *Rommel's Desert War*, 291.

30 Brighton, *Patton, Montgomery, Rommel*, 128.

31 Kitchen, *Rommel's Desert War*, 320–21; Brighton, *Patton, Montgomery, Rommel*, 141. The actual numbers vary slightly among the sources, but the ratios are consistent.

32 Clausewitz, *Vom Kriege*, Book 1, ch. 1.

10

High Command in the Desert

Niall Barr

Fritz Bayerlein once stated that a desert soldier needed "physical capacity, intelligence, mobility, nerve, pugnacity, daring and stoicism." He considered that the qualities required in a commander were even greater and had to include "toughness, devotion to his men, instinctive judgment of terrain and enemy, speed of reaction and spirit."[1] As far as Bayerlein was concerned, Field Marshal Erwin Rommel combined these traits to a greater degree than any other officer or man that he knew. This was high praise indeed and it was famously echoed by Winston Churchill, the British prime minister. On July 1, 1942, while the fighting raged in what came to be known as the First Battle of El Alamein, Churchill was also fighting for his political life in a debate of no confidence in the House of Commons. He paid Rommel a handsome tribute when he remarked: "We have a very daring and skilful opponent against us, and, may I say across the havoc of war, a great general." Churchill's compliment to an opponent who had caused him much anxiety since the start of the German intervention in the Desert War was neither entirely disingenuous nor completely altruistic. By suggesting that Rommel was a formidable military commander, Churchill was paying a generous compliment to an opponent but he was also attempting to draw some of the sting of the grievous series of defeats that the British Eighth Army had just suffered at his hands.

While Rommel had just enjoyed a string of military victories, his British counterparts were confronting the very real possibility that they would suffer a crushing military defeat which would lead to the loss of Egypt.

Fig 10.1 British troops dig in during the First Battle of El Alamein, July 1942. (IWM E 1394)

There was, however, a strange asymmetry between the high level of military success experienced by Rommel's Panzerarmee Afrika and the low level of overall importance that Adolf Hitler accorded the war in the Mediterranean theater. As far as Hitler was concerned, the war in the desert was a minor distraction from the real war—the 'clash of titans'—which he was prosecuting on the eastern front against the Soviet Union. Meanwhile, the British may have experienced military disaster at Rommel's hands, but this was not because Egypt was of little importance to the British war effort. In fact, Egypt was considered second in importance only to the defense of the United Kingdom itself in British war planning. Although it was impossible to use the Suez Canal as intended while Axis forces controlled the central Mediterranean, Egypt remained, as it had done since Britain's occupation of the country in 1882, the forward bastion of Britain's entire position in the Middle East. It was for this reason that it was considered at the time that loss of Egypt meant the loss of Britain's position in the Middle East—and that fundamentally meant, at least as far as Britain was concerned, the loss of the entire war. Yet in May and June 1942, the unthinkable had occurred. In the long and hard-fought battle of Gazala, and the subsequent fall of Tobruk, the British Eight Army had suffered a comprehensive military disaster. The remnants of the British Eighth Army had no choice but to precipitately flee into Egypt; and its commander, Lieutenant General Neil Ritchie, was now clearly overwhelmed by the turn of events. The British hold upon Egypt and the whole of her strategic position in the Middle East seemed on the verge of collapse.

It was in this desperate situation of crisis that, on June 25, 1942, General Auchinleck and Major General Eric 'Chink' Dorman-Smith boarded a Boston bomber at Cairo west airdrome to fly up to the headquarters of the Eighth Army. They had both just eaten 'a condemned man's meal' at the Mena House Hotel. Both fully expected to be dead or in an Italian prisoner-of-war cage within the week.

When the bomber landed at Maaten Baggush, Auchinleck and Dorman-Smith drove straight to Army headquarters, where Auchinleck curtly informed Ritchie that he was taking over direct command of the Eighth Army.[2] Auchinleck had succumbed to the terrible temptation felt by many strategic commanders—to push a failing subordinate aside and take over direct control. But from the moment he boarded the Boston bomber, Auchinleck had effectively surrendered his strategic command of the Middle East—no one man could effectively fill both posts. He now faced the ultimate test of his career by taking direct field command over an already beaten army.

There are few better examples of the dilemmas, strategic pressures, and difficult choices that can face a commander than those which confronted Auchinleck in Egypt in the summer of 1942. Yet Auchinleck's command of the Eighth Army in July 1942 also seems an object lesson in how not to command an army. His removal in August 1942 after Rommel had been halted remains one of the great controversies of British military history, but it also reveals the enormous importance of the political dimension of high command.

Auchinleck was (with the exception of William Slim, who commanded the Fourteenth Army in Burma) unique among the higher commanders of the British Army during the Second World War because he was an

Indian Army officer. His formative experiences as a soldier had been on the northwest frontier of India and in Iraq during the Great War, while most of his contemporaries in the British Army learned their trade on the western front. He was noted for his personal courage, his intelligence, and unshakeable character; but he possessed one flaw that could not be overcome: he had not built up the same web of connections and intimate knowledge of the British Army that every other senior British officer had developed over the course of their careers.[3] Auchinleck's ignorance of the British home army explains his often-criticized choice of subordinates, including Ritchie, but most especially Eric Dorman-Smith. When he relieved Ritchie of command, Auchinleck took 'Chink' with him because he admired his fertile brain and his boundless confidence and enthusiasm—which certainly were important assets in the middle of a crisis.

Dorman-Smith was considered by some, including General Archibald Wavell, to be the most brilliant staff officer of his generation, but by others, including General Alan Brooke, Chief of the Imperial General Staff, to be a dangerous 'menace.' Chink possessed a mercurial and lightning-fast intelligence that thrived on complexity. But although he might come up with ten solutions to a problem, only one of these might be brilliant and the other nine were often positively dangerous. He seized on staff problems and worked out their 'solutions' faster than anyone else, but he became less and less concerned with the difficulties that subordinate commanders might face in translating those orders into reality. Dorman-Smith was only too aware of his intelligence and made no attempt to suffer fools gladly.[4] It took careful handling and judgment to make the most of Dorman-Smith. Not surprisingly, Chink was delighted with his new role as Auchinleck's eminence grise—or as some claimed, his evil genius. Yet although Auchinleck and Dorman-Smith knew and trusted each other, having first become friends in India during the 1930s, their relationship eventually proved extremely damaging to the Eighth Army.

During the flight to Maaten Baggush, Auchinleck and Dorman-Smith thrashed out a series of decisions that they hoped would stop Rommel. Auchinleck was determined that he must keep the Eighth Army in being and would not risk its destruction by fighting a last-ditch battle at Marsa Matruh. If the Eighth Army was encircled and destroyed by Rommel, then the entire British position in the Middle East would collapse. Auchinleck had correctly identified that the continued existence of the Eighth Army remained Britain's 'center of gravity' in the region.

Fig 10.2 Troops manning a sandbagged defense position near El Alamein, August 17, 1942. (IWM E 14575)

Thus he decided that the army should withdraw to the positions at El Alamein, only sixty-four kilometers from Alexandria, where the salt marsh of the Qattara Depression narrowed the Western Desert into a natural choke point. It was there that Auchinleck would turn to fight. The two men made a host of other important decisions—to reverse the disastrous infantry brigade tactics of Gazala, to reconcentrate the artillery, and to husband their few remaining tanks. It took real courage and determination—as well as inspiration—to make these risky decisions in the middle of a fast-moving and fluid retreat. Yet it is not too much to say that these decisions saved the Eighth Army from destruction. Nonetheless, Auchinleck's assumption of command was not sufficient to prevent another fiasco during the fighting at Marsa Matruh, and when Rommel's attack began on the Alamein position on July 1, 1942, the situation looked bleak. It was only after three days of intense and confused fighting that it was clear that Auchinleck and the Eighth Army had indeed stemmed the tide at El Alamein. Rommel's army had been held at the very gates of Egypt. It has been said that turning a defeated army around at the end of a long retreat is the severest test of generalship—and also the least practiced. Auchinleck had certainly passed that test.

Meanwhile, Rommel found that Alexandria and Cairo, which seemed so close on the map, were beyond his grasp. Worse, he now found he was trapped in a situation of his own making. Rommel depended on victory for Hitler's favor, and to withdraw would signal defeat. There was more—after his rapid advance, Rommel had burned all his petrol to reach El Alamein. He could not go forward, but nor could he go back. He was literally stranded in the desert.

Yet as the two armies confronted each other at El Alamein in the searing July heat, Auchinleck also faced an intractable dilemma. The German offensive in Russia had begun in June and, at that time, it looked like the Red Army might collapse under its hammer blows. Auchinleck knew that if the Germans succeeded, they could soon threaten Britain's position in the Middle East from the north. Like so many commanders before and since, Auchinleck looked to his political master to provide grand strategic guidance. In the worst-possible case, what was more important—Egypt or Iraq? Like so many politicians before and since, Churchill refused to make a hard and fast decision.[5] Enormous risks would still have to be taken.

This dilemma meant that Auchinleck had to attempt to destroy Rommel's army while it lay stranded in the desert. Only when the threat to Egypt had been removed could the British shift forces north. Failure to do so would mean that, in the event of a German attack from the Caucasus, there would be no troops available to protect Iraq and its oil. Such a disaster would cost Britain the war.

This strategic imperative bore down hard upon the Eighth Army during July 1942 and illustrated the full peril of combining the strategic responsibilities of the Middle East with the operational demands of the Eighth Army into one man's burden. Without any insulation from these strategic imperatives, the Eighth Army was pushed to make highly ambitious attacks that were simply beyond its strength.

To persuade an already exhausted army to make an all-out effort to destroy its opponent required command and leadership skills of the highest order. Unfortunately, it is not clear that Auchinleck possessed these. Auchinleck has been called the 'lonely soldier,' and nothing illustrates this better than his choice of location for his headquarters at El Alamein. The new headquarters was located at the junction of some camel tracks just nineteen kilometers behind the front and in the middle of the army. Auchinleck insisted that all of the staff should share the same rations and hardships of the men in the frontline. Throughout his time at El Alamein, Auchinleck slept in the open beside his operations caravan. One staff officer explained that the HQ "was liberally supplied with camel dung and the attendant clouds of flies."[6] It seems that this simply enhanced the air of austerity which hung around the place.

While Auchinleck shared the spartan conditions of his soldiers, he remained a 'lonely soldier' in every sense of the word. His HQ was completely isolated even though it was in the middle of the army. He did not get to know the officers and men of the Eighth Army or attempt to explain properly why the Eighth Army had to keep stretching to the limit in order to destroy Rommel's army. This lack of contact meant that Auchinleck was unable to grip the army or focus its efforts. His style may have suited the demands of theater command, but seemed unable to adapt to the demands of commanding an army in the field. He was also unable to manage his HQ effectively. As the battles continued, Auchinleck relied increasingly upon Dorman-Smith. Each evening, Auchinleck had an 'evening prayers' session in his caravan, where the staff discussed the day's events and developed future plans. Charles Richardson, nominally in charge of plans, found his role usurped by Dorman-Smith. He lamented: "The prayer meetings were very depressing; nothing constructive by way of seizing the initiative ever emerged. . . . I could offer nothing and felt totally impotent."[7] This was not the way to manage an efficient staff. Dorman-Smith, whom Richardson regarded as a "dangerous supernumerary adviser," was actually operating as Auchinleck's chief inspiration and, albeit informally, as the principal staff officer of the Eighth Army. Ultimately, Dorman-Smith's informal post offered him power without responsibility. He produced a constant stream of voluminous plans for the Eighth Army operations—and many changed on a daily basis, making lower-level planning impossible. But he never took on the full responsibilities of a chief of staff, which would have included ensuring that every commander involved in operations understood his role and had the time to prepare his formations properly. This

Fig 10.3 Winston Churchill visiting the El Alamein area. Here he is seen shaking hands with Lieutenant General Ramsden, commander, Thirtieth Corps, August 7, 1942. (IWM E 15295)

arrangement, exacerbated by Chink's personality, led to confusion and enmity at Eighth Army Headquarters. No one, with the exception of Auchinleck and Chink, understood the complex and ambiguous relations that existed at Army Headquarters.

The breakdown in the staff system led to a series of increasingly violent arguments between the Eighth Army's commanders, who began to query the orders they were being given in what Montgomery later called "bellyaching." Perhaps the best example of this occurred between Lieutenant General Leslie Morshead, the commander of the fresh and sorely needed Ninth Australian Division, and Auchinleck, even before the Australian force had reached the front. When Auchinleck demanded the use of the first available Australian brigade to shore up the line, Morshead used his 'red card' as a Dominion commander. The interview was brusque

Auchinleck: I want that brigade right away.

Morshead: You can't have that brigade.

Auchinleck: Why?

Morshead: Because they are going to fight as a formation with the rest of the division.

Auchinleck: Not if I give you orders?

Morshead: Give me the orders and you'll see.

Auchinleck: So you're being like Blamey, you're wearing his mantle.[8]

The use of Dominion 'red cards' became such a habit during this period that when Major General Douglas Wimberley, the newly arrived commander of the Fifty-First Highland Division, witnessed one such scene, he joked that he should refer orders to the Secretary of State for Scotland![9]

Increasingly violent arguments among Eighth Army commanders revealed that Auchinleck's command over the army had fundamentally broken down. It was not surprising then that armor, infantry, and artillery found it impossible to cooperate properly with each other at the tactical level. All of these problems led to a doleful result. During July, the Eighth Army mounted three major attempts to destroy the Panzerarmee. All failed at a cost of some thirteen thousand casualties. Hasty planning and continued misunderstandings between units meant that each attack dissolved into disaster. The soldiers of Eighth Army displayed courage and determination but were let down by faulty tactics, poor planning, and a fundamental failure of command. Auchinleck had pushed an exhausted army too far.

Yet it was after the last disappointing failure that Auchinleck had what was arguably his finest hour. On July 27, Dorman-Smith wrote his last staff appreciation for Auchinleck.[10] This appreciation, which detailed the Eighth Army's defensive posture and forecast the future course of the battle of Alam al-Halfa with remarkable accuracy, has become well-known; but Auchinleck's own final appreciations, written on August 1 and 2, without any input from Dorman-Smith, have been entirely forgotten.

His first appreciation dealt not only with the short-term posture for the Eighth Army but also with the need for a coordinated campaign against the vulnerable Axis supply lines across the Mediterranean, which was to prove instrumental in the later success of the Eighth Army. Auchinleck's final appreciation of August 2, which has been lost or ignored for sixty years, was an inspired piece of military thought. The plan was unconventional, at least as far as expectations of desert warfare went, and was designed to maximize the Eighth Army's advantages in an offensive timed for mid-September. The plan was

> (i) To make all preparations for a deliberate attack on the extreme NORTH of the enemy's position.
> (ii) To disguise this intention by inducing the enemy to believe that when able to resume the offensive we intend to attack in the SOUTH.
> (iii) To attack and harass the enemy communications to the greatest possible extent.
> (iv) To perfect the organisation of our main defensive zone in the rear of the EL ALAMEIN position and be ready to meet an enemy attempt to turn or by-pass our SOUTHERN FLANK.
> (v) To train and rehearse intensively for the main operation against the enemy NORTHERN flank.
> (vi) To prepare our motorised and armoured forces to take immediate advantage of the break through when made.[11]

This plan proved that, for all his faults as a commander, Auchinleck was an original and clear-sighted military thinker. His appreciations established the framework for the rest of the Alamein campaign and formed the blueprint for the Eighth Army's subsequent success. Every single element of Auchinleck's plan was later followed by the Eighth Army under Montgomery's leadership. Montgomery's much-vaunted master plan for 'his' battle of El Alamein actually originated with Auchinleck—a fact that Montgomery never admitted and indeed has been strenuously denied to this day.

Auchinleck was a committed professional soldier with an inventive mind and deep sense of duty. The final tragedy of his command was that, for all of his talent as a strategic thinker, he lacked the ability to command an army in the field. The South African official historian, Agar-Hamilton, gave the harsh assessment that

> Auchinleck as a commander was hopeless but not because he was a fool. He possessed in fact both a first-class military brain and good fighting spirit. What he lacked was leadership. He never seemed able to get anyone to obey him. . . . His intellect and his understanding of his trade were alike excellent—his powers of command were nil.[12]

This evaluation of Auchinleck seems fair in the light of the July fighting. There is no question that Auchinleck could identify what needed to be done, but he had encountered real difficulty in translating those ideas into practice. He made too many poor choices in subordinates and proved unable to control Dorman-Smith. By the end of July 1942, Auchinleck had lost not only control of his army but also the confidence of Winston Churchill. Churchill had become convinced that something was very wrong with his desert army, and he became determined to visit Egypt in person to 'shake up' the Middle East Command.[13]

Churchill and Brooke arrived in Egypt on August 3, 1942, and after two days of 'fact finding' in Cairo, flew to Burg al-Arab where they were met by Auchinleck. Dorman-Smith sensed Churchill's hostility immediately. Churchill and Auchinleck sat in separate cars on the drive to Eighth Army HQ and once there, the atmosphere became distinctly frosty. Churchill did not approve of the flies, camel dung, or the unappetizing fried breakfast which was offered to him. He was "hot and unhappy."[14] Auchinleck had already made a terrible mistake: he was meeting Churchill in the morning and offered him no drink stronger than tea to soften the prime minister's mood. When Auchinleck and Dorman-Smith gave Churchill a briefing alone in the operations caravan, the prime minister paid no attention and instead, as Dorman-Smith later related,

> quickly began to demand that the Eighth Army should attack afresh. He thrust stubby fingers against the talc; 'Here,' he said, 'or here.' We were alone with him and it was a little like being caged with a gorilla. Eventually Auchinleck said quietly and finally, 'No, Sir, we cannot attack again yet.' Churchill, rose, grunted, stumped down from the caravan and stood alone in the sand, back turned to us.[15]

Auchinleck's and Dorman-Smith's fates were sealed by this disastrous briefing. They hadn't been able to explain their plans to meet a future offensive by Rommel, or their offensive planned for September. Churchill needed a victory and he needed it now. If Auchinleck would not deliver this, then Churchill would find someone who would. Auchinleck had handled this crucial visit very badly—unlike the RAF, which entertained the prime minister with a specially prepared lunch brought from Shepheard's Hotel in Cairo. When Auchinleck waved farewell to the prime minister, he was also essentially waving goodbye to his military career.

Fig 10.4 Winston Churchill with General Alexander and Lieutenant General Bernard Montgomery, commander in chief, Eighth Army, during his second visit to the Western Desert, August 23, 1942. (IWM E 15905)

The very next day, Churchill and Brooke decided to replace Auchinleck with General Harold Alexander.[16] Churchill later said that sacking Auchinleck was like "killing a magnificent stag"; but that suggests he sacked Auchinleck in person, when he in fact sent Col. Ian Jacob in his stead to deliver the letter of doom. Jacob later recalled that "it was like going to murder an unsuspecting friend."[17] Auchinleck was sacked and offered a truncated Iraq–Persia command. This he refused, but instead eventually replaced Wavell as Commander in Chief India. Meanwhile, Dorman-Smith was sent back to the United Kingdom and dropped from his wartime rank of major general to his substantive rank of lieutenant colonel, and thus experienced true military oblivion.[18] There is no doubt that the bitterness engendered by the 'Cairo purge' lasted for the rest of their lives.

Yet the same day as Auchinleck's disastrous briefing, Churchill believed he had found a new commander for the Eighth Army in the person of Lieutenant General William 'Strafer' Gott. Tragically, he had no chance to prove himself as just two days later, the plane carrying him to Cairo on leave was shot down and Gott was killed. Brooke then insisted that his protégé, Lieutenant General Bernard Law Montgomery, be given the job. It was thus only by chance that Montgomery gained the post that was to make his reputation.

General Harold Alexander, the new commander in chief Middle East, was a suave, immaculately turned-out Guardsman with a strong reputation for courage, tactical skill, and an acute sense of diplomacy. He had first come to prominence during the Dunkirk and Rangoon evacuations. Churchill selected Alexander as "the best possible fighting soldier" and expected him to take direct personal charge of the operations against Rommel; but Alexander had no intention of falling into the trap that had ruined Auchinleck. It was Alexander's good fortune to take command of a greatly truncated Middle East Command. His responsibilities were focused on the campaign in Egypt. There was no war in East Africa, no threat to Palestine or Syria as there had been in 1941. The looming menace of a German attack into Persia was not his concern. But Alexander's remit could only be as seemingly simple and straightforward because Wavell and Auchinleck had wrestled with, and overcome, so many dilemmas and difficulties in the previous two years of war.

Meanwhile, Brigadier Freddie De Guingand, the newly appointed brigadier general staff of the Eighth Army, was dismayed and rather worried. Auchinleck had returned to Cairo and Gott was dead. De Guingand was left with a contradictory array of forward plans, and the Eighth Army had lacked a commander for almost a week. What Dorman-Smith later called the "fortnight of confusion" caused by Churchill's sweeping command changes, combined with Gott's death, produced a dangerous interregnum at Eighth Army Headquarters.

It was into this uncertain situation that Montgomery appeared at the Eighth Army. It is difficult in hindsight to disentangle the triumphant 'Monty' of post-1942 fame from the white-kneed lieutenant general who came to command the Eighth Army. Montgomery's last experience of command in action had been with the Third Infantry Division during the retreat to Dunkirk. He had developed a powerful reputation as an energetic trainer of troops and an unconventional commander who drove his men hard. But, although everyone recognized Montgomery as a consummate professional, his abrasive personality had also made him unpopular within the home army.[19]

When Montgomery arrived in Egypt he received a full briefing on the situation from Auchinleck, but claimed in his *Memoirs* that Auchinleck was planning to retreat if Rommel attacked. This was at best highly mendacious; but Montgomery, both at the time and when writing his *Memoirs*, needed to distance himself from Auchinleck.[20] He had been selected as the 'new broom' that would sweep clean; he could not acknowledge any possible debt to a discredited predecessor.

Montgomery drove up to the Eighth Army on August 13 and took command immediately. That night he addressed the staff and gave the clear direction that was most certainly needed. He told them that the bad old days were over, and nothing but good was in store for them. He insisted that the HQ move to Burg al-Arab to join the RAF. De Guingand later recalled that the effect of Montgomery's address was "electric—it was terrific! And we all went to bed that night with a new hope in our hearts, and a great confidence in the future of our Army."[21]

His most important announcement was the appointment of De Guingand as his chief of staff, which meant that he now acted as the main conduit for all of Montgomery's decisions. The 'chief of staff' system functioned brilliantly under his direction. Early every morning, De Guingand met with the staff to discuss matters for attention that day. Unlike Auchinleck's 'evening prayers,' De Guingand's system ensured that the entire staff knew exactly what they were responsible for and could work to achieve it immediately. Every evening, Freddie reported to Montgomery on the actions executed that day and discussed the program for the next. Although Montgomery and De Guingand had very different personalities and tastes—indeed perhaps because of this—they made a highly efficient team.

Right from the start, Montgomery reenergized the staff of the Eighth Army. He also began to execute the 'projection of personality' which had been one of his key tenets of command since he taught at Staff College in the 1920s. He projected confidence, determination, and a clear direction that was bound to be appealing to a rather jaded and confused group of staff officers. But Montgomery did not stop at his headquarters. Montgomery had long craved publicity and recognition, and he purposefully developed a distinctive image. His first, not entirely successful, attempt was to wear an Australian bush hat decorated with badges from all of the units that he visited. However, it was when his Royal Tank Regiment sergeant driver tossed him his black beret that Montgomery hit upon the image that he was to make world-famous. It is, however, just possible that Montgomery might have been infuriated to learn that 'Chink' and his friend Ernest Hemingway had first worn Basque berets, which became the model for the RTR beret, when climbing in the Pyrenees in 1924![22]

Perhaps the most powerful element of Montgomery's concept of the projection of personality was his insistence on visiting as many of the officers and men of the Eighth Army as possible. He was not the first commander of the army to be well-known by the troops (an accolade that can also be claimed for Richard O'Connor, Jock Campbell, and 'Strafer' Gott). However, through his punishing rounds of visits and countless pep talks to the troops, Montgomery energized the Eighth Army and gave it a clear focus and direction. Most importantly of all, through his 'projection of personality,' and by enacting the intense training recommended by Auchinleck, he restored the Eighth Army's will to win.

Churchill returned to Cairo from Moscow on August 17 and could not resist the temptation to revisit the Eighth Army under its new commander. The next day he and Brooke drove out to Burg al-Arab to visit Montgomery at his new HQ. Churchill certainly preferred this HQ, "drawn up amid the sand-dunes by the sparkling waves."[23] Brooke and Churchill went for a swim after their long drive and "the troops were delighted to see their Prime Minister wading into the water in the untanned nude."[24] After dinner, Churchill was only too happy to listen to Montgomery's "masterly exposition of the situation."[25] The contrast with Auchinleck's last briefing of the prime minister could not have been greater.

While the Eighth Army was being transformed into a winning team, the complex aero–naval battle in the Mediterranean wrecked Rommel's supply lines. Ultra intelligence enabled the British to target their limited resources on the highest-value targets—the tankers carrying Rommel's fuel. By the end of August, Rommel was a sick man. He was also so desperate to finally break through to the Delta that he launched his attack even though he knew that he did not have enough petrol to reach Alexandria.

Fig. 10.5 A line of Sherman tanks, the Queen's Bays (Second Dragoon Guards, First Armored Division) at El Alamein, October 24, 1942. (IWM E 18377)

Montgomery's first battle in the desert, which was known to the Axis troops as the 'six days race' but which became known to the British as the Battle of Alam al-Halfa, was rigidly defensive as he refused to allow any pursuit—even when Rommel's armor lay immobilized in the desert for want of fuel. Montgomery's greatest achievement at Alam al-Halfa was that he did not make any serious mistakes. It was later said that the Army held the ring and the RAF gave the punch inside the ring.[26] This time, it was Rommel who was punished severely.

In fact, Montgomery was fortunate indeed that Rommel attacked at the end of August, because he soon realized that the preparations for his own offensive would not be ready until late October. Auchinleck had planned for an offensive in mid-September but even this delay had infuriated Churchill. It would have been very difficult for Montgomery to resist Churchill's insistent demands for an "immediate offensive" without his reassuring defensive victory at Alam al-Halfa.

In the event, it was Alexander's reputation and standing with Churchill that proved vital in gaining the political assent for postponement. For once, Churchill's new commander in chief Middle East had all the political capital he needed to stave off demands for an immediate offensive. The command changes of August, combined with the defensive victory of Alam al-Halfa, made it impossible for Churchill to threaten further changes to 'encourage' his generals.[27] Churchill had little choice but to accept the delay. Alexander won this political battle with consummate skill and Montgomery reaped the benefits in full.

Oliver Leese later claimed that the October Battle of El Alamein "was fought by one man—the Army Commander. It was conceived and carried out by him and was a great personal triumph for him"; and Montgomery would have readily agreed with this point of view.[28] In fact, the strength of the plan for Lightfoot lay in the fact that there were multiple authors and contributors. Montgomery provided the clear overall framework, but much of the detailed work was done further down the command chain. Eighth Army Headquarters worked rapidly and efficiently under De Guingand. Sidney Kirkman, the artillery commander, and Frederick Kisch, the chief engineer, were given complete freedom by Montgomery to develop their plans, and both succeeded brilliantly. The corps commanders translated Montgomery's intentions into practical plans, and the divisional commanders then worked out the fine details. Morshead and Freyberg (the Dominion commanders who had 'bellyached' under Auchinleck) also put their considerable weight behind the plan. The exception lay in the armored division of the Tenth Corps, where personal animosity between its commanders created friction. And unlike many previous British commanders, Montgomery also ensured that, by the time the offensive opened, every soldier in the Eighth Army knew his part in the plan. Montgomery's real strength as an operational commander thus lay not in the production of cast-iron, omniscient, single-authored plans, as he later claimed, but in his skill in using the talents and experience of the commanders serving under him. In doing so, Montgomery managed to focus the efforts of his entire army toward a single goal.

The opening bombardment at El Alamein on October 23, 1942 has remained one of the events of the war that has become indelibly etched

Fig. 10.6 Lieutenant General Bernard Montgomery, general officer commanding Eighth Army in North Africa, in the turret of his Grant tank, November 5, 1942. (IWM E 18980)

into the collective British memory of the war. Yet, however impressive the bombardment, or courageous the attacking Australian, Scottish, New Zealand, and South African infantry, the results of the first night of battle, fought in clouds of swirling dust, were less than Montgomery's ambitious plan had allowed for. The armored divisions, in particular, found it impossible to break out of the extensive Axis minefields in just one night. Montgomery applied what he termed "ginger" to his armored commanders on numerous occasions, and held a number of crisis meetings with them: by the end of the battle, relations between Monty and Lumsden, his Armoured Corps commander, had completely broken down. Yet no amount of Montgomery's 'ginger' could alter the fact that the Panzerarmee Afrika mounted a tenacious defense that made any progress by the Eighth Army slow and costly.

During these tense days of fierce fighting, it would appear that much of Montgomery's confidence was feigned. Liddell Hart later discussed the battle with Brigadier Ronald Briggs, who revealed . . . that Montgomery himself confessed . . . that the confident and assured way in which he had talked during the first week of the battle had been assumed, and that toward the end of the first week he had actually felt that the battle might have to be broken off, in face of the stiff resistance that he was meeting.[29]

In the event, Montgomery's 'projection of personality' served him well and he continued to infuse his subordinates with a sense of purpose and, crucially, belief in victory.

Back in London, Churchill began to have doubts as well. News of Montgomery's 'regrouping' dismayed the prime minister. On October 29, Brooke met Churchill only to be greeted with

a flow of abuse of Monty. What was my Monty doing now, allowing the battle to peter out (Monty was always my Monty when he was out of favour!) He had done nothing now for the last three days, and now he was withdrawing troops from the front. Why had he told us he would be through in seven days if all he intended to do was to fight a half-hearted battle? Had we not got a single general who could even win one single battle?[30]

Brooke defended Monty strenuously but admitted to his diary a "desperate feeling of loneliness because there was just the possibility that I was wrong and that Monty was beat."[31]

Yet it was at this moment of supreme crisis that Montgomery showed his true mettle as a commander. That same afternoon, Montgomery and De Guingand held a full-scale conference for the next breakthrough attempt, Operation Supercharge. Montgomery was under supreme pressure to achieve a breakthrough, but he did not rush the attack. The weight and intensity of the staff work was also a heavy test of De Guingand as chief of staff. After fierce fighting on November 2 and 3, Operation Supercharge finally succeeded. Rommel, who had been shocked to receive a 'stand fast' order from Hitler, had no alternative on November 4 but to order a full-scale withdrawal in order to try and rescue at least the shattered remnants of his once-formidable army.[32]

Montgomery's finest hour almost certainly arrived on November 4, 1942, when he greeted General von Thoma, the captured commander of the Afrika Korps, at his headquarters. Rommel's army had been broken and the Eighth Army was finally out into the open desert. The news that Montgomery had entertained a defeated German general caused a sensation in Britain: the British public was incensed that such gentlemanly behavior could be extended to a Nazi general. However, when Churchill heard the news, his mind was clearly fixated on the fact that Montgomery was a non-smoking teetotaler: he could only mutter, "I sympathize with General von Thoma: Defeated, in captivity . . . and dinner with Montgomery."

Rommel later called the Battle of El Alamein the "battle without hope," but in many respects this was a situation of his own making. Rommel realized only too late the importance of logistics and the necessity for calculated staff planning. Yet while Montgomery always claimed that he had beaten Rommel, the truth was that it was the combined effect of the Eighth Army, Desert Air Force, and Royal Navy—both in Egypt and in the Mediterranean—that proved too much for him.

The Eighth Army's victory at El Alamein was precisely the news that Churchill had most desperately desired. Here, finally, was a conclusive British victory which proved that Britain could actually fight and win in this war. Not surprisingly, Churchill emphasized the importance of this victory in a speech at the Mansion House on November 10, 1942, in which he said: "This is not the end. It is not even the beginning of the end. But it is, perhaps, the end of the beginning."[33] Churchill had put into a masterful phrase what was seen as the real meaning of the victory. After so many disappointments and defeats, the victory at El Alamein seemed to be a true watershed in Britain's fortunes during the war. The turn of the tide, so long expected, seemed to have finally arrived. Yet although the victory at El Alamein seemed of vital importance to the British in November 1942, even a few years later the battle seemed only one milestone on the road to victory. Michael Howard may well be right in suggesting that the battle's true importance was that it enabled the British Empire to go out with a bang rather than with a whimper.[34]

After the war, Churchill pressed the point yet further when he claimed: "It might almost be said: 'Before Alamein we never had a victory, after Alamein we never had a defeat.'"[35] Unfortunately, the hugely significant caveat 'it might almost be said' tends to be ignored in most renditions of this phrase. Churchill had a significant interest in developing and maintaining this version of events—that all was defeat before El Alamein and all was success after it, however much that might mangle historical truth—since it was Churchill who had gone to Egypt in August 1942 and shaken up Britain's Middle East Command.

Montgomery also had an interest in supporting Churchill's version of events, and his *Memoirs* convinced many that his assumption of command radically changed the fortunes of Britain's desert army.[36] Perhaps not surprisingly, the publication of Montgomery's *Memoirs* and Churchill's *The Second World War*, with their claims that Auchinleck had intended to retreat in August, provoked fury from the victims of the Cairo purge. Dorman-Smith even brought a libel action against Churchill and forced a retraction.[37]

Dorman-Smith certainly held different views about what had happened at El Alamein. He wrote to General Brian Horrocks, who served in the Eighth Army under Montgomery, many years later about the Cairo purge, arguing that

> The astonishing thing being that out of all this politico-military confusion . . . the 'common doctrine' survived; historically there is no break between a) the July 1942 'Battle for Egypt,' b) The July 27th Appreciation; c) Alam al-Halfa; d) Your Alamein. If we didn't know of the 'Fortnight of Confusion' everything would have seemed to dovetail. Which is what we all went to the Staff Colleges to ensure.[38]

Although Dorman-Smith may have gone too far in his claim of a 'common doctrine,' the controversies over the command changes have tended to obscure the fact that the Eighth Army itself was relatively unscathed by the turbulence. In many respects, the critical document was Auchinleck's appreciation of August 2, which laid out the need to defeat an offensive by the Panzerarmee and then the measures necessary for the Eighth Army's own offensive; and this 'blueprint' did indeed survive the 'Fortnight of Confusion.'

While Dorman-Smith's point might be arguable, there is perhaps a valid theme. Ultimately, the British were fortunate that the talents of Auchinleck, Montgomery, and Alexander were brought to bear during this critical period of the Second World War. All three men—or all five if we include 'Chink' and Freddie—made vital contributions to the successful outcome of the campaign. In this sense Dorman-Smith's concept of a 'common doctrine' might well extend to our thinking about High Command. It may well be more of a team activity than is normally considered. Since it is seventy years since the fighting raged at El Alamein, perhaps it is time to heal the divisions caused by the 'Cairo purge' and acknowledge the contribution of all the British generals and their staff who fought in the three battles that marked "the end of the beginning."

Notes

1   William Richardson and Freidlin Seymour, *The Fatal Decisions* (London: Michael Joseph, 1956), 162.
2   John Keegan, *Churchill's Generals* (London: Weidenfeld & Nicholson, 1991), 214.
3   For Auchinleck's life and career, see John Connell, *Auchinleck: A Biography of Field-Marshal Sir Claude Auchinleck* (London: Cassell, 1959); Phillip Warner, *Auchinleck: The Lonely Soldier* (London: Buchan & Enright, 1981); Alexander Greenwood, *Field-Marshal Auchinleck* (Durham: Pentland Press, 1990); Roger Parkinson, *The Auk: Auchinleck, Victor at Alamein* (London: Granada, 1977).
4   For an unrivalled biography of 'Chink' Dorman-Smith, see Lavinia Greacen, *Chink: A Biography* (London: MacMillan, 1989).
5   The importance of Iraq and the exchange of telegrams can be found in Auchinleck's despatch, 328, TNA WO32/10160, Churchill to Auchinleck, July 12, 1942, TNA PREM3/290/6, Auchinleck to Churchill, July 15, 1942, TNA PREM3/290/6.
6   Charles Richardson, *Flashback: A Soldier's Story* (London: William Kimber, 1985), 101.
7   Richardson, *Flashback*, 103.
8   This exchange is related in Barton Maughan, *Tobruk and Alamein* (Canberra: Australian War Memorial, 1966), 552.
9   Wimberley, "A Scottish Soldier," 33, PP/MCR/182 Wimberley MSS, Imperial War Museum, London.
10   See Corelli Barnett, *The Desert Generals* (London: William Kimber, 1960), 224–30, for a copy of this appreciation. Barnett reproduced Dorman-Smith's appreciation of July 27, 1942, which has been subsequently quoted by many authors.
11   Auchinleck, Western Front, Appreciation of Situation, Aug 2, 1942, TNA WO201/556.
12   Agar-Hamilton to Kippenberger, July 2, 1951, ANZ WA II/II/6, New Zealand National Archives.
13   Alex Danchev and Daniel Todman, eds., *War Diaries 1939–1945, Field Marshal Lord Alanbrooke* (London: Weidenfeld & Nicholson, 2001), 275.
14   Dorman O'Gowan, "A4: Liquidation in Cairo," 68, 1/2/19 Dorman O'Gowan MSS, John Rylands Library, Manchester.
15   O'Gowan, "A4: Liquidation in Cairo," 68.

16 Nigel Nicholson, *Alex: The Life of Field Marshal Earl Alexander of Tunis* (London: Weidenfeld and Nicholson, 1973), 111.

17 Lt. Col. Ian Jacob's diary, August 8, 1942, 6/2/7 Alanbrooke MSS, Liddell Hart Centre for Military Archives, London.

18 Dorman-Smith was given command of a brigade at Anzio but was removed under controversial circumstances and left the army in 1945. See Greacen, *Chink*, 246, 279–91, 294.

19 See Bernard L. Montgomery, *The Memoirs of Viscount Montgomery of Alamein* (London: Collins, 1958), 42–43; Nigel Hamilton, *Monty: The Making of a General 1887–1942* (London: Allen Lane, 1982), 215–21.

20 Montgomery, *Memoirs*, 94.

21 Francis De Guingand, *Operation Victory* (London: Hodder & Stoughton, 1947), 136–37.

22 Greacen, *Chink*, 95.

23 Winston S. Churchill, *The Second World War*, vol. 4: *The Hinge of Fate* (London: Cassell, 1951, 462.

24 De Guingand, *Operation Victory*, 151.

25 Churchill, *The Hinge of Fate*, 463.

26 Air Historical Branch, *The Middle East Campaign, July 1942–May 1942*, 193.

27 De Guingand, *Operation Victory*, 158.

28 Account by Oliver Leese, ANZ WA II/1/DA491.2/17, New Zealand National Archives.

29 Liddell Hart notes, 11/1943/74 Liddell Hart MSS, Liddell Hart Centre for Military Archives, London.

30 Danchev and Todman, *War Diaries [of] Alanbrooke*, 335.

31 Danchev and Todman, *War Diaries [of] Alanbrooke*, 336.

32 Walter Warlimont, *Inside Hitler's Headquarters 1939–45* (London: Weidenfeld and Nicholson, 1964), 268.

33 Martin Gilbert, *Churchill: A Life* (London: William Heinemann Ltd., 1991), 734.

34 Jill Edwards, *Al-Alamein Revisited: The Battle of Al-Alamein and Its Historical Implications* (Cairo: The American University in Cairo Press, 2000), 6.

35 Churchill, *The Hinge of Fate*, 354.

36 Montgomery, *Memoirs*.

37 Greacen, *Chink*, 304–309.

38 Dorman O'Gowan to Horrocks, July 11, 1959, Dorman O'Gowan MSS, John Rylands Library, Manchester.

11

Alexandrians Tell Their Story
Oral Narratives of the War in North Africa 1940–43

Mohamed Awad and Sahar Hamouda

lexandria acquires its legendary fame from the larger-than-life characters with whom its name is associated: Alexander the Great, Cleopatra, Caesar, Marc Antony, and, in more recent times, with Cavafy, Durrell, Forster, Ungaretti, and so on. During the Second World War, other legendary names made the city their headquarters while they fought the war in North Africa. As the Germans advanced upon El Alamein, Montgomery took up residence in the Cecil Hotel—one of Alexandria's landmarks on the Corniche—and conducted his war from there. Churchill was to be seen eating at the Union restaurant, at the table next to the door, and we Alexandrians were often regaled with stories from the proprietor about Churchill's presence there. Sadly, that proprietor is now dead, and nobody has recorded those invaluable stories. But all is not lost. The Bibliotheca Alexandrina—the new Library of Alexandria—has over the last seven years been collecting the oral heritage of Alexandria, in order to save from oblivion a history that is fast fading as the younger generation awakens to a different life in a distinctly different city from the one that existed a hundred years ago.[1] As we interviewed people from the many foreign communities that had made Alexandria their home, from the faiths and denominations that had worshiped in its mosques, churches, and synagogues, from all the social strata that lived in the neighborhoods of the rich and the poor, a colorful mosaic was recreated from their memories reflecting the cultural variety that was the cosmopolitan Alexandria of the first half of the twentieth century. The story of these ordinary people, leading ordinary lives, complements the grand narrative of Montgomery and

Churchill. This chapter will let the voices of Egyptians and foreigners, rich and poor, Christians, Jews, and Muslims, speak for themselves, with very little editorial intervention, to narrate the story of a city that was being bombarded and was preparing for the possibility of a German occupation.

The Second World War placed Alexandrian Italians in an anomalous position. To all intents and purposes they were Egyptians, for they had been living in Alexandria for generations, and knew no other home. But the Montreux Convention of 1937 had abolished the capitulations that gave them special privileges. They were still Italians, and so they were enemies. They remember how the war impacted their lives as children, for whom school was a prime concern:

Roberto Butta-Calice: "When the war broke out, I was fourteen. The [Italian Littorio] school was seized and closed."

Nicolette Pinto: "As a child, Italy represented, for me, the possibility of not going to school because of the demonstrations. In 1945 and 1946 the school would close down when there were demonstrations, and we would stay at home."

Others explained how the authorities dealt with Italian men. Throughout the war years, the Italian men were interned in camps in Fayed, and their families were allowed to visit once a month:

Alessandro Monti: "When the war broke out, a lot of Italians here were surprised to find themselves on the wrong side, because Egypt was allied to England. Those Italians who had reached a certain age were interned in camps—not exactly prison—in Fayed on the Red Sea. I wasn't interned. Here, the Italians who reached the age of eighteen had to present themselves to the government to be taken to the internment camp, but my birthday was on September 10 and Italy signed the Armistice on September 8. In spite of the bombings and certain episodes, it can't be said it was a very difficult war. Here in Egypt, nothing was ever missed by the Egyptians. Naturally the Italian men were interned and their families went to visit them. My father was not interned because he directed work at the port, which was in the service of Egypt, and so there was no reason to intern him."

Though the two countries were at war, and Italian property was sequestrated and the men were interned, Alexandria's tolerance extended toward its Italian population, who were allowed a certain freedom:

Roberto Butta-Chalice: "During the war, we celebrated the national fascist days by parading in the streets and in the stadium of Alexandria."

Alexandrians drew on the capital of friendship and cultural diversity they had invested in for generations, so life went on as normal for Italians:

Alessandro Monti: "There was no xenophobia. Yes, the relations were bad with the Greeks because Italy had considered invading Greece, but the personal relations were always good. Also the relations were good between the two royal houses: of the kings Fouad and Farouk, and of the House of Savoy. That is why the exiled king of Italy [King Victor Emmanuel III] and his wife came to live in Alexandria. He died here and is buried in the Church of St. Catherine."

Having signed the racist laws in Italy, though, King Emmanuel was not popular with the Italian Jews of Alexandria. Mohamed Awad has the following story to tell, which was narrated to him by the late Djemil Camel-Toueg: "King Victor Emmanuel was a collector of coins, and when he came to Alexandria he heard that Monsieur Ada, a wealthy Italian Jew of Alexandria, had an exceptional collection of coins. He therefore requested to see the famous collection. Monsieur Ada, unwilling to meet the man who had signed the racist laws, yet unable to deny his king entry into his house, agreed. So the king arrived at the appointed hour, only to be received by the butler. He was shown the collection, then shown the door. Monsieur Ada remained upstairs, and the king came and left without seeing him."

On a less royal level, there was anticipation that the Italians would enter Alexandria victorious:

Vangelis Pandelidis: "The Italians were waiting for Mussolini. My mother told me we had in our apartment blocks Italians who were painting the flag waiting for Mussolini."

And it wasn't only the Italians who were waiting excitedly for the Axis powers to sweep into Alexandria. Lucette de Saab, a Syro–Lebanese, had her very personal reasons, befitting a child, for wishing the Germans and Italians to be victorious: "I loved the Italian chauffeurs. When we thought that the Germans were going to enter Alexandria, everybody cried, but not me. I was thrilled. I wanted them to come and liberate our two Italian chauffeurs and carry off my English governess."

The war arrived at the doorsteps of Alexandrians. Bombs began to fall and sandbags went up. Esther Hardman-Zimmerli, a Swiss, recounts what happened in those days: "I remember the war years very well. In '42, when Rommel was so close, we used to spend the nights in the shelters. I also remember very well that there were sandbags in front of all the buildings.

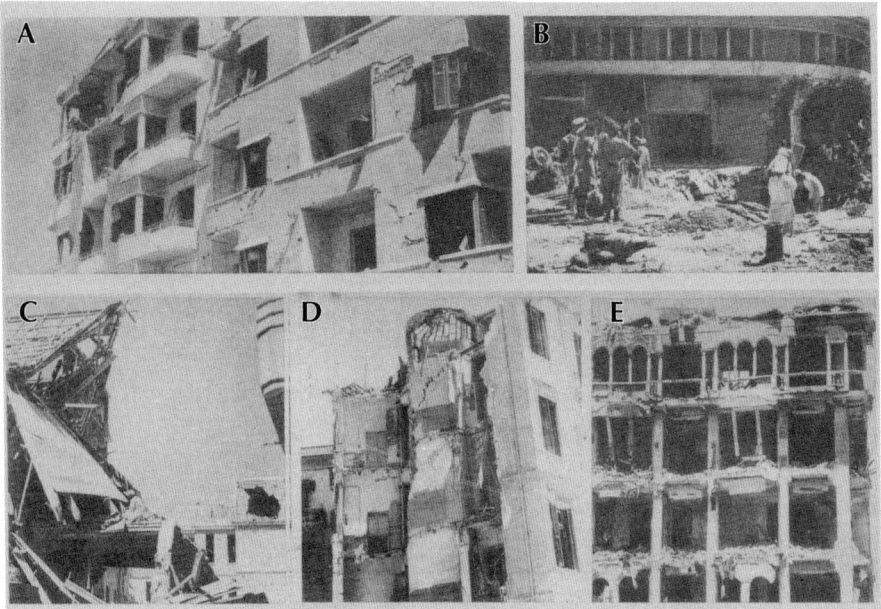

Fig. 11.1 Advice to readers for safety during air raids

All pictures in this chapter from *Images* magazine, reproduced with kind permission of Mohamed Awad.

(a). "A bomb exploded close to these two buildings. To avoid a direct hit or the blast of the explosion, it was vital, as soon as the warning siren blew, to get off the balconies and not lean out of windows."

(b). "The bomb that fell here carved out this huge crater. The fact that it exploded below ground significantly reduced destruction for various reasons. A building only fifteen meters away remained undamaged, because it was built of reinforced concrete."

(c). "A bomb fell just a few meters from this villa. The side nearest the bomb was blown off by the force of the explosion, so better to stay in the side furthest from the explosion."

(d). "This three-story block, likely made of ordinary stone, took a direct hit that shattered part of the building. Yet the building next door was untouched. Better to take cover in a building of reinforced concrete."

(e). "The upper four floors of this five-story block were destroyed by the explosion, leaving only the floors and supporting pillars. During an attack, the lower floors are clearly safer than those above."

I also remember mornings in the Swiss School, when we used to run into the garden and collect shrapnel, and compare what each had found. Some of the bombs fell pretty close, especially the German ones. The Italian bombs usually fell far wide of their target. There were those machines like locomotives which used to produce a lot of smoke, like a smoke wall, so that the German planes wouldn't see the ships."

For some, this was the most terrifying experience of their lives. Haj Mustafa el Mulla, who was to live through three more wars, considers this the worst one: "When the air raid siren sounded, all the people would go to the shelter underneath their homes till the raid was over. We would hear the bombs and raids, and the British guns that were near us in the Fort. And one day the raid lasted six hours. We spent six hours in the shelter, to the extent that the Germans sent down lanterns to light up for them their targets. When we saw the lights in the streets we were amazed at who would have switched these lights on. And then we saw those lanterns dangling in the air lighting the place up for ten minutes. These were very difficult days, of the raids. Although today there is the electronic war which is more difficult and dangerous, but in the past it was more difficult, the things we saw during the raids. We lived through the wars of 1956 and 1967 and 1973, and we didn't see the things we saw in the German war. And in the days of the Germans there wasn't the technological progress there is today. But the sight of their raids was worse than what happens now in wars."

Families began to move from their houses, fearing for their lives. Whoever had family in Ramleh (east of Alexandria, outside the city center, and in the opposite direction from El Alamein) sought shelter there. Giselle Boulad Tawa, of Syro–Lebanese origin, describes the terror of those days: "I was terrified every time I heard those bombs, so we went to my sister at Ramleh to escape them. Still we heard the sirens all night long and we often had to rush to the basement of my sister-in-law's villa, alongside many other neighbors, to evade the bombardments. We remained there till the war came to an end."

Such moves seemed to be at the owner's peril. Michel Marco, an Albanian with French nationality, recounts how they had to seek safety farther east, a few tram stations away, only to lose their home to the authorities: "My family was living in Kasr el Bustan in Glymenopoulo [Ramleh], 75 rue Bochgrenvick. It was a small castle on a hill. . . . My father was caught during the Second World War in France, and my mother got afraid, so we left the house because some bombs fell on the house of Prince Mohamed Ali in Zizinia. We went to my grandmother's place in Tharwat Pasha because it was a bit inside. So the house was empty and there was a military ordinance where you could take over a house if it was empty. Abdel Khalek Hassouna Pasha was then the governor of Alexandria. So he called the manager of my father, monsieur Fortunato André, and told him that he would like to take the house. When my father told them it was not for rent, they told him there is a military ordinance so they will take it whether he likes it or not."

For some, moving a few kilometers east was not enough. As Mary Sinadinou, a Greek, mentions, those who could leave Alexandria altogether did: "People were definitely scared and most of the Egyptians ran to the villages where they had parents, families, or friends. It became even more scary when the war was in Alamein, which was quite close to Alexandria."

Haj Mustafa el Mulla narrates how his family would 'commute' back and forth between the village and Alexandria: "The war began in November 1939, and at the beginning of 1940 we migrated. We went to Sinbillawayn. Only my father stayed in Alexandria, because of his job. We came back to Kom al-Dikka six months later. When there were bombs or air strikes we'd travel again, and spend three or four months away. So we'd come and go, so as not to leave my father on his own. In the morning each one would go to his work, and after six-thirty each one would go to his village and hide there."

Lucette de Saab remembers how her family found refuge outside Alexandria altogether: "We spent two summers in Mansurah, where my father had a house, to escape the bombing."

And for others, moving to the villages was not enough. Isabelle Tawil (French) explains that the German advance spelled danger for some more than others, and thus escape had to be to a distant destination: "As the Germans advanced upon Alamein, which was only two hundred miles [320 kilometers] away from Alexandria, those foreigners whose countries were at war with Germany fled to Cairo. They were terrified. The Jews fled as far as Luxor."

But not all Jews 'fled as far as Luxor.' Jimmy Mawas, an Egyptian Jew, recounts his memories of the war period, which sound idyllic: "I didn't do my primary education at school because of the war in 1939 and the bombardments. A judge lent us a house in a village and the whole family—mother, aunts and cousins—went there and we spent two years there. It was enchanting. My cousins and I became close to each other, like brothers, and we had a happy time together. There was a dear teacher in the village who taught us at home, and there was the governess or my mother who tried to teach us some reading and writing. But we were always playing or going on walks or visiting the neighbors, such as Mr. Nimr who had a huge agricultural property. There we learnt how to make butter and bake bread—that kind of education. We returned to Alexandria in 1943."

It is worth observing the kind of life Jews led in Egypt in the 1930s and 1940s and their total integration into the Egyptian social fabric, as opposed to their suffering in Europe in the same decades.

The war was not all doom and gloom in Alexandria, despite the very real fear of a German occupation. Alexandrians managed to continue with the lifestyle they had been used to before the war, as Mary Thomas exclaims: "Surprising as it may sound, even when the war was going on, we always had time for fun and entertainment."

Foreign soldiers and officers, arriving in the city to fight the war in North Africa, found themselves drawn into a whirlpool of activity: of dance, theater, and delicious food. Dany Leondarakis, a Greek, enumerates the kinds of entertainment offered by the lively city: "During the war, the Grand Trianon had a very big nightclub at the back, which was called Follies, where they used to bring ballets from France, Italy, and Hungary. All the officers of the Greek Navy, the Australians, and the British used to gather in the bar. The Petit Trianon was a patisserie and *confiserie* where they had *thé dansant* in the afternoon with an orchestra. Unica was a meeting point for all the ladies who used to go shopping and all the gentlemen who were in the offices of the neighborhood. Although people had fun, every night there was a blackout and Alexandria was repeatedly bombed."

While the ladies continued to shop as usual, they also started a new activity of looking after the soldiers who had come to fight in El Alamein. Anahide Meramedjian, an Armenian, describes how all joined hands in the 'war effort' in a typically Alexandrian manner: "This is a terrible thing to say, but during the war we had to amuse the soldiers who had gone to Alamein. There were clubs like 'End of 20 Club' and 'Britannia Club,' where we would all go to work. I once cooked 150 eggs in one day and handed out six hundred cups of tea. Everybody was trying to amuse the soldiers. We would take them out and give them lunches and dinners so that they would eat. The English were very young, and were looking for families to whose homes they could go and feel they were back home. It

11.2 Fleeing the bombs

(a). Within hours of the attack, roads from Alexandria became choked with the makeshift tents of refugees

(b). A camel, requisitioned and loaded with household goods, including a bed, makes its triumphal entry into the village of Abi Hemmos.

(c). Among the Alexandrian refugees, this group from the city has been fortunate to be offered sanctuary by the religious authorities of this mosque.

was all very simple and there was no segregation of races: Greeks, Armenians, Muslims, Copts, Protestants, Catholics, all were the same and there was no discrimination."

Women of different communities, including Egyptians, did more than feed the soldiers and entertain them. Mohamed Awad still keeps the Red Crescent card of his aunt Faika (who was half Egyptian, half Greek), and remembers her telling him that "whether they were in the Red Cross or the Red Crescent, Alexandrian women from all communities and faiths worked side by side to nurse the injured soldiers."

So there were hospitals and there were dinners. Obviously, those who had escaped to the villages missed out on much that was going on in Alexandria. What a contrast to a Europe living in deprivation! Alexandria's women pitched in, as Isabelle Tawil says: "The war years were the great madness. We went out every evening. First it was the age of the Poles—because of the Polish contingents one saw nothing but Poles. Then we saw nothing but Greeks, and then it was only this and then only that. And always the parties and the dances, to distract those who had been at the front. Then there were the charity dances organized by the different communities: the Greek, the Italian. It was very cosmopolitan. There was a lot of social activity, with dances left, right, and center. It was incredible."

While England tightened its belt and imposed rationing, Alexandria continued unperturbed, even though Rommel was knocking at its doors. Mary Sinadinou: "We missed nothing during the war. There was plenty of food, and life went on smoothly."

One food item was missing, however, as Esther Zimmerli-Hardman noticed: "I used to ask why we were no longer getting any potatoes, and was told that they were all taken for the English."

But there were other concerns for the young Alexandrian woman. Love remained in the air, though fate did part a couple who belonged to two countries at war with each other. Evangelia Pastroudis, a Greek, still remembers her childhood sweetheart that the war deprived her of: "I fell in love with a German boy who went to the same school as I. He wanted to take me with him to Germany, but my father refused, so I had to obey. We went on communicating by letters until recently."

Others were more fortunate. In the process of cooking for the English soldiers, some lucky Alexandrian women managed to land husbands. Lucette de Saab (who wished the Germans would carry off her English governess and liberate her Italian chauffeurs from the internment camp) felt chagrin at being too young to join the parties: "Unfortunately I was not old enough, but my sister went out a lot. She went to the clubs of the English soldiers, and so did the governess. They cooked eggs for the soldiers. Then there was the Britannia Club and there was Mrs. Baker, the wife of Baker Pasha [Valentine Baker], chief of police in Alexandria. She was a foreigner—Greek or Armenian—and every Saturday evening she would give a party, to which my sister went regularly. All the young women died of envy and would give anything to go and meet the English soldiers. There were lots of marriages. It was said that the ugliest girls, with the least chance of getting married, got married to the English."

Marriages were plentiful in Alexandria, but not all were between Alexandrian girls and English soldiers or officers. When King Victor Emmanuel III of Italy was exiled, he sought refuge in Alexandria. Mohamed Awad remembers this about the king: "Robert Gasche, a Swiss Alexandrian, told me that he married the granddaughter of King Emmanuel, the daughter of Prince Calvi del Bergolo. When the king was in exile here, he lived in the Ambron house, the house of an Italian family. This is precisely the 'house with the tower' in which Lawrence Durrell rented rooms while he was in Alexandria from 1944 to 45, and it was also in this house that King Emmanuel died."

Then there were moments of poignancy. Perhaps her love for the German boy—not destined to end in marriage—made Evangelia Pastroudis sympathize with some German prisoners and be the instrument of their release: "One day a policeman took me to the police station. I discovered they had caught three German prisoners of war, and as I was the only one in Mex who knew German, they wanted me to translate for them. Although Egypt and Greece were on the side of the Allies, I felt pity for those Germans, who had been in the police station for days. I said they were tourists, and asked the policeman to let them go."

Mohamed Awad remembers a yet more striking story concerning Germans, related to him by his father, Fouad Awad: "In class with my father at Victoria College was Hans Perkunder, son of the German consul general in Alexandria. His family lived in the Dumreicher house, in Carlton [Rushdy]. The garden wall was designed in the form of swastikas (of which one remains today). The two boys were inseparable, one reason being my grandmother's irresistible Greek meals, which he obviously preferred to the German dishes his own mother gave him. Hans enjoyed the Awad cooking to the extent that the Awad home more or less became his own and his visits were often prolonged into days. But the war disrupted their lives and separated them. Unable to go to college abroad as had been planned, my father joined his father's contracting business and set to work in Amriya, twenty-five kilometers west of Alexandria on the route to El Alamein. Hans was conscripted as an officer in the German Army in Europe. When the war came to North Africa, he was sent there, where he got excited about seeing his school friend. He somehow got hold of a British uniform and motorcycle, and crossed the lines. Because of his 'borrowed' gear and fluent English (acquired at Victoria College), he passed for an Englishman and traveled all the way to Amriya undetected, where he asked the Bedouins about Fouad Awad. Sadly, he could not find him, and went back to the 'enemy' lines. But the story does not end there. The Bedouins, when they found my father, told him his friend Hans had come looking for him. And many years later, the doorbell of the family home, where I was then living, rang. I opened the front door and found a stranger standing there, asking for Fouad Awad. It was the indomitable Hans Perkunder, come back to Alexandria for a visit (and perhaps a Greek meal). He was finally united with his friend."

The war separated Fouad Awad not just from his friend but also from his school. Mohamed Awad remembers what his father told him about the fate of Victoria College: "During the war, Victoria College was requisitioned and became the Seventeenth General Hospital. The school moved to the Hotel and Casino San Stefano where the boys had a jolly good time. They didn't do much studying, and instead spent most of their time swimming in the clear blue waters of the Mediterranean. Then they flirted with the beautiful daughter of Philippe, who was famous for his little sandwich shop on the tram, and who would chase them away with his knife. I also remember that Youssef Chahine told me he filmed his first film ever when he was a schoolboy at Victoria during the San Stefano days."

While the boys were swimming instead of studying, the Germans went on bombing Alexandria. There is the story of the bomb Lucette found on her sister's pillow, and the method by which it was defused: civilians organizing themselves into wardens to protect Alexandria: "During the war our street, rue des Pharaons, was bombarded. One night, while my sister was out dancing, a bomb landed on her bed, on her pillow. It didn't explode. The maid carried it and rushed to the edge of the garden, and put it there. Then Mani Horwitz, who was the air warden, came with his team and carried the bomb off. There were also many English air wardens, each in his neighborhood. There was Finney, for example. The principal families were charged with the civil defense of their city."

This was not the only story of a bomb being defused. The folk heritage of Alexandria includes a story that has lived in the collective consciousness and popular memory of the city, but of which there is no trace among the younger generation today. It is the story of how the holy man, Abul Dardar, rose from his shrine to embrace a bomb and defuse it so it wouldn't explode. The keeper of the shrine, Adel el Bannan, narrates the story as it was narrated to him by his father, also keeper of the shrine: "My father was the 'servant' of the shrine of Abul Dardar, and when he died in 1968, I was appointed by the Supreme Sufi Council to take over his responsibilities, although I was still a child. . . . During the Second World War, they dropped a bomb on the shrine. But Abul Dardar rose, dressed all in white, and pushed the bomb all the way to the police head-quarters. He defused it and there was no explosion. This was during my father's time."

Also in the time of Mohamed Awad's father and grandfather, there were contributions in another area. His story about his grandfather's work was as follows: "My grandfather was a contractor, and during the war construction had decreased considerably in the city, because all build-ing was directed toward the war efforts. So he moved his work to Amriya, where he built barracks and shelters for the British Army. He also built them a swimming pool to cool off in; it was decidedly a novelty in those days, and may well have been the first swimming pool to be built in Alex-andria. After the war, the British sent him a letter thanking him for his contribution to the war. My father was hit by a bullet from a German plane during those days. He told me the German planes were recogniz-able by a particular intermittent sound of their engines."

And so everybody joined in the war effort: the women fed the soldiers, and married them when the war was over, and the men detonated bombs, as did the spirits of the holy men of Alexandria. Food was plentiful, and life went on as usual. But there were also air raids, and as a consequence people moved to Ramleh east of the city, or to villages outside Alexan-dria. Jews were treated no differently from Muslims; and Italians, though interned, were not badly treated. On the contrary, they were allowed to have fascist parades. There was love, and there was friendship, and there were British governesses who were obviously not popular. Here is another story of a British governess, narrated by Zizi Niazi Badr:

"We used to have English governesses, and one of them, called Miss Griffith, would take us for a walk on the beach during sunset. And every time she'd say, 'Do you see the setting sun?' and we'd answer, 'Yes, Miss Griffith.' Then she'd go on, 'The sun is setting, but the sun never sets on the British Empire.'"

Although England was victorious in the end, the sun began setting on the British Empire after the Second World War. Within a decade, the revolution of 1952 would break out in Egypt, and soon afterward there would be demonstrations in the streets, calling for the evacuation of the British soldiers. And what would the impact of the Second World War be on Alexandria in particular? Alexandrians believed it sounded the death knell of the cosmopolitanism that had made Alexandria so special. Omar Koreich, an antique dealer, argues that the "decline of Alexandrian cosmopolitanism began with the Second World War, when the Italians were sequestrated in 1942. In our profession there were huge auctions in 1948, when people started leaving Egypt. The Averrinos, who had a superb collection, auctioned it in 1948. Then there were the Benakis; two-thirds of their famous collection in Athens came from Alexandria."

Ahmed Abou Zeid, founder of the department of anthropology in Alexandria University, offers a similar interpretation: "I consider that the Second World War was the real beginning of change. The advance of the German military forces and their arrival at Alamein was actually the reason why the foreigners, especially the Jews, left Alexandria and Egypt—and this was the real beginning of change. The Italians and the Greeks and the Jews left Egypt, and this exodus after the end of the Second World War affected cultural life and the economy. After that came the 1952 Revolution and the rise of nationalism and affiliations that led to the dismissal of most of the foreigners from Egypt. Then there was the advent of 1956, the adoption of socialist principles, and the end of a capitalist regime at that time. That is why we should not claim that the 'Revolution' was solely responsible for the change that took place."

Other Alexandrians would disagree, and date the beginning of the demise of cosmopolitanism to the First World War, when the Germans began leaving. But that is another story. For Alexandrians, El Alamein was *the* war. It, rather than the First World War, was referred to as *'al-harb al-'alameya'*—the World War. Despite the bombings, the destruction, the deaths, the fear, the immigrations, there was bonding and love and friendship. With the nursing came the parties and the entertainment.

Rich and poor, foreign and Egyptian, Christian, Muslim, and Jew, all joined in the war effort—not with tears, but with aplomb. That was the true spirit of Alexandria.

Notes

1   Some of these interviews were included in Mohamed Awad and Sahar Hamouda, eds, *Voices from Cosmopolitan Alexandria* (Alexandria: Bibliotheca Alexandrina, 2006). The other interviews have not yet been published. Thus this chapter relies on published and unpublished interviews.

12

The Battle of El Alamein
Impressions of a Young Schoolboy in Alexandria[1]

Harry Tzalas

At the end of September 1942, I was a six-year-old boy and had just started school at St. Vincent de Paul in Alexandria. The war in North Africa, with the repeated advances and retreats of the Allied and Axis forces, had been going on for over a year and Alexandria, an important naval base for the Royal Navy, was constantly under air attack. We did spend nearly every night in an ancient cistern arranged for the occasion as a shelter. This *abri* was the meeting point of our cosmopolitan neighborhood. My Greek father and my Italian mother shared the anxiety, fears, and the incertitude of what would happen next with our neighbors of different nationalities and creeds.

But war for a six-year-old boy was part of a game. We fought with toy tanks, miniature airplanes, and guns made of broomsticks; I believed this was war. It was only later that I realized that real guns, real cannons spit fire and death. But, inquisitive as I was, I did follow grown-up people's conversations and search the sites marked on a map displayed in our hall. Tobruk, Bir Hakim, Sidi Barrani, Marsa Matruh, Fuka, Qattara, Alam al-Halfa, El Alamein, mythical toponyms whispered again and again, and the constant question: "When will Rommel enter Alexandria?" Some did not much care either way, and there were some who secretly wished it. The Europeans, though, were in a panic. The bombing became more and more intense. The German and Italian bombers were aiming for the port and the army barracks. Slowly the city began to empty.

Until then Alexandrians, Europeans and locals alike, had lived quietly and peacefully far from war and confrontation. The Europeans (with

Fig 12.1 Count Aziz de Saab—an Alexandrian savoring peace. Reproduced with kind permission of Lucette de Saab.

the exception of 1882 when the English warships bombed the neighborhoods bordering on the Western Harbor, Alexandria) and all of Egypt had known many years of peace. Other than the Italian and German women and children who awaited the arrival of the Axis troops as liberators, the Europeans, including Greeks, Armenians, and Jews, now feared German occupation. Suddenly Mother announced that I would have to interrupt classes. Why? I was enjoying my initiation into the French alphabet! We had to leave our apartment in the center of Alexandria and move eastward to Sidi Bishr to the villa of Uncle Gaetano? Why? Because Rommel would soon enter Alexandria from the west. Those who could, closed up their homes, taking just a few essentials with them, and left. Rommel would enter from the Western Desert, so it would be wise to leave for the east, toward Abu Qir, Rashid, Damietta. There was chaos on the roads and at all the train stations. Even bread will soon be in short supply, said Aunt Ione. So we left.

Field Marshal Montgomery had settled on the small village and railway halt of El Alamein as the point at which to halt Rommel's advance, and the date for the commencement of the massive attack was set for late in the evening of October 23. The night was cold, as it often is in the desert. One thousand, two hundred Allied cannons thundered all night long, and all the next day, and the third day, and the fourth day without pause, and the fifth day, and the sixth. October passed, November came, and the cannons continued to spew out burning iron, hatred, and death. Twelve nights of fire. The Germans and Italians held their ground, returned fire, and did not retreat.

News of the great battle reached Alexandria with lightning speed. Uncle Gaetano's son Enrico was fighting with the Italian Brescia Brigade. My mother's family too were gathered in Sidi Bishr at the Villa Felicità in that autumn of 1942. It was a true tower of Babel. Every evening just after nightfall, the three men of Uncle Gaetano's Villa Felicità, the Italian, the Copt, and the Greek, would climb silently up onto the terrace to survey the horizon. Far away beyond the darkness, you could see flashes of light over the great battle.

It did not take long: two weeks later we were back in Alexandria; for an obscure reason, Rommel had withdrawn. Night bombardments continued, and then their intensity was reduced; finally all stopped. I remember the day when my father entered our home in a triumphal mood announcing that the war was over. I did wonder, "And now, what will become of us without a war?" We had become addicted to it.

Ten years later, as a young man, I visited El Alamein; I was curious to see for myself the mythical battlefield that kept me away from school and imposed our short self-exile in Sidi Bishr at the Villa Felicità. Reality was a traumatic shock. Endless stone steles marked burials of the victorious soldiers, mostly young lads only two or three years older than I was. The losers, Germans and Italians, had not yet found peace in their later impressive memorials, and casual burials of unidentified bodies scattered the immensity of the desert.

Most shocking was the contrast with the beauty of the sea: indigo blue at the horizon merging with light green in the shallows, and the murmur of the waves caressing the immaculate sand. And I wondered how men could have fought a war in this earthly paradise.

Notes
1   Some passages here are from Harry E. Tzalas, *Farewell to Alexandria: Eleven Short Stories* (Cairo: The American University in Cairo Press, 2004).

"Here Dead Lie We"

Here dead lie we
Because we did not choose
To live and shame the land
From which we sprung.

Life, to be sure,
Is nothing much to lose,
But young men think it is,
And we were young.

— *A.E. Housman*